Dear Reader,

Are you looking to improve your health and lose weight all while enjoying **delicious, satisfying meals** without spending hours in the kitchen? Then have I got the cookbook for you! In this book I will reveal how the Mediterranean diet and the Instant Pot® can join forces to help you eat well, save time, and relax with your loved ones. Learn about the Mediterranean lifestyle and how it can benefit you, and how the Instant Pot® can take the stress out of cooking fresh meals any night of the week.

You will find recipes that can be made ahead of time as part of your weekly meal prep—perfect to pack for lunches or for dinners on busy days. There are recipes special enough to be made for dinner parties, fun salads that can be taken along to potluck parties, and hearty main and side dishes for special events and holidays. Everything is packed with flavor and **filled with healthful ingredients**, and nearly all of them are ready in an hour or less.

One of the great joys in my life is cooking for my family and friends. I love sharing a meal with those I hold dear, and I want to provide them with food that nourishes the body as well as the spirit. The Instant Pot® and the Mediterranean diet help me do just that. I get to spend more **quality time with my loved ones** while I serve them meals I feel good about. It is my sincere hope that this book helps you on your path to a healthier, happier you.

Kelly Jaggers

Welcome to the Everything® Series!

These handy, accessible books give you all you need to tackle a difficult project, gain a new hobby, comprehend a fascinating topic, prepare for an exam, or even brush up on something you learned back in school but have since forgotten.

You can choose to read an Everything® book from cover to cover or just pick out the information you want from our four useful boxes: Questions, Facts, Alerts, and Essentials. We give you everything you need to know on the subject, but throw in a lot of fun stuff along the way too.

question	fact
Answers to common questions.	Important snippets of information.

alert	essential
Urgent warnings.	Quick handy tips.

We now have more than 600 Everything® books in print, spanning such wide-ranging categories as cooking, health, parenting, personal finance, wedding planning, word puzzles, and so much more. When you're done reading them all, you can finally say you know Everything®!

PUBLISHER Karen Cooper

MANAGING EDITOR Lisa Laing

COPY CHIEF Casey Ebert

PRODUCTION EDITOR Jo-Anne Duhamel

ACQUISITIONS EDITOR Lisa Laing

SENIOR DEVELOPMENT EDITOR Lisa Laing

EVERYTHING® SERIES COVER DESIGNER Erin Alexander

OFFICIAL
Instant Pot
BOOK

THE EVERYTHING® MEDITERRANEAN INSTANT POT® COOKBOOK

KELLY JAGGERS

300 RECIPES FOR HEALTHY MEDITERRANEAN MEALS—MADE IN MINUTES

ADAMS MEDIA

NEW YORK   LONDON   TORONTO   SYDNEY   NEW DELHI

Acknowledgments

This book would not have been possible without the team at Adams Media. Thank you for all your hard work on my behalf, and for believing in me! You make me look so good, and it is so appreciated.

To my dear friends—Torie, Tanisha, Jodi, Sonya, and Novia. You make me a better person, and you are loved.

To my mom, Carol, and to Tina. You ladies are amazing. Don't you ever forget it!

Finally, to my husband, Mark—thank you for your love and support. Without you I would not be where I am today. I love you!

Dedicated to you, dear reader. You got this!

Adams Media
An Imprint of Simon & Schuster, Inc.
57 Littlefield Street
Avon, Massachusetts 02322

An Everything® Series Book.
Everything® and everything.com® are registered trademarks of Simon & Schuster, Inc.

First Adams Media trade paperback edition February 2020

ADAMS MEDIA and colophon are trademarks of Simon & Schuster.

For information about special discounts for bulk purchases, please contact Simon & Schuster Special Sales at 1-866-506-1949 or business@simonandschuster.com.

The Simon & Schuster Speakers Bureau can bring authors to your live event. For more information or to book an event contact the Simon & Schuster Speakers Bureau at 1-866-248-3049 or visit our website at www.simonspeakers.com.

Interior design by Colleen Cunningham
Photographs by Kelly Jaggers
Mediterranean Diet Pyramid © 2009 Oldways Preservation and Exchange Trust; illustration by George Middleton

Manufactured in the United States of America

10 9 8 7 6 5 4 3 2 1

Library of Congress Cataloging-in-Publication Data
Names: Jaggers, Kelly, author.
Title: The everything® Mediterranean Instant Pot® cookbook / Kelly Jaggers.
Description: First Adams Media trade paperback edition. | Avon, Massachusetts: Adams Media, 2020.
Series: Everything®.
Includes index.
Identifiers: LCCN 2019038554 | ISBN 9781507212509 (pb) | ISBN 9781507212516 (ebook)
Subjects: LCSH: Cooking, Mediterranean. | Smart cookers. | Pressure cooking. | Diet--Mediterranean Region. | Quick and easy cooking.
Classification: LCC TX725.M35 J34 2020 | DDC 641.59/1822--dc23
LC record available at https://lccn.loc.gov/2019038554

ISBN 978-1-5072-1250-9
ISBN 978-1-5072-1251-6 (ebook)

Contains material adapted from the following titles published by Adams Media, an Imprint of Simon & Schuster, Inc.: *The Everything® Easy Instant Pot® Cookbook* by Kelly Jaggers, copyright © 2018, ISBN 978-1-5072-0940-0; *The Everything® Healthy Pressure Cooker Cookbook* by Laura D.A. Pazzaglia, copyright © 2012, ISBN 978-1-4405-4186-5; *The Everything® Mediterranean Cookbook, 2nd Edition* by Peter Minaki, copyright © 2013, ISBN 978-1-4405-6855-8; *The Everything® Mediterranean Diet Book* by Connie Diekman, MEd, RD, LD, FADA and Sam Sotiropoulos, copyright © 2010, ISBN 978-1-4405-0674-1; *The Everything® Pressure Cooker Cookbook* by Pamela Rice Hahn, copyright © 2009, ISBN 978-1-4405-0017-6; *The Everything® Vegetarian Pressure Cooker Cookbook* by Amy Snyder and Justin Snyder, copyright © 2010, ISBN 978-1-4405-0672-7; and *The "I Love My Instant Pot®" Recipe Book* by Michelle Fagone, copyright © 2017, ISBN 978-1-5072-0228-9.

Contents

Introduction

The Mediterranean region is known for its beauty, its diverse cultures from the islands of Greece to the warm beaches of Spain, the variety of fish that come from the sea, and the diet that takes its name from the region. People who live in the Mediterranean love their food, and this love is reflected in how they live their lives. Very often, family and friends gather for long, leisurely meals that can last hours. You'll find on their table artisan breads, fish, lamb, vegetables, pasta, rice, lentils, and, of course, olive oil—lots of olive oil. And they end their meals simply, with platters of fruit and a sip of *raki*, a Mediterranean liqueur flavored with aniseed.

The Mediterranean diet has been enjoyed for centuries, but recently it has been the subject of much interest. People in the southern Mediterranean countries tend to have less heart disease, even though they consume more fat than many American dietary guidelines recommend. In addition, a core element of the diet in many of the Mediterranean countries is the consumption of wine. These two factors together seem to contradict the typical concept of healthful eating, but, for people in the Mediterranean, they are a part of life. Another factor that characterizes the diet is the use of oils, nuts, and seeds. The use of oils instead of animal fats in cooking seems to provide not only more healthy fats but also a variety of phytonutrients, natural plant compounds that help prevent disease.

People in this region consume less red meat, refined grains, salt, and sugar, and enjoy more plant-based meals and daily physical activity. They prioritize time to slow down, relax, and enjoy the company of others. Mealtime is more relaxed, communal, and treasured. Instead of a quick meal while on the go, meals are a time to unwind and connect with those you love most.

Like the Mediterranean diet, pressure cooking also has a long history. For decades, it's been a way to help home cooks save time and energy in the kitchen. Long gone are the days of the clunky stovetop pressure cooker. Today's modern electric pressure cookers are safer, easier to use, and designed with convenience in mind. The most well known of these electric pressure cookers is the Instant Pot®. This machine replaces a stovetop pressure cooker, slow cooker, rice maker, steamer, electric skillet, and yogurt maker. It offers preprogrammed cooking functions so even the most novice user is more likely to have success. Meals that once took hours to make can be ready in a fraction of the time, and because the Instant Pot® offers the ability to brown and sauté in the same pot you cook in, there are fewer dishes and pans to clean up at the end of the meal. Saving time and effort makes the Instant Pot® a natural when adopting the Mediterranean lifestyle.

Your healthcare professional may have recommended the Mediterranean diet to help you lose weight, gain vitality, or achieve better overall health. Or you might have read about how a lifestyle focused on eating plant-based meals, lowering the amounts of saturated fat in your diet, and finding ways to relax and lower stress has helped many people achieve their health goals. Whatever the reason, the Instant Pot® is an invaluable tool on your Mediterranean diet journey. It makes cooking at home faster and less stressful, so you can avoid the pitfalls of eating fast food and convenience foods. It also preserves more of the nutrition in foods, so you will get more of the nutritional benefit from the meals you make. You will spend less time actively cooking and more time enjoying the activities you love. Cooking in an Instant Pot® is often as simple as putting the ingredients in, setting your cooking function, and letting the machine do the rest.

So, what can you make in your Instant Pot®? How about fresh vegetables with herbs, olive oil, and whole-grain pasta in less than 30 minutes? Steamed fish with bright lemon and garlic in less than 20 minutes? How much happier and easier would your mornings be if you could wake up to a hot, hearty pot of oatmeal flavored with fruit and nuts? All of these things are possible when you use the Instant Pot®. Making meals at home is no longer a chore. Even lunches can be made ahead of time in the Instant Pot®, divided for the week, and then grabbed on your way out the door. No muss, no fuss—just wholesome food that you will look forward to eating.

So, sit down at the table, savor a meal with those you care about, and enjoy a glass of red wine in honor of your health. With the Mediterranean diet and the Instant Pot®, you are on the road to a long, nourished, and happy life.

CHAPTER 1

The Number-One Diet Meets the Top Kitchen Appliance

The Mediterranean diet, a diet based on food traditions from the Mediterranean, is widely believed to be one of the most beneficial diets in the world for those looking to improve their health, lose weight, and boost energy. The diet encourages eating fresh, plant-based meals, adding more activity into your day, and enjoying time with friends and family. Cooking fresh, healthful meals every day might seem like a chore, especially if you are used to serving processed convenience foods, but there is an answer—the Instant Pot®! With this one appliance, you can make breakfast, lunch, and dinner a breeze. The Instant Pot® is your express pass to delicious meals, often ready in less than an hour, with less work, more nutrition, and less cleanup, so you can relax and enjoy all the benefits the Mediterranean diet has to offer.

Mediterranean Diet Basics

Studies show that the people of the Mediterranean live longer, weigh less, and suffer from fewer medical complaints, such as cardiovascular disease. Researchers looked at their lifestyles and found that the key to their abundant good health was their diet, activity level, and the amount of time they spent with friends and family. They don't count calories, they don't deprive themselves, and they don't believe in bland meals.

So, what does all this mean? Well, the Mediterranean diet is a heart-healthy eating plan that focuses on fresh, plant-based meals, healthy fats, and whole grains. Meals are made up of vegetables, whole grains, legumes, pulses (beans, lentils, and peas), pasta, fresh fruit, nuts, and rice. Healthy fats (such as olive oil) replace other fats (such as butter), dairy products are eaten in moderation, and fresh herbs and spices are used in place of most salt. Meat, fish, and seafood are enjoyed in moderation, with roughly two or three servings of fish or seafood eaten per week, poultry enjoyed about once per week, and red meat limited to one to two servings per month.

The Mediterranean Diet Pyramid

The Mediterranean diet pyramid includes a variety of fruits, vegetables, and grains with limited amounts of fish and poultry. The most famous Mediterranean diet pyramid is one developed in 1993 by the Harvard School of Public Health, the European Office of the World Health Organization, and Oldways Preservation and Exchange Trust.

Pyramid Components

As with all pyramids, the Mediterranean pyramid is built from the bottom up. The base of the pyramid consists of grains, fruits and vegetables, beans, nuts, and olive oil. If you look at the bottom of the pyramid, you'll see that this layer is in fact at least half of the entire pyramid, in order to make visually clear that plant-based foods come first.

A close look at the bottom layer shows an abundance of whole grains like wheat, oats, barley, rice, and corn. The vegetables range from dark green ones, like broccoli, asparagus, wild greens, and spinach, to dark red, orange, or purple vegetables, such as pumpkin, eggplant, and peppers. The fruits in this layer also reflect the colors of the rainbow with apricots, cherries, olives, peaches, dates, and figs among them. This layer is also where you will find beans, nuts, and seeds included in all meals. When you think of your dinner on a plate, envision at least half to three-quarters of your plate filled with dishes made with these ingredients. Planning entirely plant-based meals for one to two meals per day is ideal.

Building on top of this layer, you'll find fish and seafood, which you should enjoy at least two times per week. Salmon, cod and other white fish, clams, mussels, and shrimp are good choices. Foods to include in your diet in moderation include poultry, eggs, and dairy products. Think about using dairy and eggs in ways that give the greatest impact. Crumble a small amount of feta cheese on top of a salad, use yogurt for salad dressings or as a topping for oatmeal, or slice a hard-cooked egg and layer it on whole-grain toast with sautéed veggies and a drizzle of olive oil. Poultry should be eaten about once a week, and should be no more than one-quarter of your plate.

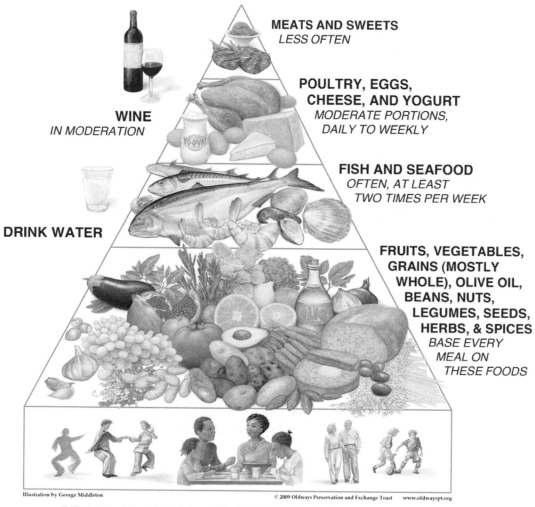

Mediterranean Diet Pyramid

A contemporary approach to delicious, healthy eating

MEATS AND SWEETS
LESS OFTEN

POULTRY, EGGS, CHEESE, AND YOGURT
MODERATE PORTIONS, DAILY TO WEEKLY

WINE
IN MODERATION

FISH AND SEAFOOD
OFTEN, AT LEAST TWO TIMES PER WEEK

DRINK WATER

FRUITS, VEGETABLES, GRAINS (MOSTLY WHOLE), OLIVE OIL, BEANS, NUTS, LEGUMES, SEEDS, HERBS, & SPICES
BASE EVERY MEAL ON THESE FOODS

Illustration by George Middleton

© 2009 Oldways Preservation and Exchange Trust   www.oldwayspt.org

BE PHYSICALLY ACTIVE; ENJOY MEALS WITH OTHERS

And finally, at the top of the pyramid, you'll find meats and sweets. Placing these foods at the top of the pyramid conveys the importance of eating them less often and in smaller amounts. In addition to the sweets at the top of the pyramid, other processed foods are generally included here as well. This placement makes it clear that these foods don't contribute to the overall health benefits of a Mediterranean diet and should be used as complements to the lower sections of the pyramid and not as first choices. In most Mediterranean countries, the use of sweets is portion appropriate, so they are used in the balance suggested by the pyramid. A common dessert in Italy is gelato, which is milk based, thus providing some protein, calcium, phosphorus, and potassium with the sweet. Fruit tarts are common throughout the region and allow for use of in-season fruits.

Red Wine

While not strictly a part of the Mediterranean pyramid, red wine is allowed in moderation on the Mediterranean diet. There are some studies that show that moderate consumption of red wine, in conjunction with a healthy diet, can benefit the cardiovascular system and help prevent heart disease. If you choose to consume wine, drink it with a meal and enjoy it slowly. The wine should enhance your meal, not be its sole focus. It is important to note that if you are unable to limit your alcohol consumption, if you have a family or personal history of alcoholism, or if you have any medical condition that makes drinking alcohol dangerous or triggering to you, you should avoid it entirely.

question

How much wine am I allowed to drink?

It is important to remember that wine should be consumed in moderation, but what does that mean exactly? Well, the definition of moderation depends on a couple of factors. In general, for women and men over the age of sixty-five, drinking 5 ounces (148 milliliters) of wine per day is an appropriate amount. For men under sixty-five years of age, consuming 10 ounces (296 milliliters) of wine per day is an appropriate amount. Keep in mind that an average bottle of wine holds 25 ounces (750 milliliters), or roughly five 5-ounce servings.

Lifestyle Changes

The Mediterranean diet encourages lifestyle changes in addition to dietary changes. The first is to add physical activity into your day. Take a long walk before or after dinner, participate in sports, or even just take the stairs at work instead of the elevator. Adding more movement into your daily routine will improve your health and your mood. Another mood enhancer is to slow down and enjoy your meals with friends and family. Spend time talking, pausing while you eat to enjoy the company of those around you. Finally, drink more water. The Mediterranean diet encourages staying hydrated with water or unsweetened drinks, like coffee or tea. Sugary drinks, like juice or sodas, should be avoided. These changes may seem small, but they can have a big impact on your health over time.

Focus on Plant-Based Foods

The Mediterranean diet has a plant-forward philosophy, meaning that the majority of your meals should be based around plants, whole grains, and healthy fats, and less on meats, dairy, and eggs. This requires that those who eat a standard American diet change the way they think about the food—in particular, meat—they consume. Filling, nutritious, and satisfying meals built around whole-food, plant-based recipes is easy on a Mediterranean diet, especially when you are using the Instant Pot® to save time and make cooking easy.

Build Meals Around Plant-Based Foods

When you plan meals on a Mediterranean diet, start the way they do in the Mediterranean—with vegetables. Whole foods (meaning foods that are minimally processed and fresh) are best. When you plan meals around whole, plant-based foods, you eliminate the risk of consuming the added sugar, fat, and salt commonly found in convenience foods. Plan your meals in advance, making a plan for breakfast, lunch, dinner, snacks, and dessert ahead of time so you can reduce your reliance on meat. For example, try Flax, Date, and Walnut Steel-Cut Oats (Chapter 2) for breakfast, Chilled Pearl Couscous Salad (Chapter 6) for lunch, Provençal Fish Soup (Chapter 11) for dinner, and Peaches Poached in Rose Water

(Chapter 14) for a refreshing dessert. Make more shopping trips to the grocery store per week to ensure you have the freshest vegetables and fruits on hand for meals.

---

essential

Preparing meals in advance is an easy way to keep on track, and it makes life easier during a busy week. Spend time on the weekend selecting a few recipes to make in advance. Cold salads, soups, and stews are all excellent make-ahead options, and you can divide them into reusable containers for lunches and dinners all week. Cooking these dishes over the weekend using your Instant Pot® will take just minutes, so you can prep for the week ahead but still enjoy a relaxing weekend.

Eat Seasonally

Fruits and vegetables taste best when they are eaten in season. Become familiar with what produce is fresh and in season where you live, and base your meal plans on those foods. Visit your local farmer's market and talk to the individuals who are selling fresh produce. Ask them what they love and how they like to prepare it. Seasonal fruits and vegetables have more flavor, pack in more nutrition, and are generally less expensive, so enjoy the finest fruits and vegetables the season has to offer.

Enjoy Healthy Fats

For cooking and making dressings, olive oil should be your go-to choice, but there are other ways to incorporate healthy fats into your diet. For example, add nuts, olives, avocados, and seeds to grain-based salads or leafy green salads;

or incorporate them into dips or dressings. For example, tahini, or sesame paste, can be added to salad dressings to give them richness and a pleasantly nutty flavor. Olives make an excellent snack alone, but can also be added to stews, salads, and egg dishes. Get creative in the ways you add healthy fats to your recipes, and remember to enjoy your fats in moderation.

Think of Meat Differently

When you are planning meals that include meat, think of it more as a supporting player than the star of the show. Red meat should be limited to one or two 3-ounce servings per month. Poultry and pork should be limited to one or two 3-ounce servings per week. Fish and seafood, in 3- to 4-ounce portions, can be enjoyed two times per week as well. There are benefits to eating moderate amounts of meat, but use meat as a complement to more healthful plant-based dishes.

> **fact**
>
> The protein from meat, fish, dairy, and eggs contains amino acids that your body uses to repair and rebuild muscle tissue. If you enjoy working out or weight lifting, or if you are looking for ways to maintain healthy muscle mass, then be sure to include moderate amounts of animal protein in your diet. Plant-based proteins contain some of these amino acids, but not in forms that are as dietarily available as those found in meat, seafood, fish, and poultry.

Remember your Mediterranean diet food pyramid when planning your meals: Build a plate that is at least 50 percent vegetables; 25 percent lentils, pasta, or starchy vegetables; and 25 percent plant-based protein such as legumes or fresh poultry, seafood, fish, or meat. The key is balance; when you find that balance, you will find the key to lifelong health.

Eat What You Love

What good is a diet if you don't eat what you crave and enjoy? Above all, cook and eat foods you love; otherwise, what is the point? Look for recipes that feature vegetables, fruits, and other plant-based ingredients that you truly enjoy, and find ways to modify recipes with ingredients you may not be as fond of. Explore the market and try new foods, and experiment with fresh herbs and spices. Remember that food is more than a way to nourish your body—it's a way to nourish your soul. Finally, try new things. If there is an ingredient in a recipe you have not used before, why not give it a try? You never know what you might like unless you give it a taste. Your new favorite ingredient may be waiting for you to discover it in your local farmer's market.

Instant Pot® Basics

The Instant Pot® is perhaps your greatest tool when it comes to saving time in the kitchen. It cooks quickly and preserves more nutrients, and, since your Instant Pot® can also brown foods, you don't need to dirty any other pots and pans. For a Mediterranean diet, your Instant Pot® is an invaluable tool for preparing pasta, grains, beans, and vegetables quickly and easily.

The Instant Pot® is programmed with a number of cooking functions that have been developed and tested by the manufacturer to cook certain foods in certain amounts. For more detailed information about each function (including cook time and pressure level) of your specific model, you will need to refer to your owner's manual.

Pressure Functions

The Instant Pot® can be used manually, allowing you to select your preferred pressure and cook time. It also comes with a number of preprogrammed function buttons that have been calibrated for cooking specific types of foods.

Manual Pressure Cooking

The Manual/Pressure button allows you to set your own pressure and time for cooking. This may be the button you use most when pressure cooking, as it is the easiest to customize for precision cooking. The Manual/Pressure setting will automatically default to high pressure, but you can manually set the pressure by pressing the -/+ buttons from Low to High, depending on what you are cooking. Once you seal the pot, you will need to set your timer using the -/+ buttons. The Instant Pot® will take about 10–15 minutes to come to full pressure. Once it reaches full pressure, the countdown timer will start and all you need to do is sit back, relax, and let the Instant Pot® do all the work. Remember: Never open the lid while the machine is coming to pressure, and do not try to open the lid once the machine has reached full pressure. If for any reason you need to end cooking early or stop the machine as it is coming to pressure, press Cancel and let any pressure release naturally.

> **essential**
>
> When using a pan or other cooking dish inside your Instant Pot®, a foil sling makes removing the dish safe and easy. Add the cooking rack and liquid to the pot. Next, fold a long piece of foil (long enough to fit over the cooking rack and come up and over the sides) in half lengthwise. Place the pan or cooking dish on the center of the foil and use the two ends to lower it into the pot. When cooking is complete, remove the lid, and use the ends of the sling to remove the cooking vessel. Be sure to use pot holders—the foil may be hot.

Preset Cooking Functions

If you choose, you can use one of the many preset functions programmed into your Instant Pot®. These functions are programmed with suggested cooking times for certain foods in certain volumes, as tested by the manufacturer. These can be a handy place to start, but please keep in mind that some manual adjustments may be needed to ensure thorough cooking. For example, the Instant Pot® does not know if you are starting with fresh or frozen foods, or how much food you are cooking by weight or volume. These buttons are meant to get you close to your desired cooking time, so they can be a good place to start when you are unsure about which pressure level and time to use. Please review your owner's manual for information about each of your specific model's programmed functions, including pressure level and cooking time. While each model is different, some of the most common programmed functions include Soup/Broth, Meat/Stew, Bean/Chili, Rice, Poultry, and Steam.

Nonpressure Functions

If you are thinking that the Instant Pot® is only a pressure cooker, think again! You may indeed use your Instant Pot® primarily for pressure cooking, but it can do so much more. The Instant Pot® has a number of nonpressure cooking options that make it a reliable replacement for small appliances like slow cookers, warming pots, yogurt makers, electric sauté pans, and rice cookers.

Sauté

Sautéing is the process of cooking food over fairly high heat with a small amount of fat, such as oil or butter, added to the pan. The Instant Pot® Sauté function allows you to brown meats, soften vegetables, and thicken sauces all inside the inner pot. This function may be the one you depend on most because browning meats and vegetables gives your food more flavor, and doing it all in the same pot will add even more flavor to your finished dishes. Depending on your model, the temperature of the Sauté setting can be changed by pressing either the Adjust button or the -/+ buttons. The machine is ready when the display reads Hot. You can also use Sauté after pressure cooking to reduce soups, stews, and pan juices, or to thicken gravy.

Slow Cook

When you use this function, your Instant Pot® will behave just like a traditional slow cooker. The default time for most models is 4 hours, but the time can be adjusted to suit your recipe. You can also adjust the temperature to Low, Normal, or High. Be sure to add about 1–2 cups of liquid to the Instant Pot® when using it as a slow cooker to help evenly distribute the heat. The lid can be used with this function, but make sure the steam release is set to Venting to avoid pressure buildup.

Yogurt

With the Instant Pot®, homemade yogurt is nearly impossible to mess up. You can make both dairy and nondairy yogurts, so you can produce yogurt for most diets. All you need is the milk of your choice, and either a live yogurt culture or unsweetened prepared yogurt with a live active culture. Use store-bought plain yogurt for an initial batch, then reserve a small amount of your own homemade yogurt to use in the future. You have the option to make the yogurt directly in the pot or in smaller heatproof jars. If you are making yogurt using the jars, make sure they are sanitized. Place the jars on a rack in the Instant Pot®, and use a small amount of water in the pot to generate heat and steam for incubating your yogurt culture.

Keep Warm

Keep Warm does exactly what the name suggests: It keeps your food at a safe temperature until you are ready to serve it. Keep Warm will start automatically after any programmed or manual cooking ends, so if your food is ready but you are not, your food will be kept warm until you're ready to eat. Keep Warm will automatically shut off after 10 hours if you do not turn off the machine. However, if you open and close the lid, it will not turn off Keep Warm—so you can use your Instant Pot® as a warming pot for a potluck or party.

Other Buttons

Along with the buttons that set cooking settings, there are a number of buttons that allow you to make adjustments and customizations to these settings. You may need to adjust the pressure you use for a certain cut of meat or increase the cooking time for rice, oats, or other foods. These settings may vary by model, but in general, they include the following options.

Pressure Level/Pressure

You may need to adjust the pressure used for cooking food based on your recipe. When that happens, press the Pressure or Pressure Level button within 10 seconds of selecting your cooking program, and then select the pressure you prefer. In general, you will use high pressure more often than low pressure. Most electric pressure cooker recipes are formulated using high pressure, so when in doubt, use high pressure. The one major exception is eggs, which come out better when cooked using low pressure.

Delay Start/Timer

This feature can be used for pressure and nonpressure cooking. Load the Instant Pot® with your ingredients, then press the cooking function you want, or use your Manual/Pressure button and set to your desired cooking time and pressure. Then, within 10 seconds, press the Delay Start or Timer button and set the time to wait before beginning cooking. Press Delay Start or Timer button once to set the hours and then press Delay Start or Timer a *second time* to set the minutes. This function is best for cooking food like grains, oats, beans, and vegetables.

Keep Warm and Keep Warm/Cancel

While there is a Keep Warm function, there is also a Keep Warm button—and on some models, a combined Keep Warm/Cancel button. The Cancel button on the Instant Pot® will cancel a program you have selected. The Keep Warm button will set your food to the Keep Warm function. For the combined Keep Warm/Cancel button, pressing it once will cancel the program currently running. If you press the button a second time it will activate Keep Warm mode.

Adjust

This button has a lot of different functions depending on what kind of cooking you are doing. When pressure cooking, press Adjust to change the cook times of the programmed cooking functions, such as Soup and Poultry, but not other functions, like Rice, which are fully automatic. If you press Adjust after pressing Sauté or Slow Cook, you can adjust the temperature of those features to Low, Normal, or High. Finally, Adjust can select different programs: Less for fermenting glutinous rice, Normal for incubating yogurt culture, and High for pasteurizing milk prior to yogurt making, in the Yogurt setting.

Preparing Foods for Pressure Cooking

The Instant Pot® makes cooking quick and easy as long as you know a few tips. First, verify that the item you intend to cook fits in the pot. Larger items like potatoes, large pieces of meat, or long vegetables like carrots or celery might not fit well if left whole, so you may need to cut them into small pieces. Smaller pieces also cook more quickly than larger ones, so you may need to make adjustments to cooking time. If you plan to use a pan or dish in the Instant Pot®, make sure that it will fit without touching the sides of the liner. Items cooked inside a second vessel should be placed on a metal rack inside the pot so that steam can form easily; make sure there is adequate space around the edges of the pot to allow for steam to circulate in the Instant Pot®.

Finally, cut vegetables of similar density into similar sizes so they will cook uniformly. When cooking firm and soft vegetables at the same time, it is a good idea to cut the firm vegetables into smaller pieces than the softer vegetables.

alert

Never fill your Instant Pot® more than two-thirds full with meat or vegetables, and never fill the pot past the indicated max fill line on the inside of the pot. Overfilling the pot clogs the pressure release and float valve, and prevents the machine from coming to pressure properly. If you do accidentally overfill the machine, make sure you allow any pressure to release naturally before opening the steam release and removing the lid.

The Importance of Browning

Browned food, in particular browned meats and poultry, have a richer, deeper flavor. If you need to save time, you can skip the browning step. Keep in mind, however, that browned food looks more appealing and simply tastes better. Since the Instant Pot® has a Sauté function, you can sear and brown meats, and soften vegetables without dirtying a second pan. The browned bits of food at the bottom of the pot are full of flavor, so add a little of the cooking liquid to the hot pot and scrape up any browned bits.

Maintenance and Cleaning

Maintaining your Instant Pot® will ensure you have many happy years of cooking ahead of you. The owner's manual has specific information for care and maintenance of your particular model, but there are a few basic things you can do to keep your machine working properly.

Maintenance

A little preventative maintenance can go a long way. Regularly inspect the power cord for damage, discoloration, or other defects. If the Instant Pot® smells like it is burning, if the power cord feels hot, or if the machine is heating abnormally, unplug it immediately and discontinue use. If the body of the machine becomes dented or damaged, if the lid is not closing properly, or if you notice any changes to the performance of the machine, you should discontinue use and contact the manufacturer for assistance.

Cleaning

The most valuable maintenance you can do is to properly and thoroughly clean your Instant Pot® after each use (once it has completely cooled). Take time to wipe down the body of the machine inside and out, and clean the lid and sealing ring with warm water and mild detergent. Never immerse the body of the Instant Pot® in water. Use a damp cloth to clean off any food or debris. Clean the steam release and float valve, taking time to inspect them for clogs or debris. Be sure the inner pot is clean, grease free, thoroughly dry, and free from dents and deep scratches. Clean the power cord and prongs to remove any dust or debris, and be sure to unplug the cord when the machine is not in use.

CHAPTER 2

Breakfast

Greek Yogurt

Per Serving:

Calories	202
Fat	11g
Protein	10g
Sodium	143mg
Fiber	0g
Carbohydrates	16g
Sugar	17g

STERILIZATION

Make sure all the utensils, as well as the cooking pot and storage container, are sterilized. When you make yogurt, you are incubating good bacteria. If there are any bad bacteria in the pot or clinging to the utensils, you run the risk of incubating them too, and the yogurt will spoil very quickly. Sterilization does not take long, and it is worth it when you enjoy your own homemade yogurt.

Homemade yogurt is easier than you might think when you have the Instant Pot® and a digital thermometer. Make it a part of your weekly meal prep routine. Yogurt will keep for up to 5 days in the refrigerator.

8 cups whole or 2% milk
2 tablespoons plain low-fat yogurt with live active cultures

1 Before starting, sterilize all equipment, including digital thermometer, whisk, storage jars, and the inner pot, by thoroughly rinsing each with boiling water.

2 Place milk in inner pot. Close lid and set steam release to Sealing. Press the Yogurt button and press the Adjust button until "Boil" is indicated. When the timer beeps, "Yogt" will display. Quick-release the pressure until the float valve drops and open lid. Check temperature with sterilized digital thermometer to ensure milk has reached 180°F.

3 Remove any skin from milk. Place inner pot in an ice water bath, whisking occasionally without scraping the bottom or sides of the pot, until milk reaches 110°F, about 5–7 minutes. Lift pot from ice water bath and dry thoroughly.

4 Whisk together 1 cup heated milk with yogurt in a small bowl, then stir yogurt mixture into pot. Place inner pot back into machine, close lid, press the Yogurt button, and set time to 10 hours. When the timer beeps, "Yogt" will display. Open lid and transfer yogurt to a storage container, and refrigerate for at least 2 hours.

5 Remove yogurt from refrigerator and spoon into a fine-mesh strainer lined with three layers of cheesecloth or a coffee filter. Place strainer over a medium bowl, cover with plastic wrap, and refrigerate overnight. The next day, transfer thickened yogurt to an airtight container and discard the water and cheesecloth.

Steel-Cut Oatmeal with Fruit

You can substitute other dried fruit according to your tastes. Try prunes, dates, and cherries for different flavors. Adding butter to this recipe gives it additional flavor and helps prevent the oatmeal from foaming, which can clog the pressure release valve. Top the oatmeal with brown sugar or maple syrup, chopped nuts, and milk or cream.

3 cups water, divided
1 cup toasted steel-cut oats
2 teaspoons unsalted butter
1 cup apple juice
1 tablespoon dried cranberries
1 tablespoon golden raisins
1 tablespoon snipped dried apricots
1 tablespoon maple syrup
¼ teaspoon ground cinnamon
⅛ teaspoon salt

1 Pour ½ cup water into the Instant Pot® and add rack. Fold a long piece of aluminum foil in half lengthwise. Lay foil over rack to form a sling.

2 In a metal bowl that fits inside pot, add remaining 2½ cups water, oats, butter, apple juice, cranberries, raisins, apricots, maple syrup, cinnamon, and salt. Stir to combine. Place bowl in the pot so it rests on the sling.

3 Close lid, set steam release to Sealing, press the Manual button, and set time to 5 minutes for chewy oatmeal or 8 minutes for creamy oatmeal.

4 When the timer beeps, let pressure release naturally, about 20 minutes. Open lid and carefully lift bowl out of the Instant Pot® using the sling. Spoon the cooked oats into bowls. Serve warm.

SERVES 2	
Per Serving:	
Calories	278
Fat	6g
Protein	6g
Sodium	179mg
Fiber	5g
Carbohydrates	51g
Sugar	22g

COOKING AHEAD

If you're not a morning person, you can make Steel-Cut Oatmeal with Fruit the night before. Once it's cooled, divide between two covered microwave-safe containers and refrigerate overnight. The next morning, microwave on high for 1 to 2 minutes or until heated through.

Almond Date Oatmeal

SERVES 4	
Per Serving:	
Calories	451
Fat	25g
Protein	14g
Sodium	320mg
Fiber	9g
Carbohydrates	52g
Sugar	16g

Dates are naturally sweet and add a caramelized flavor to this oatmeal. Add a few drops of vanilla extract after cooking if you want to further enhance the flavor of the oatmeal.

1 cup sliced almonds
4 cups water
2 cups rolled oats
1 tablespoon extra-virgin olive oil
¼ teaspoon salt
½ cup chopped pitted dates

1 Press the Sauté button on the Instant Pot® and add almonds. Toast, stirring constantly, until almonds are golden brown, about 8 minutes. Press the Cancel button and add water, oats, oil, salt, and dates to the pot. Stir well. Close lid and set steam release to Sealing. Press the Manual button and set time to 4 minutes.

2 When the timer beeps, quick-release the pressure until the float valve drops, open lid, and stir well. Serve hot.

Quinoa and Yogurt Breakfast Bowls

SERVES 8	
Per Serving:	
Calories	376
Fat	13g
Protein	16g
Sodium	105mg
Fiber	6g
Carbohydrates	52g
Sugar	18g

These breakfast bowls are wonderfully warm, but you can also prepare them in advance, layering the quinoa and fruit into jars for breakfasts on the go. Mix up the fruit and nuts for more flavors.

2 cups quinoa, rinsed and drained
4 cups water
1 teaspoon vanilla extract
¼ teaspoon salt

2 cups low-fat plain Greek yogurt
2 cups blueberries
1 cup toasted almonds
½ cup pure maple syrup

1 Place quinoa, water, vanilla, and salt in the Instant Pot®. Close lid and set steam release to Sealing. Press the Rice button and set time to 12 minutes.

2 When the timer beeps, let pressure release naturally, about 20 minutes. Open lid and fluff quinoa with a fork.

3 Stir in yogurt. Serve warm, topped with berries, almonds, and maple syrup.

Baked Eggs with Ham and Kale

Creamy kale, poached eggs, and browned ham make this a perfect dish for company but also easy enough for every day. Replace the ham with a pound of sliced mushrooms to make the dish vegetarian.

1 tablespoon olive oil
2 cups diced ham
1 medium yellow onion, peeled and chopped
2 pounds chopped kale
½ cup heavy cream
1 (8-ounce) package cream cheese
¼ teaspoon salt
¼ teaspoon ground black pepper
⅛ teaspoon ground nutmeg
6 large eggs
1 cup water

Per Serving:	
Calories	245
Fat	17g
Protein	12g
Sodium	435mg
Fiber	4g
Carbohydrates	10g
Sugar	3g

1 Spray an 8" round baking dish with nonstick cooking spray.

2 Press the Sauté button on the Instant Pot® and heat oil, then add ham. Cook until ham starts to brown, about 5 minutes. Add onion and cook until tender, about 5 minutes, then add kale and cook until wilted, about 5 minutes.

3 Add cream, cream cheese, salt, pepper, and nutmeg, and stir until cream cheese is melted and mixture thickens, about 5 minutes. Press the Cancel button and transfer mixture to prepared baking dish. Clean out pot.

4 Use a spoon to press six indentations into kale mixture. Crack eggs into indentations.

5 Place the rack in the Instant Pot® and add water. Fold a long piece of aluminum foil in half lengthwise. Lay foil over rack to form a sling. Place dish on rack so it rests on the sling and cover loosely with aluminum foil to protect eggs from condensation inside pot. Close lid, set steam release to Sealing, press the Manual button, and set time to 5 minutes.

6 When the timer beeps, quick-release the pressure until the float valve drops. Open lid. Let stand 5 minutes before carefully removing dish from pot with sling. Serve warm.

Red Pepper and Feta Egg Bites

Roasted red peppers are located near the pickles and other condiments in most grocery stores. Be sure to pat them dry with paper towels before adding to the eggs so they aren't watery.

1 tablespoon olive oil
½ cup crumbled feta cheese
¼ cup chopped roasted red peppers
6 large eggs, beaten
¼ teaspoon ground black pepper
1 cup water

1 Brush silicone muffin or poaching cups with oil. Divide feta and roasted red peppers among prepared cups. In a bowl with a pour spout, beat eggs with black pepper.

2 Place rack in the Instant Pot® and add water. Place cups on rack. Pour egg mixture into cups. Close lid, set steam release to Sealing, press the Manual button, and set time to 8 minutes.

3 When the timer beeps, quick-release the pressure until the float valve drops and open lid. Remove silicone cups carefully and slide eggs from cups onto plates. Serve warm.

SERVES 6

Per Serving:

Calories	145
Fat	11g
Protein	10g
Sodium	294mg
Fiber	1g
Carbohydrates	3g
Sugar	1g

ROASTING RED BELL PEPPERS

You can roast peppers easily in your oven. Cut large bell peppers in half and remove the stem and seeds. Place the peppers on a foil-lined baking sheet lightly brushed with olive oil. Place peppers under a preheated broiler for 10 minutes, or until the skin of the peppers is blistered and charred. Carefully transfer peppers to a medium bowl and cover with plastic wrap. Let peppers steam for 15 minutes. When cool enough to handle, rub the charred skin off the peppers. Store in the refrigerator in an airtight container for up to a week.

Egg Salad with Red Pepper and Dill

Making hard-cooked eggs in the Instant Pot® will give you consistent results each and every time. Here, those eggs are made into a refreshing breakfast egg salad, perfect as a topping on whole-grain toast.

6 large eggs
1 cup water
1 tablespoon olive oil
1 medium red bell pepper, seeded and chopped
¼ teaspoon salt
¼ teaspoon ground black pepper
½ cup low-fat plain Greek yogurt
2 tablespoons chopped fresh dill

1 Have ready a large bowl of ice water. Place rack or egg holder into bottom of the Instant Pot®.

2 Arrange eggs on rack or holder and add water to the Instant Pot®. Close lid, set steam release to Sealing, press the Manual button, and set time to 5 minutes.

3 When the timer beeps, let pressure release naturally for 5 minutes, then quick-release the remaining pressure until the float valve drops. Press the Cancel button and open lid. Carefully transfer eggs to the bowl of ice water. Let stand in ice water for 10 minutes, then peel, chop, and add eggs to a medium bowl.

4 Clean out pot, dry well, and return to machine. Press the Sauté button and heat oil. Add bell pepper, salt, and black pepper. Cook, stirring often, until bell pepper is tender, about 5 minutes. Transfer to bowl with eggs.

5 Add yogurt and dill to bowl, and fold to combine. Cover and chill for 1 hour before serving.

Peachy Oatmeal with Pecans

This oatmeal is a summertime treat. Fresh, ripe peaches are the star of the show, while toasted pecans add crunch and a rich, nutty flavor. Look for peaches that are firm, but not hard, and that have a strong peachy aroma.

4 cups water
2 cups rolled oats
1 tablespoon light olive oil
1 large peach, peeled, pitted, and diced
¼ teaspoon salt
½ cup toasted pecans
2 tablespoons maple syrup

SERVES 4	
Per Serving:	
Calories	399
Fat	27g
Protein	8g
Sodium	148mg
Fiber	7g
Carbohydrates	35g
Sugar	5g

1 Place water, oats, oil, peach, and salt in the Instant Pot®. Stir well. Close lid, set steam release to Sealing, press the Manual button, and set time to 4 minutes.

2 When the timer beeps, quick-release the pressure until the float valve drops. Press the Cancel button, open lid, and stir well. Serve oatmeal topped with pecans and maple syrup.

Buckwheat Porridge with Fresh Fruit

Buckwheat is naturally gluten-free, an excellent source of dietary fiber and protein, and a good source of minerals, such as zinc, copper, niacin, and magnesium. If you want extra-rich porridge, use almond milk in place of all or part of the water.

1 cup buckwheat groats, rinsed and drained
3 cups water
½ cup chopped pitted dates
1 tablespoon light olive oil
¼ teaspoon ground cinnamon
¼ teaspoon salt
½ teaspoon vanilla extract
1 cup blueberries
1 cup raspberries
1 cup hulled and quartered strawberries
2 tablespoons balsamic vinegar

SERVES 4	
Per Serving:	
Calories	318
Fat	5g
Protein	6g
Sodium	151mg
Fiber	9g
Carbohydrates	64g
Sugar	21g

1 Place buckwheat, water, dates, oil, cinnamon, and salt in the Instant Pot® and stir well. Close lid and set steam release to Sealing. Press the Manual button and set time to 6 minutes.

2 When the timer beeps, let pressure release naturally, about 20 minutes. Open lid and stir in vanilla.

3 While buckwheat cooks, combine blueberries, raspberries, strawberries, and vinegar in a medium bowl. Stir well. Top porridge with berry mixture. Serve hot.

Spinach and Feta Frittata

SERVES 4	
Per Serving:	
Calories	303
Fat	23g
Protein	21g
Sodium	1,096mg
Fiber	2g
Carbohydrates	7g
Sugar	2g

FETA CHEESE

Feta is a brined curd cheese from Greece. In order to be officially labeled as "feta," it must be made from sheep's milk, or a sheep and goat milk blend. It can be found in blocks, cubed, or crumbled in containers, and it is often packaged in brine to prevent it from drying out. In the Mediterranean, it is served as a table cheese with meals so people can add as much or as little as they would like to their plates. It has a salty, tangy flavor that makes it a great garnish.

Traditional frittatas require you to babysit the pan on the stove, carefully watching the eggs to keep them from burning. In the Instant Pot®, your frittata will cook to perfection while you relax.

1 tablespoon olive oil
½ medium onion, peeled and chopped
½ medium red bell pepper, seeded and chopped
2 cups chopped fresh baby spinach
1 cup water
1 cup crumbled feta cheese
6 large eggs, beaten
¼ cup low-fat plain Greek yogurt
½ teaspoon salt
½ teaspoon ground black pepper

1   Press the Sauté button on the Instant Pot® and heat oil. Add onion and bell pepper, and cook until tender, about 8 minutes. Add spinach and cook until wilted, about 3 minutes. Press the Cancel button and transfer vegetables to a medium bowl to cool. Wipe out inner pot.

2   Place the rack in the Instant Pot® and add water. Spray a 1.5-liter baking dish with nonstick cooking spray. Drain excess liquid from spinach mixture, then add to dish with cheese.

3   In a separate medium bowl, mix eggs, yogurt, salt, and black pepper until well combined. Pour over vegetable and cheese mixture. Cover dish tightly with foil, then gently lower into machine.

4   Close lid, set steam release to Sealing, press the Manual button, and set time to 15 minutes. When the timer beeps, let pressure release naturally for 10 minutes, then quick-release any remaining pressure until the float valve drops. Press the Cancel button and open lid. Let stand for 10–15 minutes before carefully removing dish from pot.

5   Run a thin knife around the edge of the frittata and turn it out onto a serving platter. Serve warm.

Tomato and Asparagus Frittata

This frittata is an excellent way to use leftover asparagus. If you don't have any on hand, you can quickly cook the asparagus in the Instant Pot® using the Sauté setting and a teaspoon of olive oil. Sauté for 3–4 minutes.

1 cup water
1 teaspoon olive oil
1 cup halved cherry tomatoes
1 cup cooked asparagus tips
¼ cup grated Parmesan cheese
6 large eggs
¼ cup low-fat plain Greek yogurt
½ teaspoon salt
½ teaspoon ground black pepper

SERVES 4	
Per Serving:	
Calories	170
Fat	11g
Protein	14g
Sodium	509mg
Fiber	1g
Carbohydrates	4g
Sugar	1g

1 Place the rack in the Instant Pot® and add water. Brush a 1.5-liter baking dish with olive oil. Add tomatoes, asparagus, and cheese to dish.

2 In a medium bowl, beat eggs, yogurt, salt, and pepper. Pour over vegetable and cheese mixture. Cover dish tightly with aluminum foil, then gently lower into machine.

3 Close lid, set steam release to Sealing, press the Manual button, and set time to 15 minutes. When the timer beeps, let pressure release naturally for 10 minutes, then quick-release any remaining pressure until the float valve drops. Press the Cancel button and open lid. Let stand for 10–15 minutes before carefully removing dish from pot.

4 Run a thin knife around the edge of the frittata and turn it out onto a serving platter. Serve warm.

Oatmeal with Apple and Cardamom

SERVES 4

Per Serving:	
Calories	249
Fat	6g
Protein	6g
Sodium	298mg
Fiber	5g
Carbohydrates	48g
Sugar	18g

ALL ABOUT CARDAMOM

Native to India, but also popular in Middle Eastern and Scandinavian dishes, cardamom is made from the pods and seeds of plants in the ginger family. While there are green and black varieties, green cardamom is most commonly found in US grocery stores. Cardamom is sold as ground seeds or whole seed pods. Its complex, citrusy flavor can be enhanced by toasting the whole seed pods before use. When cooking with whole seed pods, be sure to gently crush them to release their delicate flavor.

Cardamom has an earthy taste with a bright citrus flavor. It makes a unique change from cinnamon in your breakfast oats. It is also a powerful antioxidant, and some studies show that it may help lower blood pressure.

1 tablespoon light olive oil
1 large Granny Smith, Honeycrisp, or Pink Lady apple, peeled, cored, and diced
½ teaspoon ground cardamom
1 cup steel-cut oats
3 cups water
¼ cup maple syrup
½ teaspoon salt

1 Press the Sauté button on the Instant Pot® and heat oil. Add apple and cardamom and cook until apple is just softened, about 2 minutes. Press the Cancel button.

2 Add oats, water, maple syrup, and salt to pot, and stir well. Close lid, set steam release to Sealing, press the Manual button, and set time to 5 minutes.

3 When the timer beeps, let pressure release naturally for 10 minutes, then quick-release the remaining pressure until the float valve drops. Press the Cancel button, open lid, and stir well. Serve hot.

Eggs Poached in Tomato Sauce

SERVES 6

Per Serving:

Calories	151
Fat	10g
Protein	9g
Sodium	189mg
Fiber	1g
Carbohydrates	10g
Sugar	5g

This dish is great as part of a lazy weekend breakfast or brunch. Serve the eggs with slices of toasted whole-grain bread, creamy polenta, or a vegetable and potato hash. If you prefer your tomato sauce extra spicy, add as much crushed red pepper flakes as you like.

2 tablespoons olive oil
1 medium onion, peeled and chopped
1 clove garlic, peeled and minced
1 (15-ounce) can tomato purée
2 medium tomatoes, seeded and diced
2 tablespoons chopped fresh oregano
½ teaspoon ground fennel
¼ teaspoon salt
¼ teaspoon ground black pepper
¼ teaspoon crushed red pepper flakes
6 large eggs

1 Press the Sauté button on the Instant Pot® and heat oil. Add onion and cook until tender, about 5 minutes. Add garlic and cook until fragrant, about 30 seconds. Add tomato purée, diced tomatoes, oregano, fennel, salt, black pepper, and crushed red pepper, and stir well. Cook until mixture starts to bubble, about 3 minutes, then press the Cancel button.

2 Carefully crack eggs one at a time into a small ramekin and carefully turn out into sauce, making sure eggs are spaced out evenly. Close lid, set steam release to Sealing, press the Manual button, adjust pressure to Low, and set time to 0 minutes. When the timer beeps, quick-release the pressure until the float valve drops, press the Cancel button, open lid, and serve.

Spinach and Feta Steamed Eggs

This version of the traditional French recipe oeufs en cocotte *can be ready in a flash, and offers a healthy start to the day with sautéed spinach, garlic, and scallions. If you're not a fan of feta cheese, substitute with goat cheese or Brie. Serve with whole-grain toast for dipping into the egg.*

2 tablespoons olive oil, divided

2 cups chopped baby spinach

1 scallion, chopped

1 clove garlic, peeled and minced

¼ teaspoon salt

¼ teaspoon ground black pepper

2 tablespoons low-fat plain Greek yogurt

2 tablespoons crumbled feta cheese

2 large eggs

1 cup water

1 Press the Sauté button on the Instant Pot® and heat 1 tablespoon oil. Add spinach and scallion and cook until spinach wilts, about 3 minutes. Add garlic and cook until fragrant, about 30 seconds. Press the Cancel button.

2 Brush two 4-ounce ramekins with remaining 1 tablespoon oil. Divide spinach mixture between ramekins, then season with salt and pepper. Spread yogurt over spinach, top with feta, and crack egg over the top of each ramekin.

3 Clean and dry pot. Place rack in the pot and add water. Place ramekins on rack. Close lid, set steam release to Sealing, press the Manual button, adjust pressure to Low, and set time to 2 minutes. When the timer beeps, quick-release the pressure until the float valve drops. Press the Cancel button, open lid, and carefully transfer ramekins to plates. Serve immediately.

SERVES 2	
Per Serving:	
Calories	265
Fat	21g
Protein	13g
Sodium	665mg
Fiber	1g
Carbohydrates	6g
Sugar	1g

IN A BREAKFAST RUT?

It is easy to fall into a breakfast rut when you make the same things day after day. Cooking with the Instant Pot® can rescue you from this breakfast burnout. You can quickly and easily prepare a variety of breakfast dishes that are ready in a flash, allowing you to have a different breakfast every day of the week. When you eat a variety of foods, you are more likely to stay satisfied and stick with your new healthy lifestyle.

Quinoa Porridge with Apricots

SERVES 4	
Per Serving:	
Calories	197
Fat	2g
Protein	3g
Sodium	293mg
Fiber	4g
Carbohydrates	44g
Sugar	24g

Rose water and cardamom give this breakfast porridge a Middle Eastern flair, but if you can't find rose water or don't care for its flavor, substitute ½ teaspoon vanilla extract and ¼ teaspoon almond extract.

1½ cups quinoa, rinsed and drained
1 cup chopped dried apricots
2½ cups water
1 cup almond milk
1 tablespoon rose water
½ teaspoon cardamom
¼ teaspoon salt

1 Place all ingredients in the Instant Pot®. Stir to combine. Close lid, set steam release to Sealing, press the Rice button, and set time to 12 minutes. When the timer beeps, let pressure release naturally, about 20 minutes.

2 Press the Cancel button, open lid, and fluff quinoa with a fork. Serve warm.

Nuts and Fruit Oatmeal

SERVES 2	
Per Serving:	
Calories	362
Fat	8g
Protein	7g
Sodium	164mg
Fiber	8g
Carbohydrates	69g
Sugar	33g

Instead of waking up to plain old oatmeal, enjoy this bowl of flavors and warmth that will have you doing a jig out the door—no matter the weather. This dish is absolutely perfect for a cold morning when you need a little extra get-up-and-go.

1 cup rolled oats
1¼ cups water
¼ cup orange juice
1 medium pear, peeled, cored, and cubed
¼ cup dried cherries
¼ cup chopped walnuts
1 tablespoon honey
¼ teaspoon ground ginger
¼ teaspoon ground cinnamon
⅛ teaspoon salt

1 Place oats, water, orange juice, pear, cherries, walnuts, honey, ginger, cinnamon, and salt in the Instant Pot®. Stir to combine.

2 Close lid, set steam release to Sealing, press the Manual button, and set time to 7 minutes. When the timer beeps, let pressure release naturally, about 20 minutes. Press the Cancel button, open lid, and stir well. Serve warm.

Banana Walnut Millet Porridge

Millet is a staple across Europe, Asia, and South America, where it is served for breakfast, lunch, or dinner. The flavor is mild and nutty, and is similar to that of cornmeal. You can find millet in the bulk section of most natural food stores.

½ cup millet
½ cup rolled oats
2½ cups almond milk
2 tablespoons maple syrup
1 tablespoon unsalted butter

½ teaspoon ground cinnamon
¼ teaspoon salt
½ teaspoon vanilla extract
1 cup toasted walnuts
2 medium bananas, peeled and sliced

SERVES 4	
Per Serving:	
Calories	476
Fat	25g
Protein	9g
Sodium	242mg
Fiber	7g
Carbohydrates	57g
Sugar	17g

1 Place millet, oats, almond milk, maple syrup, butter, cinnamon, and salt in the Instant Pot® and stir well. Close lid, set steam release to Sealing, press the Manual button, and set time to 6 minutes.

2 When the timer beeps, let pressure release naturally, about 20 minutes. Press the Cancel button, open lid, and stir in vanilla. Serve hot, topped with walnuts and bananas.

Flax, Date, and Walnut Steel-Cut Oats

A tablespoon of flax contains 1,597 milligrams of omega-3 fatty acids, which are linked to a reduced risk of heart disease. To get the maximum nutritional benefit from flax, it's best to eat the ground version. For extra crunch, sprinkle a few whole flaxseeds on top as a garnish.

1 tablespoon light olive oil
1 cup steel-cut oats
3 cups water
⅓ cup chopped pitted dates
¼ cup ground flax
¼ teaspoon salt
½ cup toasted chopped walnuts

SERVES 4	
Per Serving:	
Calories	322
Fat	18g
Protein	10g
Sodium	150mg
Fiber	8g
Carbohydrates	42g
Sugar	10g

1 Place oil, oats, water, dates, flax, and salt in the Instant Pot® and stir well. Close lid, set steam release to Sealing, press the Manual button, and set time to 5 minutes.

2 When the timer beeps, let pressure release naturally for 10 minutes, then quick-release the remaining pressure until the float valve drops. Press the Cancel button, open lid, and stir in walnuts. Serve hot.

Chickpea Hash with Eggs

If you prefer, poach the eggs or fry them in a little olive oil in a skillet on the stove rather than using sliced hard-cooked eggs. You can also use soft-cooked eggs instead, but those should be left whole or simply sliced in half.

1 cup dried chickpeas

4 cups water

2 tablespoons extra-virgin olive oil, divided

1 medium onion, peeled and chopped

1 medium zucchini, trimmed and sliced

1 large red bell pepper, seeded and chopped

1 teaspoon minced garlic

½ teaspoon ground cumin

½ teaspoon ground black pepper

¼ teaspoon salt

4 large hard-cooked eggs, peeled and halved

½ teaspoon smoked paprika

1 Place chickpeas, water, and 1 tablespoon oil in the Instant Pot®. Close lid, set steam release to Sealing, press the Manual button, and set time to 30 minutes.

2 When the timer beeps, quick-release the pressure until the float valve drops, press the Cancel button, and open lid. Drain chickpeas well, transfer to a medium bowl, and set aside.

3 Clean and dry pot. Return to machine, press the Sauté button, and heat remaining 1 tablespoon oil. Add onion, zucchini, and bell pepper. Cook until tender, about 5 minutes. Add garlic, cumin, black pepper, and salt and cook for 30 seconds. Add chickpeas and turn to coat.

4 Transfer chickpea mixture to a serving platter. Top with eggs and paprika and serve immediately.

SERVES 4	
Per Serving:	
Calories	274
Fat	14g
Protein	15g
Sodium	242mg
Fiber	16g
Carbohydrates	36g
Sugar	5g

BREAKFAST HASH

Most people think of corned beef hash when they think of a breakfast hash, but a hash can be made of just about any ingredients you like. A hash usually includes a type of protein, chopped vegetables, and some form of onion. While meat is traditional, you can replace it with a healthy plant-based protein like legumes or tofu. Eggs are also traditionally served with hash but are totally optional. Hash can be enjoyed any time of day; in fact, it makes a hearty and filling dinner.

Amaranth Breakfast Bowl with Chocolate and Almonds

If you love chocolate, this breakfast recipe is for you. Topping hot amaranth with a sprinkle of miniature chocolate chips gives the chocolate a bigger impact so you do not need as much to be satisfied. You can substitute toasted pecans for the almonds, if you prefer.

SERVES 6	
Per Serving:	
Calories	263
Fat	12g
Protein	5g
Sodium	212mg
Fiber	5g
Carbohydrates	35g
Sugar	21g

2 cups amaranth, rinsed and drained
2 cups almond milk
2 cups water
¼ cup maple syrup
3 tablespoons cocoa powder
1 teaspoon vanilla extract
¼ teaspoon salt
½ cup toasted sliced almonds
⅓ cup miniature semisweet chocolate chips

1 Place amaranth, almond milk, water, maple syrup, cocoa powder, vanilla, and salt in the Instant Pot®. Stir to combine. Close lid, set steam release to Sealing, press the Rice button, and set time to 6 minutes. When the timer beeps, quick-release the pressure until the float valve drops, press the Cancel button, open lid, and stir well.

2 Serve hot, topped with almonds and chocolate chips.

Breakfast Quinoa with Figs and Walnuts

Fresh figs are available from August to October. Look for figs that are slightly wrinkled but still plump, with stems that bend a bit when pressed. Figs pair well with tangy yogurt and nuts, both of which are featured in this unusual breakfast.

SERVES 4	
Per Serving:	
Calories	413
Fat	25g
Protein	10g
Sodium	275mg
Fiber	7g
Carbohydrates	52g
Sugar	37g

1½ cups quinoa, rinsed and drained
2½ cups water
1 cup almond milk
2 tablespoons honey
1 teaspoon vanilla extract
½ teaspoon ground cinnamon
¼ teaspoon salt
½ cup low-fat plain Greek yogurt
8 fresh figs, quartered
1 cup chopped toasted walnuts

1 Place quinoa, water, almond milk, honey, vanilla, cinnamon, and salt in the Instant Pot®. Stir to combine. Close lid, set steam release to Sealing, press the Rice button, and set time to 12 minutes. When the timer beeps, let pressure release naturally, about 20 minutes.

2 Press the Cancel button, open lid, and fluff quinoa with a fork. Serve warm with yogurt, figs, and walnuts.

Banana Nut Bread Oatmeal

Bananas are high in potassium. Walnuts contain anti-inflammatory omega-3 essential fatty acids. And cinnamon contains manganese and fiber, and is an excellent source of calcium.

1 cup rolled oats
1 cup water
1 cup whole milk
2 ripe bananas, peeled and sliced
2 tablespoons pure maple syrup

2 teaspoons ground cinnamon
¼ teaspoon vanilla extract
2 tablespoons chopped walnuts
⅛ teaspoon salt

SERVES 2	
Per Serving:	
Calories	448
Fat	11g
Protein	11g
Sodium	203mg
Fiber	10g
Carbohydrates	72g
Sugar	39g

1 Place all ingredients in the Instant Pot®. Stir to combine.

2 Close lid, set steam release to Sealing, press the Manual button, and set time to 7 minutes. When the timer beeps, let pressure release naturally, about 20 minutes. Press the Cancel button, open lid, and stir well. Serve warm.

Breakfast Farro with Dried Fruit and Nuts

Farro is a powerhouse grain. A ½-cup serving of cooked farro offers 5–7 grams of fiber and 7 grams of protein. It is also a good source of niacin, magnesium, iron, calcium, and zinc. Farro cooks up with a slightly chewy texture, and has a flavor that is similar to barley, which complements the dried fruit.

16 ounces farro, rinsed and drained
4½ cups water
¼ cup maple syrup
¼ teaspoon salt

1 cup dried mixed fruit
½ cup chopped toasted mixed nuts
2 cups almond milk

SERVES 8	
Per Serving:	
Calories	347
Fat	7g
Protein	9g
Sodium	145mg
Fiber	9g
Carbohydrates	65g
Sugar	17g

1 Place farro, water, maple syrup, and salt in the Instant Pot® and stir to combine. Close lid, set steam release to Sealing, press the Multigrain button, and set time to 20 minutes. When the timer beeps, let pressure release naturally, about 30 minutes.

2 Press the Cancel button, open lid, and add dried fruit. Close lid and let stand on the Keep Warm setting for 20 minutes. Serve warm with nuts and almond milk.

Enjoy-Your-Veggies Breakfast

SERVES 4	
Per Serving:	
Calories	224
Fat	5g
Protein	6g
Sodium	159mg
Fiber	5g
Carbohydrates	41g
Sugar	5g

Add toasted almonds or sunflower seeds to boost the protein in this savory breakfast. If you want even more protein, stir in some diced tofu when you add the water. This vegetable mixture can be rolled up in a whole-wheat tortilla for a handy, portable breakfast.

1 tablespoon olive oil
1 small sweet onion, peeled and diced
2 large carrots, peeled and diced
2 medium potatoes, peeled and diced
1 stalk celery, diced
1 large red bell pepper, seeded and diced
1 tablespoon low-sodium soy sauce
¼ cup water
1 cup diced peeled zucchini or summer squash
2 medium tomatoes, peeled and diced
2 cups cooked brown rice
½ teaspoon ground black pepper

1 Press the Sauté button on the Instant Pot® and heat oil. Add onion and cook until just tender, about 2 minutes.

2 Stir in carrots, potatoes, celery, and bell pepper and cook until just tender, about 2 minutes. Add soy sauce and water. Press the Cancel button.

3 Close lid, set steam release to Sealing, press the Manual button, and set time to 2 minutes. When the timer beeps, quick-release the pressure until the float valve drops. Press the Cancel button.

4 Open lid and add squash and tomatoes, and stir. Close lid, set steam release to Sealing, press the Manual button, and set time to 1 minute. When the timer beeps, quick-release the pressure until the float valve drops. Press the Cancel button and open lid.

5 Serve over rice and sprinkle with black pepper.

CHAPTER 3

Dips and Appetizers

Classic Hummus

Hummus is a nutritious, plant-based snack that is rich in fiber, loaded with good fats, and a good source of nutrients and vitamins. Serve it as a dip for crisp carrots, celery, and cucumber; a topping for grilled fish or chicken; or a side dish with roasted or grilled vegetables.

1 cup dried chickpeas
4 cups water
1 tablespoon plus ¼ cup extra-virgin olive oil, divided
⅓ cup tahini
1½ teaspoons ground cumin
¾ teaspoon salt
½ teaspoon ground black pepper
½ teaspoon ground coriander
⅓ cup lemon juice
1 teaspoon minced garlic

1. Place chickpeas, water, and 1 tablespoon oil in the Instant Pot®. Close the lid, set steam release to Sealing, press the Manual button, and set time to 30 minutes.

2. When the timer beeps, quick-release the pressure until the float valve drops and open lid. Press the Cancel button and open lid. Drain, reserving the cooking liquid.

3. Place chickpeas, remaining ¼ cup oil, tahini, cumin, salt, pepper, coriander, lemon juice, and garlic in a food processor and process until creamy. If hummus is too thick, add reserved cooking liquid 1 tablespoon at a time until it reaches desired consistency. Serve at room temperature.

Roasted Garlic Hummus

Roasted garlic is a delicious condiment to have on hand. Spread it on toast, mix it into sauces, add it to soups, or, in this case, use it to flavor hummus. If you want even more garlic, add 1–2 tablespoons of roasted garlic as a garnish to your hummus along with a drizzle of extra-virgin olive oil.

1 cup dried chickpeas
4 cups water
1 tablespoon plus ¼ cup extra-virgin olive oil, divided
⅓ cup tahini
1 teaspoon ground cumin
½ teaspoon onion powder
¾ teaspoon salt
½ teaspoon ground black pepper
⅓ cup lemon juice
3 tablespoons mashed roasted garlic
2 tablespoons chopped fresh parsley

1   Place chickpeas, water, and 1 tablespoon oil in the Instant Pot®. Close the lid, set steam release to Sealing, press the Manual button, and set time to 30 minutes.

2   When the timer beeps, quick-release the pressure until the float valve drops. Press the Cancel button and open lid. Drain, reserving the cooking liquid.

3   Place chickpeas, remaining ¼ cup oil, tahini, cumin, onion powder, salt, pepper, lemon juice, and roasted garlic in a food processor and process until creamy. If hummus is too thick, add reserved cooking liquid 1 tablespoon at a time until it reaches desired consistency. Top with parsley. Serve at room temperature.

MAKES 2 CUPS

Per Serving (2 tablespoons):

Calories	104
Fat	6g
Protein	4g
Sodium	120mg
Fiber	2g
Carbohydrates	8g
Sugar	1g

ROASTING GARLIC

Roasting garlic at home is easy, and you can roast a few heads of garlic on the weekends for use all week long. Roasted garlic has a sweet, almost buttery flavor, and can be used in all sorts of recipes as a spread or mixed into sauces. To roast garlic, preheat oven to 350°F. Rub the papery skin off the garlic head, slice off the top, and place on a piece of aluminum foil. Drizzle with 1 tablespoon olive oil, season with ⅛ teaspoon each salt and pepper, and wrap in the foil. Bake for about 1 hour, or until the garlic is golden and soft. Cool, then squeeze the garlic cloves into an airtight container. Use immediately or refrigerate for up to 7 days.

Red Pepper Hummus

MAKES 2 CUPS

**Per Serving
(2 tablespoons):**

Calories	96
Fat	8g
Protein	2g
Sodium	122mg
Fiber	4g
Carbohydrates	10g
Sugar	0g

THE HISTORY OF HUMMUS

There is some debate as to the origins of hummus, with both the Greeks and Arabs claiming it as their own. The Arabs may have the more solid claim, as the Arabic word for chickpea is "hummus." There is evidence that a dish very similar to modern-day hummus was eaten as far back as the thirteenth century. While we may never know its true origins, we do know that hummus is a delicious and nutritious part of a balanced diet. Serve it as a dip with toasted pita bread and raw vegetables or use it as a condiment for grilled vegetables and meats.

Roasted red bell peppers have a smoky yet sweet flavor that is enhanced by the creamy chickpeas and tahini in this recipe. If you like spicy foods, add a bit of cayenne pepper. Start with ⅛ teaspoon and add more until it is as spicy as you like.

1 cup dried chickpeas
4 cups water
1 tablespoon plus ¼ cup extra-virgin olive oil, divided
½ cup chopped roasted red pepper, divided
⅓ cup tahini
1 teaspoon ground cumin
¾ teaspoon salt
½ teaspoon ground black pepper
¼ teaspoon smoked paprika
⅓ cup lemon juice
½ teaspoon minced garlic

1 Place chickpeas, water, and 1 tablespoon oil in the Instant Pot®. Close the lid, set steam release to Sealing, press the Manual button, and set time to 30 minutes.

2 When the timer beeps, quick-release the pressure until the float valve drops. Press the Cancel button and open lid. Drain, reserving the cooking liquid.

3 Place chickpeas, ⅓ cup roasted red pepper, remaining ¼ cup oil, tahini, cumin, salt, black pepper, paprika, lemon juice, and garlic in a food processor and process until creamy. If hummus is too thick, add reserved cooking liquid 1 tablespoon at a time until it reaches desired consistency. Serve at room temperature, garnished with reserved roasted red pepper on top.

White Bean Hummus

Dress up hummus by adding minced roasted red peppers, pesto, or just a drizzle of olive oil and smoked paprika to the top. Use carrots and cucumbers for dippers.

SERVES 12	
Per Serving:	
Calories	57
Fat	5g
Protein	1g
Sodium	99mg
Fiber	1g
Carbohydrates	3g
Sugar	0g

⅔ cup dried white beans, rinsed and drained

3 cloves garlic, peeled and crushed

¼ cup olive oil

1 tablespoon lemon juice

½ teaspoon salt

1 Place beans and garlic in the Instant Pot® and stir well. Add enough cold water to cover ingredients. Close lid, set steam release to Sealing, press the Manual button, and set time to 30 minutes.

2 When the timer beeps, let pressure release naturally, about 20 minutes. Press the Cancel button and open lid. Use a fork to check that beans are tender. Drain off excess water and transfer beans to a food processor.

3 Add oil, lemon juice, and salt to the processor and pulse until mixture is smooth with some small chunks. Transfer to a storage container and refrigerate for at least 4 hours. Serve cold or at room temperature. Store in the refrigerator for up to one week.

Kidney Bean Dip with Cilantro, Cumin, and Lime

This dip is perfect as a spread for warm pita bread or crusty bread, but is also lovely served with crisp cucumber slices and carrots. The lime juice and zest give this dip a refreshing quality, but if you find it too strong, reduce the lime juice and zest by half.

SERVES 16	
Per Serving:	
Calories	65
Fat	3g
Protein	2g
Sodium	75mg
Fiber	2g
Carbohydrates	7g
Sugar	0g

1 cup dried kidney beans, soaked overnight and drained

4 cups water

3 cloves garlic, peeled and crushed

¼ cup roughly chopped cilantro, divided

¼ cup extra-virgin olive oil

1 tablespoon lime juice

2 teaspoons grated lime zest

1 teaspoon ground cumin

½ teaspoon salt

1 Place beans, water, garlic, and 2 tablespoons cilantro in the Instant Pot®. Close the lid, set steam release to Sealing, press the Bean button, and cook for the default time of 30 minutes.

2 When the timer beeps, let pressure release naturally, about 20 minutes. Press the Cancel button, open lid, and check that beans are tender. Drain off excess water and transfer beans to a medium bowl. Gently mash beans with potato masher or fork until beans are mashed but chunky. Add oil, lime juice, lime zest, cumin, salt, and remaining 2 tablespoons cilantro and stir to combine. Serve warm or at room temperature.

White Bean Dip with Garlic and Herbs

This dip lets the fresh herbs shine. To get the most flavor from this dip, it is best to serve it after chilling for at least 4 hours, or overnight if you have time. As it chills, the herbs and garlic will infuse the dip, so each bite bursts with flavor.

1 cup dried white beans, rinsed and drained

3 cloves garlic, peeled and crushed

8 cups water

¼ cup extra-virgin olive oil

¼ cup chopped fresh flat-leaf parsley

1 tablespoon chopped fresh oregano

1 tablespoon chopped fresh tarragon

1 teaspoon chopped fresh thyme leaves

1 teaspoon grated lemon zest

¼ teaspoon salt

¼ teaspoon ground black pepper

SERVES 16	
Per Serving:	
Calories	47
Fat	3g
Protein	1g
Sodium	38mg
Fiber	1g
Carbohydrates	3g
Sugar	1g

1 Place beans and garlic in the Instant Pot® and stir well. Add water, close lid, set steam release to Sealing, press the Manual button, and set time to 30 minutes.

2 When the timer beeps, let pressure release naturally, about 20 minutes. Open lid and check that beans are tender. Press the Cancel button, drain off excess water, and transfer beans and garlic to a food processor with olive oil. Pulse until mixture is smooth with some small chunks. Add parsley, oregano, tarragon, thyme, lemon zest, salt, and pepper, and pulse 3–5 times to mix. Transfer to a storage container and refrigerate for 4 hours or overnight. Serve cold or at room temperature.

Black Bean Dip

SERVES 16

Per Serving:	
Calories	60
Fat	2g
Protein	3g
Sodium	96mg
Fiber	2g
Carbohydrates	8g
Sugar	1g

Anyone can buy a black bean dip, but nothing compares to this quick homemade version. Top it with a dollop of sour cream and surround it with a sea of tortilla chips, and this dip will be the hit of the party.

1 tablespoon olive oil

2 slices bacon, finely diced

1 small onion, peeled and diced

3 cloves garlic, peeled and minced

1 cup low-sodium chicken broth

1 cup dried black beans, soaked overnight and drained

1 (14.5-ounce) can diced tomatoes, including juice

1 small jalapeño pepper, seeded and minced

1 teaspoon ground cumin

½ teaspoon smoked paprika

1 tablespoon lime juice

½ teaspoon dried oregano

¼ cup minced fresh cilantro

¼ teaspoon sea salt

1 Press the Sauté button on the Instant Pot® and heat oil. Add bacon and onion. Cook until onion is very tender, about 5 minutes. Add garlic and cook until fragrant, about 30 seconds. Add broth and scrape any browned bits from bottom of pot. Add beans, tomatoes, jalapeño, cumin, paprika, lime juice, oregano, cilantro, and salt. Press the Cancel button.

2 Close lid, set steam release to Sealing, press the Bean button, and cook for the default time of 30 minutes. When the timer beeps, let pressure release naturally for 10 minutes. Quick-release any remaining pressure until the float valve drops. Press the Cancel button and open lid.

3 Use an immersion blender, or work in batches in a food processor, to blend the ingredients until desired smoothness is achieved. Serve warm.

Salsa Verde

Salsa Verde ("green sauce") is terrific on chicken enchiladas or fish tacos. Use it also as a quick go-to dip served with tortilla chips.

1 pound tomatillos, outer husks removed
2 small jalapeño peppers, seeded and chopped
1 small onion, peeled and diced
½ cup chopped fresh cilantro
1 teaspoon ground coriander
1 teaspoon sea salt
1½ cups water

SERVES 8	
Per Serving:	
Calories	27
Fat	1g
Protein	1g
Sodium	1mg
Fiber	1g
Carbohydrates	5g
Sugar	3g

1 Cut tomatillos in half and place in the Instant Pot®. Add enough water to cover.

2 Close lid, set steam release to Sealing, press the Manual button, and set time to 2 minutes. When the timer beeps, let pressure release naturally, about 20 minutes. Press the Cancel button and open lid.

3 Drain off excess water and transfer tomatillos to a food processor or blender, and add jalapeños, onion, cilantro, coriander, salt, and water. Pulse until well combined, about 20 pulses.

4 Transfer to a serving dish, cover, and refrigerate for at least 2 hours before serving.

Melitzanosalata (Greek Eggplant Dip)

This soft eggplant dip is wonderful with baked pita chips, served alongside grilled chicken or fish, or used as a topping for veggie bowls and salads.

1 cup water
1 large eggplant, peeled and chopped
1 clove garlic, peeled
½ teaspoon salt
1 tablespoon red wine vinegar
½ cup extra-virgin olive oil
2 tablespoons minced fresh parsley

SERVES 8	
Per Serving:	
Calories	134
Fat	14g
Protein	1g
Sodium	149mg
Fiber	2g
Carbohydrates	3g
Sugar	2g

1 Add water to the Instant Pot®, add the rack to the pot, and place the steamer basket on the rack.

2 Place eggplant in steamer basket. Close lid, set steam release to Sealing, press the Manual button, and set time to 3 minutes. When the timer beeps, quick-release the pressure until the float valve drops. Press the Cancel button and open lid.

3 Transfer eggplant to a food processor and add garlic, salt, and vinegar. Pulse until smooth, about 20 pulses.

4 Slowly add oil to the eggplant mixture while the food processor runs continuously until oil is completely incorporated. Stir in parsley. Serve at room temperature.

Baba Ghanoush

This traditional appetizer dip, or meze, is perfect for eggplant lovers. Eggplant is combined with tahini and olive oil to make a luscious dip that is typically served with pita bread. To add more flavor, stir in a dash or two of cumin for a deeper, earthy taste.

SERVES 8	
Per Serving:	
Calories	79
Fat	6g
Protein	2g
Sodium	149mg
Fiber	2g
Carbohydrates	5g
Sugar	2g

2 tablespoons extra-virgin olive oil, divided
1 large eggplant, peeled and diced
3 cloves garlic, peeled and minced
½ cup water
3 tablespoons chopped fresh flat-leaf parsley
½ teaspoon salt
¼ teaspoon smoked paprika
2 tablespoons lemon juice
2 tablespoons tahini

1 Press the Sauté button on the Instant Pot® and add 1 tablespoon oil. Add eggplant and cook until it begins to soften, about 5 minutes. Add garlic and cook 30 seconds, or until very fragrant.

2 Add water and close lid, set steam release to Sealing, press the Manual button, and set time to 6 minutes. When the timer beeps, quick-release the pressure until the float valve drops. Press the Cancel button and open lid.

3 Strain cooked eggplant and garlic and add to a food processor or blender along with parsley, salt, smoked paprika, lemon juice, and tahini. Pulse to process, scraping down the sides of the food processor or blender if necessary. Add remaining 1 tablespoon oil and process until smooth. Serve warm or at room temperature.

Chickpea, Parsley, and Dill Dip

Try any combination of fresh herbs, such as basil, thyme, or mint, in this versatile dip.

8 cups plus 2 tablespoons water, divided
1 cup dried chickpeas
3 tablespoons olive oil, divided
2 garlic cloves, peeled and minced
2 tablespoons chopped fresh parsley
2 tablespoons chopped fresh dill
1 tablespoon lemon juice
¼ teaspoon salt

MAKES 2 CUPS	
Per Serving (2 tablespoons):	
Calories	76
Fat	4g
Protein	2g
Sodium	44mg
Fiber	2g
Carbohydrates	8g
Sugar	0g

1 Add 4 cups water and chickpeas to the Instant Pot®. Close lid, set steam release to Sealing, press the Manual button, and set time to 1 minute. When the timer beeps, quick-release the pressure until the float valve drops, press the Cancel button, and open lid.

2 Drain water, rinse chickpeas, and return to pot with 4 cups fresh water. Set aside to soak for 1 hour.

3 Add 1 tablespoon oil to pot. Close lid, set steam release to Sealing, press the Manual button, and set time to 20 minutes. When the timer beeps, let pressure release naturally, about 20 minutes. Press the Cancel button, open lid, and drain chickpeas.

4 Transfer chickpeas to a food processor or blender, and add garlic, parsley, dill, lemon juice, and remaining 2 tablespoons water. Blend for about 30 seconds.

5 With the processor or blender lid still in place, slowly add remaining 2 tablespoons oil while still blending, then add salt. Serve warm or at room temperature.

Instant Pot® Salsa

If you like your salsa hot and spicy, substitute one or more of the jalapeños with habañero peppers. If you don't want any heat, replace the jalapeños with a bell pepper.

SERVES 12	
Per Serving:	
Calories	68
Fat	0g
Protein	2g
Sodium	406mg
Fiber	3g
Carbohydrates	15g
Sugar	10g

12 cups seeded diced tomatoes
6 ounces tomato paste
2 medium yellow onions, peeled and diced
6 small jalapeño peppers, seeded and minced

4 cloves garlic, peeled and minced
¼ cup white vinegar
¼ cup lime juice
2 tablespoons granulated sugar
2 teaspoons salt
¼ cup chopped fresh cilantro

1 Place tomatoes, tomato paste, onions, jalapeños, garlic, vinegar, lime juice, sugar, and salt in the Instant Pot® and stir well. Close lid, set steam release to Sealing, press the Manual button, and set time to 20 minutes.

2 When the timer beeps, quick-release the pressure until the float valve drops. Open lid, stir in cilantro, and press the Cancel button.

3 Let salsa cool to room temperature, about 40 minutes, then transfer to a storage container and refrigerate overnight.

Sfougato

For Greeks, eggs are not limited to breakfast food and often make an appearance at the lunch or dinner table as an appetizer or main course.

SERVES 4	
Per Serving:	
Calories	274
Fat	14g
Protein	17g
Sodium	962mg
Fiber	2g
Carbohydrates	20g
Sugar	4g

½ cup crumbled feta cheese
¼ cup bread crumbs
1 medium onion, peeled and minced
4 tablespoons all-purpose flour
2 tablespoons minced fresh mint

½ teaspoon salt
½ teaspoon ground black pepper
1 tablespoon dried thyme
6 large eggs, beaten
1 cup water

1 In a medium bowl, mix cheese, bread crumbs, onion, flour, mint, salt, pepper, and thyme. Stir in eggs.

2 Spray an 8" round baking dish with nonstick cooking spray. Pour egg mixture into dish.

3 Place rack in the Instant Pot® and add water. Fold a long piece of foil in half lengthwise. Lay foil over rack to form a sling and top with dish. Cover loosely with foil. Close lid, set steam release to Sealing, press the Manual button, and set time to 8 minutes.

4 When the timer beeps, quick-release the pressure until the float valve drops. Open lid. Let stand 5 minutes, then remove dish from pot.

Skordalia

Skordalia is a dip made with lots of fresh garlic, a generous amount of olive oil, and tangy wine vinegar mixed into a hearty base of potatoes. Serve it with veggies for dipping, or use it as a garnish for grilled or pan-cooked fish and vegetables.

1 pound russet potatoes, peeled and quartered

3 cups plus ¼ cup water, divided

2 teaspoons salt, divided

8 cloves garlic, peeled and minced

¾ cup blanched almonds

½ cup extra-virgin olive oil

2 tablespoons lemon juice

2 tablespoons white wine vinegar

½ teaspoon ground black pepper

SERVES 16	
Per Serving:	
Calories	115
Fat	10g
Protein	2g
Sodium	292mg
Fiber	1g
Carbohydrates	5g
Sugar	0g

1 Place potatoes, 3 cups water, and 1 teaspoon salt in the Instant Pot® and stir well. Close lid, set steam release to Sealing, press the Manual button, and set time to 10 minutes.

2 While potatoes cook, place garlic and remaining 1 teaspoon salt on a cutting board. With the side of a knife, press garlic and salt until it forms a paste. Transfer garlic paste into a food processor along with almonds and olive oil. Purée into a paste. Set aside.

3 When the timer beeps, quick-release the pressure until the float valve drops. Press the Cancel button and open lid. Drain potatoes and transfer to a medium bowl. Add garlic mixture and mash with a potato masher until smooth. Stir in lemon juice, vinegar, and pepper. Stir in ¼ cup water a little at a time until mixture is thin enough for dipping. Serve warm or at room temperature.

Pinto Bean Dip with Avocado Pico

The avocado pico topping should be made just before serving to preserve the vibrant green color of the avocado, but the bean dip can be made a day or two ahead.

1 cup dried pinto beans, soaked overnight and drained
4 cups water
4 tablespoons roughly chopped cilantro, divided
3 tablespoons extra-virgin olive oil
1 teaspoon ground cumin
1 clove garlic, peeled and minced
½ teaspoon salt
1 medium avocado, peeled, pitted, and diced
1 large ripe tomato, seeded and diced
1 small jalapeño pepper, seeded and minced
½ medium white onion, peeled and chopped
2 teaspoons lime juice

1 Place beans, water, and 2 tablespoons cilantro in the Instant Pot®. Close lid, set steam release to Sealing, press the Bean button, and cook for the default time of 30 minutes.

2 When the timer beeps, let pressure release naturally, about 20 minutes. Open lid and check that beans are tender. Drain off excess water and transfer beans to a medium bowl. Gently mash beans with potato masher or fork until beans are crushed but chunky. Add oil, cumin, garlic, and salt and mix well. Transfer to a serving dish.

3 In a medium bowl, combine remaining 2 tablespoons cilantro with avocado, tomato, jalapeño, onion, and lime juice. Gently toss to combine. Spoon topping over bean dip in serving bowl. Serve warm or at room temperature.

Steamed Artichokes with Herbs and Olive Oil

Artichokes are a prebiotic food, meaning they feed your good gut flora. They are also really tasty when simply steamed. Here, they are doused in an herby olive oil mixture for extra richness and flavor.

3 medium artichokes with stems cut off
1 medium lemon, halved
1 cup water
¼ cup lemon juice
⅓ cup extra-virgin olive oil
1 clove garlic, peeled and minced
¼ teaspoon salt
1 teaspoon chopped fresh oregano
1 teaspoon chopped fresh rosemary
1 teaspoon chopped fresh flat-leaf parsley
1 teaspoon fresh thyme leaves

SERVES 6	
Per Serving:	
Calories	137
Fat	13g
Protein	2g
Sodium	158mg
Fiber	4g
Carbohydrates	7g
Sugar	1g

1 Run artichokes under running water, making sure water runs between leaves to flush out any debris. Slice off top ⅓ of artichoke and pull away any tough outer leaves. Rub all cut surfaces with lemon.

2 Add water and lemon juice to the Instant Pot®, then add rack. Place artichokes upside down on rack. Close lid, set steam release to Sealing, press the Manual button, and set time to 10 minutes. When the timer beeps, let pressure release naturally, about 20 minutes.

3 Press the Cancel button and open lid. Remove artichokes, transfer to a cutting board, and slice in half. Place halves on a serving platter.

4 In a small bowl, combine oil, garlic, salt, oregano, rosemary, parsley, and thyme. Drizzle half of mixture over artichokes, then serve remaining mixture in a small bowl for dipping. Serve warm.

Stuffed Grape Leaves

Also called dolmas, *stuffed grape leaves are a traditional Mediterranean and Middle Eastern dish. The grape leaves in some versions of this recipe are stuffed with meat, seafood, or even fruit, but this version is made with flavorful herbs and rice.*

SERVES 16	
Per Serving:	
Calories	179
Fat	6g
Protein	5g
Sodium	180mg
Fiber	7g
Carbohydrates	29g
Sugar	4g

⅓ cup extra-virgin olive oil
½ medium onion, peeled and diced
¼ cup minced fresh mint
¼ cup minced fresh dill
3 cloves garlic, peeled and minced
1 cup long-grain white rice
2 cups vegetable broth
½ teaspoon salt
¼ teaspoon ground black pepper
½ teaspoon grated lemon zest
1 (16-ounce) jar grape leaves
2 cups water
½ cup lemon juice

1 Press the Sauté button on the Instant Pot® and heat oil. Add onion, mint, and dill and cook until tender, about 4 minutes. Add garlic and cook until fragrant, about 30 seconds. Add rice and turn to coat. Add broth, salt, pepper, and lemon zest, and stir well. Close lid, set steam release to Sealing, press the Manual button, and set time to 8 minutes.

2 When the timer beeps, quick-release the pressure until the float valve drops, press the Cancel button, and open lid. Transfer rice mixture to a medium bowl.

3 Drain grape leaves, then rinse well in warm water. Arrange leaves rib side up on a work surface. Spoon about 2 teaspoons rice mixture on each grape leaf. Fold sides of a leaf over the filling and then roll it from the bottom to top. Repeat with each leaf. Arrange stuffed leaves, seam side down, in a single layer in the Instant Pot® steamer basket insert.

4 Pour water into the Instant Pot®. Set steamer basket insert in pot and pour lemon juice over stuffed grape leaves. Close lid, set steam release to Sealing, and press the Steam button and cook for the default time of 10 minutes.

5 When the timer beeps, quick-release the pressure until the float valve drops and open lid. Lift steamer basket out of pot and set aside stuffed leaves to rest for 5 minutes. Serve hot or cold.

Marinated Mushrooms and Pearl Onions

This dish also makes an excellent side dish for grilled meats and seafood.

3 pounds button mushrooms, trimmed

1 (15-ounce) bag frozen pearl onions, thawed

3 cloves garlic, peeled and minced

1 cup vegetable broth

¼ cup balsamic vinegar

¼ cup red wine

2 tablespoons olive oil

2 sprigs fresh thyme

½ teaspoon ground black pepper

¼ teaspoon crushed red pepper flakes

SERVES 10	
Per Serving:	
Calories	90
Fat	3g
Protein	4g
Sodium	92mg
Fiber	2g
Carbohydrates	9g
Sugar	4g

1 Place all ingredients in the Instant Pot® and mix well.

2 Close lid, set steam release to Sealing, press the Manual button, and set time to 4 minutes.

3 When the timer beeps, quick-release the pressure until the float valve drops and open lid. Transfer mixture to a bowl and serve warm.

Savory Lentil Dip

This simple dip allows the earthy flavor of the lentils and garlic to shine. For even more flavor, add your favorite fresh herbs, such as thyme, rosemary, dill, or oregano.

2 tablespoons olive oil

½ medium yellow onion, peeled and diced

3 cloves garlic, peeled and minced

2 cups dried red lentils, rinsed and drained

4 cups water

1 teaspoon salt

¼ teaspoon ground black pepper

2 tablespoons minced fresh flat-leaf parsley

SERVES 16	
Per Serving:	
Calories	76
Fat	2g
Protein	5g
Sodium	145mg
Fiber	2g
Carbohydrates	11g
Sugar	1g

1 Press the Sauté button on the Instant Pot® and heat oil. Add onion and cook 2–3 minutes, or until translucent. Add garlic and cook until fragrant, about 30 seconds. Add lentils, water, and salt to pot, and stir to combine. Close lid, set steam release to Sealing, press the Bean button, and cook for the default time of 30 minutes.

2 When the timer beeps, let pressure release naturally for 10 minutes. Quick-release any remaining pressure until the float valve drops, then open lid. Transfer lentil mixture to a food processor and blend until smooth. Season with pepper and garnish with parsley. Serve warm.

Mediterranean Deviled Eggs

These savory deviled eggs are lighter than the traditional version because they are made with less mayonnaise, but they pack in a lot of flavor with the addition of minced olives and capers. Olive oil mayonnaise is available in most grocery stores, but if you are unable to locate it, you can replace it with plain Greek yogurt.

6 large eggs
1 cup water
2 tablespoons olive oil mayonnaise
½ teaspoon Dijon mustard
2 tablespoons chopped fresh dill
1 tablespoon chopped capers
1 tablespoon minced Kalamata olives
¼ teaspoon ground black pepper

1 Have ready a large bowl of ice water. Place rack or egg holder into the bottom of the Instant Pot®. Arrange eggs on rack or holder and add water. Close lid and set steam release to Sealing. Press the Manual button and set time to 8 minutes.

2 When the timer beeps, let pressure release naturally for 10 minutes, then quick-release the remaining pressure. Press the Cancel button and open lid. Carefully remove eggs and transfer to the bowl of ice water. Let stand in ice water for 10 minutes, then remove shells.

3 Slice eggs in half, remove yolks, and place yokes in a medium bowl. Mash with a fork until crumbled and stir in mayonnaise and mustard. Fold in dill, capers, olives, and pepper.

4 Fill egg whites with yolk mixture, then chill for at least 2 hours before serving.

SERVES 6

Per Serving:

Calories	87
Fat	7g
Protein	6g
Sodium	105mg
Fiber	0g
Carbohydrates	1g
Sugar	0g

COOKING EGGS IN THE INSTANT POT®

Your Instant Pot® will quickly become your favorite tool for making perfectly cooked eggs. Each model of Instant Pot® cooks slightly differently, so you may need to add or subtract a minute or two to get your eggs exactly the way you like them. But in general, 8–10 minutes will yield hard-boiled eggs; medium eggs will take 5–6 minutes; and soft-boiled eggs are ready in 3–4 minutes.

Dandelion and White Bean Soup

SERVES 6

Per Serving:

Calories	146
Fat	4g
Protein	6g
Sodium	922mg
Fiber	7g
Carbohydrates	24g
Sugar	8g

DANDELION GREENS

Dandelions grow in the Mediterranean countryside. Many people forage for the young, tender plants in the spring when they are not too bitter. Try dandelions in your salads or boil them and toss them in a little olive oil and lemon juice.

If you like the taste of dandelion greens in a soup, try them raw in a salad. They're an excellent source of vitamin A, folate, vitamin K, and vitamin C, and a good source of calcium and potassium.

1 tablespoon olive oil

2 medium onions, peeled and chopped

3 medium carrots, peeled and chopped

3 stalks celery, chopped

4 cloves garlic, peeled and minced

1 bay leaf

¼ cup chopped fresh parsley

2 teaspoons fresh thyme leaves

1 teaspoon salt

½ teaspoon ground black pepper

8 cups vegetable stock

2 cups fresh dandelion greens, steamed until wilted

1 (15-ounce) can cannellini beans, drained and rinsed

¼ cup grated Parmesan cheese

1 Press the Sauté button on the Instant Pot® and heat oil. Add onions, carrots, celery, and garlic. Cook until vegetables soften, about 5 minutes. Add bay leaf, parsley, thyme, salt, and pepper and cook until thyme is fragrant, about 30 seconds. Press the Cancel button.

2 Add stock and stir well. Close lid, set steam release to Sealing, press the Soup button, and cook for the default time of 20 minutes.

3 When the timer beeps, quick-release the pressure until the float valve drops, and press the Cancel button. Open lid and stir in dandelion greens and beans. Close lid, set steam release to Sealing, press the Manual button, and set time to 1 minute. When the timer beeps, quick-release the pressure until the float valve drops, and press the Cancel button. Open lid and remove and discard bay leaf.

4 Serve soup with a sprinkle of cheese on top.

Fresh Tomato Chutney

For a change of pace, spread this chutney over pita bread, flatbread, or pizza crust; top it with goat cheese and bake at 350°F for 10–12 minutes.

4 pounds ripe tomatoes, peeled

1 (1") piece fresh ginger, peeled

3 cloves garlic, peeled and chopped

1¾ cups sugar

1 cup red wine vinegar

2 medium onions, peeled and diced

¼ cup golden raisins

¾ teaspoon ground cinnamon

½ teaspoon ground coriander

¼ teaspoon ground cloves

¼ teaspoon ground nutmeg

¼ teaspoon ground ginger

1 teaspoon chili powder

⅛ teaspoon paprika

1 tablespoon curry paste

MAKES 4 CUPS	
Per Serving (2 tablespoons):	
Calories	58
Fat	0g
Protein	0g
Sodium	4mg
Fiber	0g
Carbohydrates	14g
Sugar	14g

1 Purée tomatoes and fresh ginger in a blender or food processor.

2 Pour tomato mixture into the Instant Pot®. Stir in remaining ingredients. Close lid, set steam release to Sealing, press the Manual button, set time to 10 minutes, and adjust pressure to Low. When the timer beeps, let pressure release naturally, about 25 minutes. Open lid and stir.

3 Transfer to a storage container and refrigerate until ready to use. Serve chilled or at room temperature.

Black-Eyed Pea "Caviar"

This dish is filled with flavor, and it's great for a party. It takes a little time, and it is worth planning ahead so that it can be served chilled. Prepare up to two days in advance and store in a covered container in the refrigerator.

1 cup dried black-eyed peas

4 cups water

1 pound cooked corn kernels

½ medium red onion, peeled and diced

½ medium green bell pepper, seeded and diced

2 tablespoons minced pickled jalapeño pepper

1 medium tomato, diced

2 tablespoons chopped fresh cilantro

¼ cup red wine vinegar

2 tablespoons extra-virgin olive oil

1 teaspoon salt

½ teaspoon ground black pepper

½ teaspoon ground cumin

MAKES 5 CUPS	
Per Serving (½ cup):	
Calories	28
Fat	1g
Protein	1g
Sodium	51mg
Fiber	1g
Carbohydrates	4g
Sugar	1g

1 Add black-eyed peas and water to the Instant Pot®. Close lid, set steam release to Sealing, press the Manual button, and set time to 30 minutes.

2 When the timer beeps, let pressure release naturally, about 25 minutes, and open lid. Drain peas and transfer to a large mixing bowl. Add all remaining ingredients and stir until thoroughly combined. Cover and refrigerate for 2 hours before serving.

Savory Sun-Dried Tomato Cheesecake

You can freeze this cheesecake for up to 3 months, so it is the perfect make-ahead addition for a cheese plate. Thaw a wedge of the cheesecake in the refrigerator and then serve at room temperature, spread on crackers or thin slices of crusty bread.

SERVES 12	
Per Serving:	
Calories	165
Fat	14g
Protein	3g
Sodium	138mg
Fiber	0g
Carbohydrates	7g
Sugar	3g

3 tablespoons unsalted butter, melted

⅓ cup bread crumbs

½ cup sun-dried tomatoes in oil, drained, leaving 1 tablespoon oil

6 cloves garlic, peeled and minced

1 teaspoon dried oregano

3 large eggs

3 tablespoons all-purpose flour

2 (8-ounce) packages cream cheese

¾ cup sour cream, divided

½ cup diced scallions

2 cups hot water

1 Coat the sides and bottom of a 7" springform pan with butter. Evenly distribute bread crumbs over the bottom and sides of the pan. Place a 16" × 16" piece of plastic wrap on top of an equal-sized piece of aluminum foil. Put the pan in the center of the plastic wrap; form and crimp the foil around the springform pan to seal the bottom of the pan.

2 Add tomatoes to a food processor along with garlic, oregano, eggs, flour, cream cheese, and ¼ cup sour cream. Purée until smooth. Stir in scallions. Pour into prepared pan. Cover with foil; crimp to seal.

3 Place rack on the bottom of the Instant Pot®. Pour in water. Fold a long piece of foil in half lengthwise and lay over rack to form a sling. Place pan in the pot so it rests on the sling.

4 Close lid, set steam release to Sealing, press the Manual button, and set time to 20 minutes. When the timer beeps, let pressure release naturally for 10 minutes, then quick-release any remaining pressure until the float valve drops. Open the lid and let cheesecake continue to cool in the pot until all of the steam has dissipated.

5 Lift the pan from pot with sling. Remove foil lid and use a paper towel to dab away any accumulated moisture. Cool cheesecake completely.

6 Spread remaining ½ cup sour cream over the top. Serve at room temperature or refrigerate for at least 4 hours.

CHAPTER 4

Rice

Lemon and Garlic Rice Pilaf

RINSING RICE

Well-cooked rice always starts with the same first step: Rinse well and drain. While it may be tempting to skip this step, rinsing the rice will ensure that you have a superior outcome. Rinsing removes the starches from the outside of the grains. These outer starches form a glue that binds together the grains, making them clumpy and sticky. Also, rice can get a little dusty during processing, so rinsing gives it a fresher taste. Put rice in a strainer, rinse it for 20–30 seconds under cool water, and let the excess water drain for about 10 minutes before cooking.

This zesty rice dish makes a refreshing side dish for grilled or baked fish. Fresh lemon juice and zest yields the most aromatic flavor. If you prefer to cook without wine, add extra vegetable broth in its place.

2 tablespoons olive oil
1 medium yellow onion, peeled and chopped
4 cloves garlic, peeled and minced
1 tablespoon grated lemon zest
½ teaspoon ground black pepper
1 teaspoon dried thyme
1 teaspoon dried oregano
¼ teaspoon salt
2 tablespoons white wine
2 tablespoons lemon juice
2 cups brown rice
2 cups vegetable broth

1 Press the Sauté button on the Instant Pot® and heat oil. Add onion and cook until soft, about 6 minutes. Add garlic and cook until fragrant, about 30 seconds. Add lemon zest, pepper, thyme, oregano, and salt. Cook until fragrant, about 1 minute.

2 Add wine and lemon juice and cook, stirring well, until liquid has almost evaporated, about 1 minute. Add rice and cook, stirring constantly, until coated and starting to toast, about 3 minutes. Press the Cancel button.

3 Stir in broth. Close lid, set steam release to Sealing, press the Manual button, and set time to 22 minutes.

4 When the timer beeps, let pressure release naturally for 10 minutes, then quick-release the remaining pressure until the float valve drops. Open lid and fluff rice with a fork. Serve warm.

Pesto Rice with Olives and Goat Cheese

Fresh pesto can be found in most grocery stores in the refrigerated section where fresh pasta is kept. Refrigerated pesto has a better flavor than the jarred version, and leftover pesto can be used as a dipping sauce for crusty bread or tossed into pasta.

2 cups brown basmati rice
2¼ cups vegetable broth
½ cup pesto
½ cup chopped mixed olives
¼ cup chopped fresh basil
¼ cup crumbled goat cheese

1 Place rice, broth, and pesto in the Instant Pot® and stir well. Close lid, set steam release to Sealing, press the Manual button, and set time to 22 minutes.

2 When the timer beeps, let pressure release naturally for 10 minutes, then quick-release the remaining pressure. Open lid, add olives and basil, and fluff rice with a fork. Serve warm, topped with goat cheese.

SERVES 8	
Per Serving:	
Calories	219
Fat	6g
Protein	6g
Sodium	148mg
Fiber	1g
Carbohydrates	36g
Sugar	0g

Wild Rice with Hazelnuts and Dried Apricots

This soothing recipe can be the perfect dish to end a day spent apple picking, pumpkin picking, or just enjoying a walk in the crisp fall air. Feel free to garnish with snipped chives and serve with a glass of red wine to take this dish up a notch and impress your guests.

2 cups wild rice
3 cups vegetable broth
2½ cups water
1 teaspoon sea salt
1 tablespoon unsalted butter
½ cup chopped hazelnuts
½ cup chopped dried apricots

1 Place all ingredients in the Instant Pot® and stir to combine. Close lid, set steam release to Sealing, press the Manual button, and set time to 30 minutes.

2 When the timer beeps, let pressure release naturally for 5 minutes. Quick-release the remaining pressure until the float valve drops and open lid. Transfer to a dish and serve warm.

SERVES 8	
Per Serving:	
Calories	242
Fat	9g
Protein	7g
Sodium	302mg
Fiber	3g
Carbohydrates	46g
Sugar	8g

Wild Rice and Mushroom Soup

SERVES 8

Per Serving:

Calories	141
Fat	4g
Protein	4g
Sodium	722mg
Fiber	3g
Carbohydrates	24g
Sugar	4g

WILD RICE

Wild rice isn't really a rice at all; it's the seed of an aquatic grass. It is high in protein and fiber, and it's naturally gluten-free. Wild rice is a good source of both magnesium and lysine, which are good for digestion and beneficial for your nervous system. Because it's minimally processed, wild rice retains most of its nutrients. With a toasty, nutty flavor, and a slightly chewy texture, wild rice is delicious on its own but can be added to other grain dishes to enhance flavor and texture.

This soup is a light yet satisfying combination of savory mushrooms and nutty brown rice. For a pretty presentation, garnish each bowl of soup with a sprinkle of chopped fresh herbs, like parsley, thyme, or oregano.

2 tablespoons olive oil
2 medium carrots, peeled and chopped
2 stalks celery, chopped
1 medium yellow onion, peeled and chopped
2 (8-ounce) containers sliced button mushrooms
3 cloves garlic, peeled and minced
1 teaspoon dried thyme
1 teaspoon dried oregano
½ teaspoon salt
½ teaspoon ground black pepper
1 cup wild rice blend
6 cups vegetable broth

1 Press the Sauté button on the Instant Pot® and heat oil. Add carrots, celery, and onion. Cook until vegetables are just tender, about 5 minutes. Add mushrooms and cook until they begin to release their juices, about 4 minutes.

2 Add garlic, thyme, oregano, salt, pepper, and rice, and sauté until garlic is fragrant, about 1 minute. Press the Cancel button, add broth, and stir well. Close lid, set steam release to Sealing, press the Manual button, and set time to 25 minutes.

3 When the timer beeps, quick-release the pressure until the float valve drops, open lid, and stir well. Serve hot.

Brown Rice Salad with Zucchini and Tomatoes

SERVES 6

Per Serving:

Calories	209
Fat	12g
Protein	5g
Sodium	380mg
Fiber	2g
Carbohydrates	21g
Sugar	2g

This salad is perfect to take along to potlucks or picnics.

1 cup brown basmati rice
1¼ cups vegetable broth
5 tablespoons olive oil, divided
2 cups chopped zucchini
2 cups sliced cherry tomatoes
¼ cup minced red onion

2 tablespoons lemon juice
¼ teaspoon salt
¼ teaspoon ground black pepper
¼ cup chopped fresh flat-leaf parsley
¼ cup toasted slivered almonds
¼ cup crumbled feta cheese

1 Place rice, broth, and 1 tablespoon olive oil in the Instant Pot® and stir well. Close lid, set steam release to Sealing, press the Manual button, and set time to 22 minutes.

2 When the timer beeps, let pressure release naturally for 10 minutes, then quick-release the remaining pressure. Open lid and fluff rice with a fork. Transfer to a large bowl and set aside to cool to room temperature.

3 Add zucchini, tomatoes, and onion to rice. In a small bowl, whisk remaining 4 tablespoons olive oil, lemon juice, salt, and pepper. Pour over rice and toss. Top with parsley, almonds, and feta. Serve warm or at room temperature.

Brown Rice with Dried Fruit

SERVES 6

Per Serving:

Calories	192
Fat	5g
Protein	3g
Sodium	272mg
Fiber	4g
Carbohydrates	34g
Sugar	10g

To dice a large carrot, quarter the carrot lengthwise and then slice the resulting strips into small pieces. Easy!

2 tablespoons olive oil
2 stalks celery, thinly sliced
2 large carrots, peeled and diced
1 large sweet potato, peeled and diced
1½ cups brown rice
⅓ cup chopped prunes

⅓ cup chopped dried apricots
½ teaspoon ground cinnamon
2 teaspoons grated orange zest
3 cups water
1 bay leaf
½ teaspoon salt

1 Press the Sauté button on the Instant Pot® and heat oil. Add celery, carrots, sweet potato, and rice. Cook until vegetables are just tender, about 3 minutes. Stir in prunes, apricots, cinnamon, and orange zest. Cook until cinnamon is fragrant, about 30 seconds. Add water, bay leaf, and salt.

2 Press the Cancel button, close lid, set steam release to Sealing, press the Manual button, and set time to 16 minutes. When the timer beeps, let pressure release naturally for 10 minutes. Quick-release any remaining pressure until the float valve drops and open the lid. Fluff rice with a fork.

3 Remove and discard bay leaf. Transfer to a serving bowl. Serve hot.

Risotto Primavera

Risotto is easy to make, but standing over a stove, stirring the rice, and waiting for it to absorb the broth can be time-consuming. This Instant Pot® recipe combines ease and speed to make a delicious dish.

2 tablespoons olive oil

2 medium carrots, peeled and finely diced

1 stalk celery, finely diced

2 large shallots, peeled and diced

1 clove garlic, peeled and minced

½ teaspoon dried basil

1 teaspoon dried parsley

2 cups Arborio rice

½ cup dry white wine

5 cups vegetable broth, divided

½ pound asparagus, trimmed and chopped into 1" pieces

1 cup frozen green peas, thawed

1 cup shredded snow peas

1 cup diced zucchini

1 cup shredded Fontina cheese

½ cup grated Parmesan cheese

1 Press the Sauté button on the Instant Pot® and heat oil. Add carrots and celery and cook until tender, about 3 minutes. Add shallots and garlic and cook until fragrant, about 30 seconds. Add basil and parsley, and stir well.

2 Stir in rice and cook for 4 minutes or until rice becomes translucent. Add wine. Cook, stirring constantly for 3 minutes or until the liquid is absorbed. Stir in 4½ cups broth. Press the Cancel button.

3 Close lid, set steam release to Sealing, press the Manual button, and set time to 6 minutes. When the timer beeps, quick-release the pressure until the float valve drops and open the lid.

4 Stir in remaining ½ cup broth. Press the Cancel button, then press the Sauté button. Stir until broth is absorbed. Add asparagus, green peas, snow peas, and zucchini. Stir and cook until vegetables are bright green and cooked through, about 5 minutes. Stir in Fontina and Parmesan. Serve immediately.

SERVES 8	
Per Serving:	
Calories	277
Fat	11g
Protein	13g
Sodium	706mg
Fiber	2g
Carbohydrates	32g
Sugar	4g

RECIPE VERSATILITY

You can use whatever vegetables you have on hand; just dice or slice the vegetable pieces according to the length of time it takes that vegetable to cook. The more time you need to cook a vegetable, the smaller the dice. For example, butternut squash and carrots are slow cookers, so you should dice them into pieces that are smaller than the onions and celery.

Brown Rice Vegetable Bowl with Roasted Red Pepper Dressing

SERVES 2	
Per Serving:	
Calories	561
Fat	23g
Protein	10g
Sodium	505mg
Fiber	5g
Carbohydrates	86g
Sugar	12g

If you want to make this rice bowl for lunch at work, keep the rice in a separate container so you can reheat it in the microwave for 15–20 seconds before assembling. Or, toss all the vegetables and dressing into the rice and serve it as a side dish for dinner.

¼ cup chopped roasted red bell pepper
2 tablespoons extra-virgin olive oil
1 tablespoon red wine vinegar
1 teaspoon honey
2 tablespoons light olive oil
2 cloves garlic, peeled and minced
½ teaspoon ground black pepper
¼ teaspoon salt
1 cup brown rice
1 cup vegetable broth
¼ cup chopped fresh flat-leaf parsley
2 tablespoons chopped fresh chives
2 tablespoons chopped fresh dill
½ cup diced tomato
½ cup chopped red onion
½ cup diced cucumber
½ cup chopped green bell pepper

1 Place roasted red pepper, extra-virgin olive oil, red wine vinegar, and honey in a blender. Purée until smooth, about 1 minute. Refrigerate until ready to serve.

2 Press the Sauté button on the Instant Pot® and heat light olive oil. Add garlic and cook until fragrant, about 30 seconds. Add black pepper, salt, and rice and stir well. Press the Cancel button.

3 Stir in broth. Close lid, set steam release to Sealing, press the Manual button, and set time to 22 minutes.

4 When the timer beeps, let pressure release naturally for 10 minutes, then quick-release the remaining pressure. Open lid and fluff rice with a fork. Transfer to a large bowl and set aside to cool to room temperature, about 20 minutes, then fold in parsley, chives, and dill.

5 To assemble bowls, divide rice between two bowls. Top with tomato, onion, cucumber, and green bell pepper. Drizzle roasted red pepper sauce over vegetables. Serve immediately.

Three-Grain Pilaf

Millet is a good source of protein and B vitamins. Protein makes you feel fuller longer, and it helps your muscles recover more quickly after working out.

2 tablespoons extra-virgin olive oil
½ cup sliced scallions
1 cup jasmine rice
½ cup millet

½ cup quinoa, rinsed and drained
2½ cups vegetable stock
¼ teaspoon salt
¼ teaspoon ground black pepper

SERVES 6	
Per Serving:	
Calories	346
Fat	7g
Protein	8g
Sodium	341mg
Fiber	4g
Carbohydrates	61g
Sugar	1g

1 Press the Sauté button on the Instant Pot® and heat oil. Add scallions and cook until just tender, 2 minutes. Add rice, millet, and quinoa and cook for 3 minutes to toast. Add stock and stir well. Press the Cancel button.

2 Close lid, set steam release to Sealing, press the Manual button, and set time to 4 minutes. When the timer beeps, quick-release the pressure until the float valve drops and open the lid. Fluff pilaf with a fork and stir in salt and pepper. Serve warm.

Cranberry and Pecan Pilaf

This pilaf calls to mind a crisp autumn afternoon, but it makes a great light dish any time of year. Try sprinkling in ground ginger or cloves to add more flavor. To make a hearty vegetarian main dish, add tofu or meatless crumbles.

1 cup long-grain white rice
2 cups vegetable broth
⅔ cup dried cranberries
1 teaspoon dried thyme leaves
1 bay leaf

1 cup chopped raw pecans
2 tablespoons olive oil
¼ teaspoon salt
¼ teaspoon ground black pepper

SERVES 6	
Per Serving:	
Calories	485
Fat	18g
Protein	6g
Sodium	368mg
Fiber	5g
Carbohydrates	75g
Sugar	21g

1 Add rice, broth, cranberries, thyme, and bay leaf to the Instant Pot®. Close lid, set steam release to Sealing, press the Rice button, and cook for the default time.

2 When the timer beeps, let pressure release naturally, about 20 minutes, then open lid. Remove and discard bay leaf. Stir in pecans, oil, salt, and pepper. Serve warm.

Spinach and Feta Risotto

Let the flavors of Greece and Italy marry together in this creamy, savory dish. Kalamata olives make the perfect finishing touch.

SERVES 6	
Per Serving:	
Calories	285
Fat	13g
Protein	9g
Sodium	536mg
Fiber	1g
Carbohydrates	34g
Sugar	2g

3 tablespoons olive oil
1 small onion, peeled and minced
2 cloves garlic, peeled and minced
1½ cups Arborio rice
4 cups low-sodium chicken broth, divided

3 tablespoons grated Parmesan cheese
½ teaspoon salt
¼ teaspoon ground black pepper
½ cup julienned spinach
¼ cup crumbled feta cheese
¼ cup minced Kalamata olives

1 Press the Sauté button on the Instant Pot® and heat oil. Add onion and sauté 3 minutes. Add garlic and rice and cook for 1 minute. Add 1 cup broth and stir for 2–3 minutes until absorbed. Add remaining 3 cups broth, cheese, salt, and pepper. Press the Cancel button.

2 Close lid, set steam release to Sealing, press the Manual button, and set time to 10 minutes. When the timer beeps, let pressure release naturally for 10 minutes. Quick-release any remaining pressure until the float valve drops and then open lid.

3 Stir in spinach and feta. Transfer to a serving dish and top with olives.

Brown Rice and Chickpea Salad

Look at the label for balsamic vinegar—if the first ingredient isn't "cooked grape must," put it back on the shelf and keep looking.

SERVES 8	
Per Serving:	
Calories	417
Fat	21g
Protein	13g
Sodium	366mg
Fiber	7g
Carbohydrates	45g
Sugar	6g

2 cups brown rice
2¼ cups vegetable broth
2 tablespoons light olive oil
1 (15-ounce) can chickpeas, drained and rinsed
½ cup diced tomato
½ cup chopped red onion

½ cup diced cucumber
¼ cup chopped fresh basil
3 tablespoons extra-virgin olive oil
2 tablespoons balsamic vinegar
½ teaspoon ground black pepper
¼ teaspoon salt
¼ cup crumbled feta cheese

1 Place rice, broth, and light oil in the Instant Pot®. Close lid, set steam release to Sealing, press the Manual button, and set time to 22 minutes.

2 When the timer beeps, let pressure release naturally for 10 minutes, then quick-release the remaining pressure. Open lid, transfer rice to a large bowl, and set aside for 20 minutes. Fold in chickpeas, tomato, onion, cucumber, and basil.

3 In a small bowl, whisk together extra-virgin olive oil, balsamic vinegar, pepper, and salt. Pour over rice mixture and toss to coat. Top with feta. Serve at room temperature or refrigerate for at least 2 hours.

Simple Herbed Rice

This easy-to-make rice dish is a versatile and tasty side dish for just about any meal.

2 tablespoons extra-virgin olive oil
½ medium yellow onion, peeled and chopped
4 cloves garlic, peeled and minced
¼ teaspoon salt
½ teaspoon ground black pepper

2¼ cups brown rice
2 cups water
¼ cup chopped fresh flat-leaf parsley
¼ cup chopped fresh basil
2 tablespoons chopped fresh oregano
2 teaspoons fresh thyme leaves

SERVES 8	
Per Serving:	
Calories	102
Fat	4g
Protein	2g
Sodium	96mg
Fiber	1g
Carbohydrates	15g
Sugar	1g

1 Press the Sauté button on the Instant Pot® and heat oil. Add onion and cook until soft, about 6 minutes. Add garlic, salt, and pepper and cook until fragrant, about 30 seconds. Add rice and cook, stirring constantly, until well-coated and starting to toast, about 3 minutes. Press the Cancel button.

2 Stir in water. Close lid, set steam release to Sealing, press the Manual button, and set time to 22 minutes. When the timer beeps, let pressure release naturally for 10 minutes, then quick-release the remaining pressure. Open lid and fold in parsley, basil, oregano, and thyme. Serve warm.

Confetti Rice

For a healthy, fiber-rich alternative to white rice, use brown rice instead. It's the same thing as white rice, except the bran layer and all of its nutrients have not been removed.

3 tablespoons olive oil
1 small red onion, peeled and diced
2 cloves garlic, peeled and minced
1 cup long-grain white rice
1 (16-ounce) bag frozen mixed vegetables (carrots, corn, peas, and green beans), thawed

1 (14.5-ounce) can low-sodium chicken broth
¼ cup lemon juice
1 tablespoon ground cumin
½ teaspoon salt
½ teaspoon ground black pepper

SERVES 6	
Per Serving:	
Calories	328
Fat	8g
Protein	6g
Sodium	223mg
Fiber	2g
Carbohydrates	57g
Sugar	3g

1 Press the Sauté button on the Instant Pot® and heat oil. Add onion and sauté 3 minutes. Add garlic and cook 30 seconds.

2 Add rice and cook until grains become translucent, about 5 minutes. Add mixed vegetables, broth, lemon juice, cumin, salt, and pepper, and stir to mix. Press the Cancel button.

3 Close lid, set steam release to Sealing, press the Manual button, and set time to 7 minutes. When the timer beeps, let pressure release naturally, about 20 minutes. Open lid, fluff rice with a fork, and serve hot.

Wild Rice Pilaf with Pine Nuts

SERVES 8	
Per Serving:	
Calories	314
Fat	18g
Protein	10g
Sodium	93mg
Fiber	4g
Carbohydrates	41g
Sugar	2g

The easiest way to toast pine nuts is in a dry pan over medium heat. Cook, stirring frequently, until they are golden brown, about 3 minutes.

2 tablespoons extra-virgin olive oil
1 medium white onion, peeled and chopped
2 cups chopped baby bella mushrooms
3 cloves garlic, peeled and minced
2 cups wild rice

2½ cups vegetable broth
½ cup toasted pine nuts
¼ cup chopped fresh flat-leaf parsley
2 tablespoons chopped fresh chives
¼ teaspoon salt
½ teaspoon ground black pepper

1 Press the Sauté button on the Instant Pot® and heat oil. Add onion and mushrooms. Cook until soft, about 8 minutes. Add garlic and cook until fragrant, about 30 seconds. Add rice and press the Cancel button.

2 Stir in broth. Close lid, set steam release to Sealing, press the Manual button, and set time to 20 minutes. When the timer beeps, let pressure release naturally for 10 minutes, then quick-release the remaining pressure. Open lid and fluff rice with a fork. Fold in pine nuts, parsley, and chives. Season with salt and pepper. Serve warm.

Herbed Wild Rice Dressing

SERVES 8	
Per Serving:	
Calories	356
Fat	13g
Protein	9g
Sodium	147mg
Fiber	5g
Carbohydrates	50g
Sugar	10g

Served with roasted turkey or baked ham, this dressing is a tasty and healthful addition to your holiday table.

2 tablespoons extra-virgin olive oil
2 stalks celery, chopped
1 medium white onion, peeled and chopped
1 medium carrot, peeled and chopped
2 cups sliced baby bella mushrooms
2 cloves garlic, peeled and minced
1 tablespoon chopped fresh rosemary

1 tablespoon chopped fresh sage
¼ teaspoon salt
½ teaspoon ground black pepper
2 cups wild rice
2½ cups vegetable broth
½ cup dried cranberries
½ cup chopped toasted pecans

1 Press the Sauté button on the Instant Pot® and heat oil. Add celery, onion, carrot, and mushrooms. Cook until soft, about 10 minutes. Add garlic, rosemary, sage, salt, and pepper. Cook until fragrant, about 1 minute. Add rice and mix well. Press the Cancel button.

2 Stir in broth. Close lid, set steam release to Sealing, press the Manual button, and set time to 20 minutes. When the timer beeps, let pressure release naturally for 10 minutes, then quick-release the remaining pressure. Open lid and fold in cranberries and pecans. Serve warm.

Sun-Dried Tomato Rice

Sun-dried tomatoes are surprisingly good for you because drying them helps retain their nutritional content. The process also boosts the amount of antioxidant lycopene in tomatoes, which is believed to help prevent cancer.

2 tablespoons extra-virgin olive oil
½ medium yellow onion, peeled and chopped
2 cloves garlic, peeled and minced
1 cup chopped sun-dried tomatoes in oil, drained
1 tablespoon tomato paste
2 cups brown rice
2¼ cups water
½ cup chopped fresh basil
¼ teaspoon salt
½ teaspoon ground black pepper

SERVES 8	
Per Serving:	
Calories	114
Fat	4g
Protein	2g
Sodium	112mg
Fiber	2g
Carbohydrates	18g
Sugar	4g

1 Press the Sauté button on the Instant Pot® and heat oil. Add onion and cook until soft, about 6 minutes. Add garlic and sun-dried tomatoes and cook until fragrant, about 30 seconds. Add tomato paste, rice, and water, and stir well. Press the Cancel button.

2 Close lid, set steam release to Sealing, press the Manual button, and set time to 22 minutes. When the timer beeps, let pressure release naturally for 10 minutes, then quick-release the remaining pressure. Open lid and fold in basil. Season with salt and pepper. Serve warm.

Cilantro Lime Rice

Top this rice with salmon seasoned with cumin and lime, or with a simple grilled chicken breast, along with a crisp green salad for a complete meal.

2 tablespoons extra-virgin olive oil
½ medium yellow onion, peeled and chopped
2 cloves garlic, peeled and minced
½ cup chopped fresh cilantro, divided
2 cups brown rice
2¼ cups water
2 tablespoons lime juice
1 tablespoon grated lime zest
¼ teaspoon salt
½ teaspoon ground black pepper

SERVES 8	
Per Serving:	
Calories	95
Fat	4g
Protein	1g
Sodium	94mg
Fiber	1g
Carbohydrates	14g
Sugar	1g

1 Press the Sauté button on the Instant Pot® and heat oil. Add onion and cook until soft, about 6 minutes. Add garlic and ¼ cup cilantro and cook until fragrant, about 30 seconds. Add rice and cook, stirring constantly, until well coated and starting to toast, about 3 minutes. Press the Cancel button.

2 Stir in water. Close lid, set steam release to Sealing, press the Manual button, and set time to 22 minutes. When the timer beeps, let pressure release naturally for 10 minutes, then quick-release the remaining pressure. Open lid and fluff rice with a fork. Fold in remaining ¼ cup cilantro, lime juice, lime zest, salt, and pepper. Serve warm.

Rice with Olives and Basil

Kalamata olives are grown in Greece. They have a dark purple color and a soft texture. In most grocery stores, they are sold in jars packed in either brine or olive oil, and they come both whole and pitted.

2 tablespoons extra-virgin olive oil

1 medium yellow onion, peeled and chopped

2 cloves garlic, peeled and minced

2 cups brown rice

2¼ cups water

1 cup pitted Kalamata olives

½ cup torn basil

1 tablespoon lemon juice

2 teaspoons grated lemon zest

½ teaspoon ground black pepper

1 Press the Sauté button on the Instant Pot® and heat oil. Add onion and cook until soft, about 6 minutes. Add garlic and cook until fragrant, about 30 seconds. Add rice and cook, stirring constantly, until well coated and starting to toast, about 3 minutes. Press the Cancel button.

2 Stir in water. Close lid, set steam release to Sealing, press the Manual button, and set time to 22 minutes. When the timer beeps, let pressure release naturally for 10 minutes, then quick-release the remaining pressure until the float valve drops. Open lid and fluff rice with a fork. Fold in olives, basil, lemon juice, lemon zest, and pepper. Serve warm.

SERVES 8

Per Serving:	
Calories	182
Fat	11g
Protein	1g
Sodium	355mg
Fiber	1g
Carbohydrates	18g
Sugar	1g

OLIVES

For thousands of years, olives have been a part of the human diet. Olives are drupes (fruits with a stone or pit inside) grown on trees in many Mediterranean countries. Their color is largely due to the time of harvest. Green olives are picked when they are not yet ripe, while black olives are picked later in the growing season. Once harvested, olives are cured to soften their naturally bitter flavor. The cure also adds the salty flavor commonly associated with olives. Your local grocery store likely has an olive bar where you can sample some of the many different varieties—green or black, whole or pitted, briny or spicy.

Domatorizo (Greek Tomato Rice)

Add a few golden raisins and pine nuts to this recipe for some extra texture and little bursts of sweetness.

SERVES 6

Per Serving:

Calories	184
Fat	9g
Protein	6g
Sodium	537mg
Fiber	1g
Carbohydrates	20g
Sugar	2g

2 tablespoons extra-virgin olive oil
1 large onion, peeled and diced
1 cup Arborio rice
1 cup tomato juice
3 tablespoons dry white wine
2 cups water
1 tablespoon tomato paste
½ teaspoon salt
½ teaspoon ground black pepper
½ cup crumbled or cubed feta cheese
⅛ teaspoon dried Greek oregano
1 scallion, thinly sliced

1 Press the Sauté button on the Instant Pot® and heat oil. Add onion and cook until just tender, about 3 minutes. Stir in rice and cook for 2 minutes.

2 Add tomato juice and wine to rice. Cook, stirring often, until the liquid is absorbed, about 1 minute.

3 In a small bowl, whisk together water and tomato paste. Add to pot along with salt and pepper and stir well. Press the Cancel button.

4 Close lid, set steam release to Sealing, press the Manual button, and set time to 5 minutes. When the timer beeps, let pressure release naturally for 10 minutes, then quick-release any remaining pressure until the float valve drops.

5 Open lid and stir well. Spoon rice into bowls and top with feta, oregano, and scallion. Serve immediately.

Spinach Rice

Spinach Rice makes a hearty meal all by itself, but it can also be paired with grilled chicken, fish, or shrimp as a flavorful side dish.

2 tablespoons extra-virgin olive oil
1 large onion, peeled and diced
2 pounds chopped fresh spinach
1 tablespoon tomato paste
2½ cups water

1 cup Arborio rice
¼ cup minced fresh mint
½ teaspoon salt
¼ teaspoon ground black pepper
2 tablespoons lemon juice

SERVES 6	
Per Serving:	
Calories	158
Fat	5g
Protein	7g
Sodium	373mg
Fiber	4g
Carbohydrates	23g
Sugar	2g

1 Press the Sauté button on the Instant Pot® and heat oil. Add onion and sauté 3 minutes. Add spinach and cook until wilted, about 2 minutes.

2 Dilute tomato paste in water. Add to pot along with rice, mint, salt, and pepper and stir thoroughly. Press the Cancel button.

3 Close lid, set steam release to Sealing, press the Rice button and cook for the default time. When the timer beeps, let pressure release naturally for 5 minutes, then quick-release any remaining pressure until the float valve drops. Open lid and let rice stand 10 minutes. Serve hot or cold with a sprinkling of lemon juice over the top.

Brown Rice and Vegetables

For more flavor, add an Italian, Spanish, or a Mediterranean herbal seasoning blend to the rice and water in Step 1.

1 cup brown rice
1½ cups water
1 small turnip, peeled and diced
1 pound butternut squash, peeled and diced
½ cup quartered baby carrots
1 small zucchini, trimmed, quartered lengthwise, and sliced

3 stalks Swiss chard, leafy greens chopped and stems diced
1 cup coarsely chopped broccoli florets
⅓ cup diced water chestnuts
½ teaspoon salt
½ teaspoon ground black pepper

SERVES 8	
Per Serving:	
Calories	73
Fat	0g
Protein	2g
Sodium	187mg
Fiber	3g
Carbohydrates	16g
Sugar	3g

1 Place rice and water in the Instant Pot®. Close lid, set steam release to Sealing, press the Rice button, and cook for the default time. When the timer beeps, let pressure release naturally, about 20 minutes. Press the Cancel button. Open lid.

2 Stir in remaining ingredients.

3 Close lid, set steam release to Sealing, press the Manual button, and set time to 1 minute. When the timer beeps, quick-release the pressure until the float valve drops. Open lid and fluff with a fork. Serve.

Vegetable Risotto with Beet Greens

SERVES 6	
Per Serving:	
Calories	261
Fat	12g
Protein	9g
Sodium	544mg
Fiber	5g
Carbohydrates	30g
Sugar	5g

You can substitute water or vegetable broth for the chicken broth and make this a vegetarian meal. If you are serving this to vegans, replace the cheese with nutritional yeast.

¼ cup light olive oil
1 clove garlic, peeled and minced
1 small Asian eggplant, sliced
1 small zucchini, trimmed and sliced
1 large red bell pepper, seeded and cut in quarters
1 large portobello mushroom, gills and stem removed, cap sliced
1 medium onion, peeled and thickly sliced
½ teaspoon salt
½ teaspoon ground black pepper
1 cup Arborio rice
½ cup dry white wine
2 cups low-sodium chicken broth
2 cups sliced young beet greens
¼ cup sliced fresh basil
½ cup grated Parmesan cheese

1 Combine oil and garlic in a small bowl. Stir to mix and set aside 10 minutes to infuse.

2 Preheat a grill or a grill pan over medium-high heat.

3 Brush all sides of eggplant slices, zucchini slices, bell pepper quarters, mushroom slices, and onion slices with garlic-infused oil, making sure to reserve 1 tablespoon of the oil.

4 Place vegetables on the grill rack or in the grill pan. Sprinkle with salt and black pepper.

5 Grill vegetables for several minutes on each side or until softened and slightly charred, about 1 minute per side. Set aside to cool, and then coarsely chop.

6 Press the Sauté button on the Instant Pot® and heat reserved 1 tablespoon garlic-infused oil. Add rice and stir it to coat it in oil. Stir in wine and broth. Press the Cancel button.

7 Close lid, set steam release to Sealing, press the Manual button, and set time to 7 minutes. When the timer beeps, quick-release the pressure until the float valve drops and open the lid.

8 Add chopped grilled vegetables, beet greens, and basil. Cover the Instant Pot® (but do not lock the lid into place). Set aside for 5 minutes or until greens are wilted. Stir in cheese and serve hot.

CHAPTER 5

Grains

Buckwheat and Halloumi Bowl with Mint Dressing

Halloumi is a sheep's milk cheese made on the Greek island of Cyprus. Similar cheeses are produced in North America under the names "grilling cheese" or "bread cheese," and can usually be found in the deli department's specialty cheese section.

MORE ABOUT HALLOUMI

Halloumi only melts under very high temperatures, making it suitable for grilling and panfrying. It has a flavor similar to feta cheese, and the cheese achieves its best flavor when it is heated and well browned. For best results, be sure to add a little olive oil to the grill or pan to encourage browning and to prevent sticking. You can serve warm pieces of Halloumi as an appetizer along with almonds, olives, and vegetables; as part of a salad or vegetable bowl; or as they do in Cyprus, with cool hunks of watermelon.

1 cup raw buckwheat groats, rinsed and drained
1¼ cups water
¼ teaspoon salt
2 tablespoons light olive oil, divided
8 ounces Halloumi, cut into ¼" slices
4 cups chopped kale or spinach
½ medium red onion, peeled and diced
½ large English cucumber, chopped
1 cup halved cherry tomatoes
½ cup pitted Kalamata olives
¼ cup lemon juice
¼ cup extra-virgin olive oil
¼ cup fresh mint leaves
1 teaspoon honey
1 teaspoon Dijon mustard
¼ teaspoon ground black pepper

1. Place buckwheat, water, salt, and 1 tablespoon light olive oil in the Instant Pot® and stir well. Close lid and set steam release to Sealing. Press the Manual button and set time to 6 minutes.

2. When the timer beeps, let pressure release naturally, about 20 minutes, then open lid and transfer buckwheat to a separate medium bowl. Clean and dry pot. Press the Cancel button.

3. Press the Sauté button and heat remaining 1 tablespoon light olive oil. Add Halloumi slices and brown for 3 minutes per side.

4. To assemble, place a layer of greens in four bowls. Top with buckwheat, Halloumi slices, onion, cucumber, tomatoes, and olives.

5. Place lemon juice, extra-virgin olive oil, mint, honey, Dijon mustard, and pepper in a blender. Blend until completely combined, about 30 seconds. Pour dressing over bowls and serve immediately.

Farro Salad with Tomatoes and Olives

Before you add salt to this salad, be sure to taste it first. The olives provide plenty of salty flavor, and the balsamic vinegar adds a sweet yet tart punch.

10 ounces farro, rinsed and drained
4 cups water
4 Roma tomatoes, seeded and chopped
4 scallions, green parts only, thinly sliced
½ cup sliced black olives
¼ cup minced fresh flat-leaf parsley
¼ cup extra-virgin olive oil
2 tablespoons balsamic vinegar
¼ teaspoon ground black pepper

1 Place farro and water in the Instant Pot®. Close lid and set steam release to Sealing. Press the Multigrain button and set time to 20 minutes. When the timer beeps, let pressure release naturally, about 30 minutes.

2 Open lid and fluff with a fork. Transfer to a bowl and cool 30 minutes. Add tomatoes, scallions, black olives, and parsley and mix well.

3 In a small bowl, whisk together oil, balsamic vinegar, and pepper. Pour over salad and toss to evenly coat. Refrigerate for at least 4 hours before serving. Serve chilled or at room temperature.

Amaranth Salad

This salad is best served alongside grilled fish or seafood. Spoon it onto beds of crisp greens for a more elegant presentation.

2 cups water
1 cup amaranth
1 teaspoon dried Greek oregano
½ teaspoon salt
½ teaspoon ground black pepper
1 tablespoon extra-virgin olive oil
2 teaspoons red wine vinegar

1 Add water and amaranth to the Instant Pot®. Close lid, set steam release to Sealing, press the Manual button, and set time to 6 minutes. When the timer beeps, quick-release the pressure until the float valve drops.

2 Open lid and fluff amaranth with a fork. Add oregano, salt, and pepper. Mix well. Drizzle with olive oil and wine vinegar. Serve hot.

Quinoa Tabbouleh

Quinoa contains flavonoids, which are linked to improved heart health, as well as antioxidants, which studies show reduce inflammation.

1 cup quinoa, rinsed and drained
2 cups water
¼ cup olive oil
2 tablespoons lemon juice
1 clove garlic, peeled and minced
½ teaspoon salt

½ teaspoon ground black pepper
2 medium tomatoes, seeded and chopped
1 large English cucumber, chopped
1 cup thinly sliced scallions
½ cup minced fresh mint
½ cup chopped fresh flat-leaf parsley

SERVES 6	
Per Serving:	
Calories	117
Fat	3g
Protein	4g
Sodium	199mg
Fiber	2g
Carbohydrates	19g
Sugar	0g

1 Add quinoa and water to the Instant Pot® and stir well. Close lid, set steam release to Sealing, press the Manual button, and set time to 20 minutes. When the timer beeps, let pressure release naturally, about 20 minutes, then open lid. Fluff quinoa with a fork. Transfer to a medium bowl and set aside to cool to room temperature, about 40 minutes.

2 Add oil, lemon juice, garlic, salt, pepper, tomatoes, cucumber, scallions, mint, and parsley to quinoa and toss well. Refrigerate for 4 hours before serving.

Wheat Berry Salad

To make a healthy and delicious party appetizer, put a teaspoon of Wheat Berry Salad on individual sections of baby romaine hearts.

1½ tablespoons vegetable oil
6¾ cups water
1½ cups wheat berries
1½ teaspoons Dijon mustard
1 teaspoon sugar
1 teaspoon salt
½ teaspoon ground black pepper
¼ cup white wine vinegar
½ cup extra-virgin olive oil

½ small red onion, peeled and diced
1⅓ cups frozen corn, thawed
1 medium zucchini, trimmed, grated, and drained
2 stalks celery, finely diced
1 medium red bell pepper, seeded and diced
4 scallions, diced
¼ cup diced sun-dried tomatoes
¼ cup chopped fresh parsley

SERVES 12	
Per Serving:	
Calories	158
Fat	10g
Protein	2g
Sodium	268mg
Fiber	2g
Carbohydrates	16g
Sugar	3g

1 Add vegetable oil, water, and wheat berries to the Instant Pot®. Close lid, set steam release to Sealing, press the Manual button, and set time to 50 minutes. When the timer beeps, quick-release the pressure until the float valve drops and open lid. Fluff wheat berries with a fork. Drain any excess liquid, transfer to a large bowl, and set aside to cool.

2 Purée mustard, sugar, salt, black pepper, vinegar, olive oil, and onion in a blender. Stir dressing into wheat berries. Stir in rest of ingredients. Serve.

Prassorizo (Leeks and Rice)

For a little extra tangy flavor, sprinkle crumbled feta cheese over the top of this dish when serving.

SERVES 6	
Per Serving:	
Calories	224
Fat	12g
Protein	4g
Sodium	408mg
Fiber	4g
Carbohydrates	28g
Sugar	16g

6 large leeks
5 cups water
4 scallions, chopped
⅓ cup minced fresh dill
¼ cup minced fresh mint
½ tablespoon dried thyme

½ teaspoon salt
¼ teaspoon ground black pepper
1 cup Arborio rice
⅓ cup extra-virgin olive oil
3 tablespoons lemon juice

1 Cut white ends of leeks into thick slices. Discard green part of leeks.

2 Place leeks, water, scallions, dill, mint, thyme, salt, and pepper in the Instant Pot®. Stir well. Add rice and stir to combine.

3 Close lid, set steam release to Sealing, press the Rice button, and set time to 12 minutes. When the timer beeps, let pressure release naturally for 10 minutes, then quick-release the remaining pressure.

4 Open lid and stir well. Add olive oil and lemon juice. Serve hot.

Mediterranean Bulgur Medley

Petimezi is a Greek concentrated grape must syrup. If you can't find it in your grocery store, Greek thyme honey is a good substitute.

SERVES 6	
Per Serving:	
Calories	129
Fat	1g
Protein	3g
Sodium	219mg
Fiber	2g
Carbohydrates	28g
Sugar	3g

2 tablespoons extra-virgin olive oil
1 medium onion, peeled and diced
½ cup chopped button mushrooms
½ cup golden raisins (sultanas)
¼ cup pine nuts
2 cups vegetable stock
1 teaspoon ground cumin

½ teaspoon salt
½ teaspoon ground black pepper
1 cup medium bulgur wheat
1 tablespoon *petimezi* or honey
12 chestnuts, roasted, peeled, and halved
1 teaspoon sesame seeds

1 Press the Sauté button on the Instant Pot® and heat oil. Add onion and sauté 3 minutes. Add mushrooms, raisins, and pine nuts and cook 2 minutes.

2 Add stock, cumin, salt, pepper, bulgur, and *petimezi*. Cook, stirring, for 3 minutes. Add chestnuts, then press the Cancel button.

3 Close lid, set steam release to Sealing, press the Rice button, and set time to 12 minutes. When the timer beeps, quick-release the pressure until the float valve drops and open lid. Stir well, then let stand, uncovered, on the Keep Warm setting for 10 minutes. Sprinkle with sesame seeds and serve.

Farro and Mushroom Risotto

With its chewy texture and nutty flavor, farro makes a lovely change from traditional rice in this risotto. Combine with savory mushrooms and a sprinkle of salty Parmesan, and you have a meal that is as comforting as it is filling.

2 tablespoons olive oil

1 medium yellow onion, peeled and diced

16 ounces sliced button mushrooms

½ teaspoon salt

½ teaspoon ground black pepper

½ teaspoon dried thyme

½ teaspoon dried oregano

1 clove garlic, peeled and minced

1 cup farro, rinsed and drained

1½ cups vegetable broth

¼ cup grated Parmesan cheese

2 tablespoons minced fresh flat-leaf parsley

SERVES 6	
Per Serving:	
Calories	215
Fat	8g
Protein	11g
Sodium	419mg
Fiber	3g
Carbohydrates	24g
Sugar	2g

1 Press the Sauté button on the Instant Pot® and heat oil. Add onion and mushrooms and sauté 8 minutes. Add salt, pepper, thyme, and oregano and cook 30 seconds. Add garlic and cook for 30 seconds. Press the Cancel button.

2 Stir in farro and broth. Close lid, set steam release to Sealing, press the Manual button, and set time to 10 minutes. When timer beeps, let pressure release naturally for 10 minutes, then quick-release the remaining pressure until the float valve drops.

3 Top with cheese and parsley before serving.

Creamy Thyme Polenta

If you want to substitute the dried thyme with fresh thyme, increase the amount to 1 tablespoon chopped thyme leaves.

3½ cups water

½ cup coarse polenta

½ cup fine cornmeal

1 cup corn kernels

1 teaspoon dried thyme

1 teaspoon salt

SERVES 6	
Per Serving:	
Calories	74
Fat	1g
Protein	2g
Sodium	401mg
Fiber	2g
Carbohydrates	14g
Sugar	2g

1 Add all ingredients to the Instant Pot® and stir.

2 Close lid, set steam release to Sealing, press the Manual button, and set time to 10 minutes. When the timer beeps, quick-release the pressure until the float valve drops and open lid. Serve immediately.

Quinoa with Kale, Carrots, and Walnuts

This versatile salad is simple, fresh, and light. Enjoy it alone as a main dish or as a side dish with grilled seafood, fish, or chicken. It's a great make-ahead dish, so you can whip it up early in the week to enjoy later.

1 cup quinoa, rinsed and drained
2 cups water
¼ cup olive oil
2 tablespoons apple cider vinegar
1 clove garlic, peeled and minced
½ teaspoon ground black pepper
½ teaspoon salt
2 cups chopped kale
1 cup shredded carrot
1 cup toasted walnut pieces
½ cup crumbled feta cheese

1 Add quinoa and water to the Instant Pot® and stir well. Close lid, set steam release to Sealing, press the Manual button, and set time to 20 minutes. When the timer beeps, let pressure release naturally, about 20 minutes, then open lid. Fluff quinoa with a fork, then transfer to a medium bowl and set aside to cool to room temperature, about 40 minutes.

2 Add oil, vinegar, garlic, pepper, salt, kale, carrot, walnuts, and feta to quinoa and toss well. Refrigerate for 4 hours before serving.

SERVES 4

Per Serving:

Calories	625
Fat	39g
Protein	19g
Sodium	738mg
Fiber	10g
Carbohydrates	47g
Sugar	8g

DON'T LIKE KALE?

Kale is very popular and can be found in salads, in smoothies, and as a side dish in many restaurants. But what if you don't like kale? Collard greens, mustard greens, Swiss chard, and even spinach can be substituted for kale in most recipes. If you choose to replace kale with spinach, be sure to use regular spinach and not baby spinach—tender baby leaves will not hold up as well to cooking.

Bulgur Salad with Cucumbers, Olives, and Dill

SERVES 4

Per Serving:

Calories	290
Fat	27g
Protein	2g
Sodium	352mg
Fiber	2g
Carbohydrates	11g
Sugar	1g

Bulgur wheat needs gentle cooking as most brands sold in the store are cracked and partially cooked. You will need to adjust the pressure to Low, and for the best results, use the Rice setting.

1 cup bulgur wheat
2 cups water
1/4 cup olive oil
2 tablespoons balsamic vinegar
1 clove garlic, peeled and minced
1/2 teaspoon ground black pepper

1/2 teaspoon salt
1 large English cucumber, chopped
1/2 medium red onion, peeled and diced
1/4 cup chopped salt-cured olives
1/4 cup chopped fresh dill

1 Add bulgur and water to the Instant Pot® and stir well. Close lid, set steam release to Sealing, press the Rice button, adjust pressure to Low, and set time to 12 minutes. When the timer beeps, quick-release the pressure until the float valve drops. Open lid and fluff bulgur with a fork. Transfer to a medium bowl and set aside to cool to room temperature, about 40 minutes.

2 Stir in oil, vinegar, garlic, pepper, salt, cucumber, onion, olives, and dill, and toss well. Refrigerate for 4 hours before serving.

Barley Risotto

SERVES 6

Per Serving:

Calories	175
Fat	9g
Protein	10g
Sodium	447mg
Fiber	2g
Carbohydrates	13g
Sugar	2g

If you're not a fan of Parmesan cheese, you can substitute crumbled blue cheese or grated Cheddar cheese.

2 tablespoons olive oil
1 large onion, peeled and diced
1 clove garlic, peeled and minced
1 stalk celery, finely minced
1 1/2 cups pearl barley, rinsed and drained
1/3 cup dried mushrooms

4 cups low-sodium chicken broth
2 1/4 cups water
1 cup grated Parmesan cheese
2 tablespoons minced fresh parsley
1/4 teaspoon salt

1 Press the Sauté button on the Instant Pot® and heat oil. Add onion and sauté 5 minutes. Add garlic and cook 30 seconds. Stir in celery, barley, mushrooms, broth, and water. Press the Cancel button.

2 Close lid, set steam release to Sealing, press the Manual button, and set time to 18 minutes. When the timer beeps, quick-release the pressure until the float valve drops and open the lid.

3 Drain off excess liquid, leaving enough to leave the risotto slightly soupy. Press the Cancel button, then press the Sauté button and cook until thickened, about 5 minutes. Stir in cheese, parsley, and salt. Serve immediately.

Quinoa with Artichokes

Low in fat and rich in fiber, artichokes make a delicious addition to salads, casseroles, and soups. Look for artichoke hearts marinated in oil and herbs for the best flavor.

2 tablespoons light olive oil

1 medium yellow onion, peeled and diced

2 cloves garlic, peeled and minced

½ teaspoon salt

½ teaspoon ground black pepper

1 cup quinoa, rinsed and drained

2 cups vegetable broth

1 cup roughly chopped marinated artichoke hearts

½ cup sliced green olives

½ cup minced fresh flat-leaf parsley

2 tablespoons lemon juice

SERVES 4	
Per Serving:	
Calories	270
Fat	13g
Protein	6g
Sodium	718mg
Fiber	4g
Carbohydrates	33g
Sugar	3g

1 Press the Sauté button on the Instant Pot® and heat oil. Add onion and cook until tender, about 5 minutes. Add garlic, salt, and pepper, and cook until fragrant, about 30 seconds. Press the Cancel button.

2 Stir in quinoa and broth. Close lid, set steam release to Sealing, press the Manual button, and set time to 20 minutes. When the timer beeps, let pressure release naturally, about 20 minutes, then open lid. Fluff quinoa with a fork, then stir in remaining ingredients. Serve immediately.

Quinoa Pilaf with Almonds and Raisins

The crunch of the almonds and the slightly chewy raisins make this sweet and savory pilaf almost addictive. Serve as a side dish with grilled fish, seafood, or chicken, or enjoy it alone as a light meal.

2 tablespoons light olive oil

1 medium yellow onion, peeled and diced

2 cloves garlic, peeled and minced

½ teaspoon ground black pepper

½ teaspoon salt

1 cup quinoa, rinsed and drained

2 cups water

1 cup golden raisins (sultanas)

½ cup toasted slivered almonds

½ cup minced fresh flat-leaf parsley

½ cup crumbled feta cheese

SERVES 4	
Per Serving:	
Calories	502
Fat	21g
Protein	16g
Sodium	641mg
Fiber	6g
Carbohydrates	65g
Sugar	28g

1 Press the Sauté button on the Instant Pot® and heat oil. Add onion and cook until tender, about 5 minutes. Add garlic, pepper, and salt, and cook until fragrant, about 30 seconds. Press the Cancel button.

2 Add quinoa and water to the Instant Pot® and stir well. Close lid, set steam release to Sealing, press the Manual button, and set time to 20 minutes. When the timer beeps, let pressure release naturally, about 20 minutes, then open lid. Fluff quinoa with a fork, add raisins, almonds, and parsley, and toss well. Top with feta and serve immediately.

Quinoa Salad with Tomatoes

SERVES 4	
Per Serving:	
Calories	223
Fat	10g
Protein	6g
Sodium	586mg
Fiber	3g
Carbohydrates	29g
Sugar	0g

The combination of tomato, garlic, and parsley goes well with any grain, so if you're not in a quinoa mood, try couscous or even rice instead.

2 tablespoons olive oil
2 cloves garlic, peeled and minced
1 cup diced fresh tomatoes
¼ cup chopped fresh Italian flat-leaf parsley

1 tablespoon lemon juice
1 cup quinoa, rinsed and drained
2 cups water
1 teaspoon salt

1 Press the Sauté button on the Instant Pot® and heat oil. Add garlic and cook 30 seconds, then add tomatoes, parsley, and lemon juice. Cook an additional 1 minute. Transfer mixture to a small bowl and set aside. Press the Cancel button.

2 Add quinoa and water to the Instant Pot®. Close lid, set steam release to Sealing, press the Multigrain button, and set time to 20 minutes.

3 When timer beeps, let pressure release naturally, about 20 minutes, then open lid. Fluff with a fork and stir in tomato mixture and salt. Serve immediately.

Mushroom and Barley Soup

SERVES 6	
Per Serving:	
Calories	120
Fat	7g
Protein	3g
Sodium	126mg
Fiber	3g
Carbohydrates	13g
Sugar	2g

This is a vegetarian soup. If you want the soup to complement a meat entrée, substitute chicken or beef broth for the water.

3 tablespoons olive oil
2 stalks celery, diced
1 large carrot, peeled and diced
1 large sweet onion, peeled, halved, and sliced
2 cloves garlic, peeled and minced
1 portobello mushroom cap, diced

8 ounces mushrooms, sliced
1 bay leaf
½ cup pearl barley, rinsed and drained
6 cups water
2 tablespoons vermouth
¼ teaspoon salt
¼ teaspoon ground black pepper

1 Press the Sauté button on the Instant Pot® and heat oil. Add celery and carrot, and sauté 2 minutes. Add onion and sauté 3 minutes. Stir in garlic and mushrooms and cook until mushrooms release their moisture and onion begins to turn golden, about 10 minutes.

2 Stir in bay leaf, barley, water, vermouth, salt, and pepper. Press the Cancel button. Close lid, set steam release to Sealing, press the Manual button, and set time to 20 minutes. When the timer beeps, let pressure release naturally, about 20 minutes.

3 Open lid and remove and discard bay leaf. Serve hot.

Quinoa Salad with Chicken, Chickpeas, and Spinach

Chickpeas and chicken pack this salad with protein, so it will help fill you up and give you plenty of energy to tackle the second half of your work-day. Make this salad on Sunday and use it for grab-and-go lunches all week.

4 tablespoons olive oil, divided
1 medium yellow onion, peeled and chopped
2 cloves garlic, peeled and minced
4 cups fresh baby spinach leaves
½ teaspoon salt
¼ teaspoon ground black pepper
1½ cups quinoa, rinsed and drained
2 cups vegetable broth
1⅓ cups water
1 tablespoon apple cider vinegar
1 (15-ounce) can chickpeas, drained and rinsed
1 (6-ounce) boneless, skinless chicken breast, cooked and shredded

1 Press the Sauté button on the Instant Pot® and heat 2 tablespoons olive oil. Add onion and cook until tender, about 3 minutes. Add garlic, spinach, salt, and pepper and cook 3 minutes until spinach has wilted. Transfer spinach mixture to a large bowl. Press the Cancel button.

2 Add quinoa, broth, and water to the Instant Pot®. Close lid, set steam release to Sealing, press the Rice button, and set time to 12 minutes.

3 While quinoa cooks, add remaining 2 tablespoons olive oil, vinegar, chickpeas, and chicken to spinach mixture and toss to coat. Set aside.

4 When the timer beeps, let pressure release naturally, about 20 minutes.

5 Open lid and fluff quinoa with a fork. Press the Cancel button and let quinoa cool 10 minutes, then transfer to the bowl with chicken mixture. Mix well. Serve warm, at room temperature, or cold.

SERVES 6

Per Serving:	
Calories	232
Fat	12g
Protein	14g
Sodium	463mg
Fiber	6g
Carbohydrates	20g
Sugar	4g

CHICKPEAS

Despite the name, chickpeas are actually legumes. You can find them sold either canned or dried. They are also ground into a flour (called gram flour), but are best known as the base for hummus. Rich in nutrients, chickpeas are an excellent source of fiber, protein, iron, and phosphorus for people on vegetarian and vegan diets.

Quinoa Salad in Endive Boats

SERVES 4	
Per Serving:	
Calories	536
Fat	35g
Protein	13g
Sodium	657mg
Fiber	13g
Carbohydrates	46g
Sugar	8g

With endive, nature has created a little boat ready for you to fill. The simplicity of the seasoned quinoa stuffing and the crunchiness and nuttiness of the pecan garnish temper the slight bitterness of the endive to make a well-rounded bite.

1 tablespoon walnut oil
1 cup quinoa, rinsed and drained
2½ cups water
2 cups chopped jarred artichoke hearts
2 cups diced tomatoes
½ small red onion, peeled and thinly sliced
2 tablespoons olive oil
1 tablespoon balsamic vinegar
4 large Belgian endive leaves
1 cup toasted pecans

1 Press the Sauté button on the Instant Pot® and heat walnut oil. Add quinoa and toss for 1 minute until slightly browned. Add water and stir. Press the Cancel button.

2 Close lid, set steam release to Sealing, press the Manual button, and set time to 2 minutes. When the timer beeps, let pressure release naturally for 10 minutes. Quick-release any remaining pressure until the float valve drops and open lid. Drain liquid and transfer quinoa to a serving bowl.

3 Add artichoke hearts, tomatoes, onion, olive oil, and vinegar to quinoa and stir to combine. Cover and refrigerate mixture for 1 hour or up to overnight.

4 Place endive leaves on four plates. Top each with ¼ cup quinoa mixture. Sprinkle toasted pecans over the top of each endive boat and serve.

Vegetable Barley Soup

A big pot of soup is great to have on hand to serve for lunches during the week, especially when it's accompanied by a sandwich or green salad.

2 tablespoons olive oil
½ medium yellow onion, peeled and chopped
1 medium carrot, peeled and chopped
1 stalk celery, chopped
2 cups sliced button mushrooms
2 cloves garlic, peeled and minced
½ teaspoon dried thyme
½ teaspoon ground black pepper
1 large russet potato, peeled and cut into ½" pieces
1 (14.5-ounce) can fire-roasted diced tomatoes, undrained
½ cup medium pearl barley, rinsed and drained
4 cups vegetable broth
2 cups water
1 (15-ounce) can corn, drained
1 (15-ounce) can cut green beans, drained
1 (15-ounce) can Great Northern beans, drained and rinsed
½ teaspoon salt

1 Press the Sauté button on the Instant Pot® and heat oil. Add onion, carrot, celery, and mushrooms. Cook until just tender, about 5 minutes. Add garlic, thyme, and pepper. Cook 30 seconds. Press the Cancel button.

2 Add potato, tomatoes, barley, broth, and water to pot. Close lid, set steam release to Sealing, press the Soup button, and cook for the default time of 20 minutes.

3 When the timer beeps, let pressure release naturally, about 15 minutes. Open lid and stir soup, then add corn, green beans, and Great Northern beans. Close lid and let stand on the Keep Warm setting for 10 minutes. Stir in salt. Serve hot.

SERVES 8	
Per Serving:	
Calories	190
Fat	4g
Protein	7g
Sodium	548mg
Fiber	8g
Carbohydrates	34g
Sugar	7g

KITCHEN SINK SOUP

Have you ever looked in the refrigerator and found you have half a bell pepper, one quarter of a zucchini, a half cup of chopped squash, and perhaps a quarter of an onion? Vegetable soup is a perfect place to use up all of these odds and ends.

Bulgur with Red Pepper and Goat Cheese

SERVES 4	
Per Serving:	
Calories	123
Fat	7g
Protein	4g
Sodium	227mg
Fiber	4g
Carbohydrates	12g
Sugar	3g

CEREAL GRAINS

Cereal grains provide an excellent way to add more plant-based protein to your diet. Varieties of cereal grains include wheat, millet, rice, rye, oats, barley, and corn. They are among the world's oldest cultivated crops, with evidence that humans were growing and harvesting them as early as 10,000 B.C. Today, cereal grains are still vital, accounting for as much as 50 percent of the calories consumed by humans.

Goat cheese is lower in fat and cholesterol than cow's milk cheeses, but don't think for a second it is bland. Goat cheese is creamy, and the flavor ranges from tangy to mildly sweet. For an extra flavor boost, try an herb-crusted goat cheese.

1 tablespoon light olive oil
1 medium red bell pepper, seeded and chopped
½ medium yellow onion, peeled and chopped
1 clove garlic, peeled and minced
½ teaspoon ground black pepper
¼ teaspoon salt
1 cup bulgur wheat
2 cups water
¼ cup chopped fresh chives
¼ cup chopped fresh flat-leaf parsley
2 ounces crumbled goat cheese

1 Press the Sauté button on the Instant Pot® and heat oil. Add bell pepper and onion, and cook until just softened, about 3 minutes. Add garlic, black pepper, and salt. Cook until garlic is fragrant, about 30 seconds. Press the Cancel button.

2 Add bulgur and water to the Instant Pot® and stir well. Close lid, set steam release to Sealing, press the Rice button, adjust pressure to Low, and set time to 12 minutes. When the timer beeps, quick-release the pressure until the float valve drops. Open lid and fluff bulgur with a fork.

3 Add chives and parsley to pot and toss. Transfer rice mixture to a serving dish and top with goat cheese. Serve warm.

Millet Tabbouleh

This twist on tabbouleh (which is traditionally made with bulgur) can easily be served as a side dish to a main meal, a vegetarian main dish with grape leaves, or as a chilled lunch salad.

1½ cups chopped fresh parsley
¼ cup chopped fresh mint leaves
1 cup diced red onion
¼ cup diced zucchini
½ cup peeled, seeded, and diced cucumber
4 small Roma tomatoes, seeded and diced
¼ cup plus 2 teaspoons olive oil, divided
¼ cup lemon juice
1 teaspoon grated lemon zest
¾ teaspoons salt, divided
¼ teaspoon ground black pepper
1 cup millet
2 cups vegetable broth

1. In a medium bowl, combine parsley, mint, onion, zucchini, cucumber, tomatoes, ¼ cup olive oil, lemon juice, lemon zest, ½ teaspoon salt, and pepper. Cover and refrigerate for at least 30 minutes.

2. Add remaining 2 teaspoons olive oil to the Instant Pot®. Add millet in an even layer. Add broth and remaining ¼ teaspoon salt and stir to combine.

3. Close lid, set steam release to Sealing, and press the Rice button and cook for the default time. When the timer beeps, let pressure release naturally for 5 minutes. Quick-release any remaining pressure until the float valve drops, then open lid.

4. Transfer millet to a serving bowl and set aside to cool for 30 minutes. Add to refrigerated mixture and stir. Serve cold or at room temperature.

Quinoa and Artichoke Hearts Salad

The amount of dressing called for in this recipe is a suggestion. Use more or less dressing, depending on how strongly it is seasoned. If you need to refrigerate the quinoa for more than 1 hour before serving, leave the cherry tomatoes whole rather than halving them.

1 cup raw pecan halves

1 cup quinoa, rinsed and drained

2½ cups water

2 cups frozen artichoke hearts, thawed and drained

2 cups halved cherry tomatoes

½ small red onion, peeled and thinly sliced

¼ cup Italian salad dressing

4 large Belgian endive leaves

1 Press the Sauté button on the Instant Pot®. Roughly chop pecans and add them to the Instant Pot®. Dry-roast for several minutes, stirring continuously to prevent burning. Pecans are sufficiently toasted when they're fragrant and slightly brown. Transfer to a medium bowl and set aside to cool. Press the Cancel button.

2 Clean and dry pot. Add quinoa and water to the Instant Pot®. Close lid, set steam release to Sealing, press the Manual button, and set time to 2 minutes. When the timer beeps, let pressure release naturally for 10 minutes. Quick-release any remaining pressure until the float valve drops and open lid. Transfer to a colander, drain excess liquid, and rinse under cold water. Drain well and transfer to a large bowl.

3 While quinoa is cooking, cook artichoke hearts according to package directions and then plunge into cold water to cool and stop the cooking process. Drain and cut into quarters.

4 Stir artichoke hearts into quinoa along with tomatoes and red onion. Toss with salad dressing. Cover and refrigerate for 1 hour before serving.

5 Place endive leaves on four plates. Top each with ¼ cup quinoa mixture. Sprinkle toasted pecans over the top of each endive boat and serve.

SERVES 4	
Per Serving:	
Calories	414
Fat	24g
Protein	11g
Sodium	327mg
Fiber	10g
Carbohydrates	42g
Sugar	6g

SWITCH UP THE DRESSING

Customize this dish to your liking by choosing your favorite dressing in place of the Italian dressing. A creamy dressing, such as a Caesar or creamy dill ranch, is a delicious option.

Spiced Quinoa Salad

SERVES 6

Per Serving:	
Calories	215
Fat	7g
Protein	7g
Sodium	486mg
Fiber	4g
Carbohydrates	32g
Sugar	2g

RINSING QUINOA

The outer coating of quinoa is naturally bitter. Though it is removed during processing, a little of that bitter flavor is sometimes left behind. It's always a good idea to rinse quinoa in a fine-mesh strainer under warm water and allow it to drain thoroughly before cooking. Despite claims from some brands that their quinoa is prewashed, it is probably wise to rinse that too.

Baby spinach is added to warm quinoa to wilt slightly, but you can wait until the quinoa is cool and serve it over the crisp, fresh leaves. It is entirely up to you.

2 tablespoons vegetable oil
1 medium white onion, peeled and chopped
2 cloves garlic, peeled and minced
½ teaspoon ground cumin
½ teaspoon ground coriander
½ teaspoon smoked paprika
½ teaspoon salt
¼ teaspoon ground black pepper
1½ cups quinoa, rinsed and drained
2 cups vegetable broth
1⅓ cups water
2 cups fresh baby spinach leaves
2 plum tomatoes, seeded and chopped

1 Press the Sauté button on the Instant Pot® and heat oil. Add onion and cook until tender, about 3 minutes. Add garlic, cumin, coriander, paprika, salt, and pepper, and cook 30 seconds until garlic and spices are fragrant.

2 Add quinoa and toss to coat in spice mixture. Cook 2 minutes to lightly toast quinoa. Add broth and water, making sure to scrape bottom and sides of pot to loosen any brown bits. Press the Cancel button.

3 Close lid and set steam release to Sealing. Press the Rice button and set time to 12 minutes.

4 When the timer beeps, let pressure release naturally, about 20 minutes. Open lid, add spinach and tomatoes, and fluff quinoa with a fork. Serve warm, at room temperature, or cold.

CHAPTER 6

Pasta

Toasted Orzo Salad

Per Serving:

Calories	120
Fat	4g
Protein	4g
Sodium	586mg
Fiber	1g
Carbohydrates	17g
Sugar	3g

VEGAN FETA CHEESE

For a vegan version of this salad, look in your grocery store's produce department for feta made with soy, or try making your own. Mix crumbled firm tofu with olive oil, vinegar, salt, and herbs, such as basil and oregano.

Toasting orzo takes just a few minutes, but gives the pasta a deeper, nutty flavor. If you want to crank up the fun factor, use tri-color orzo. This doesn't change the flavor, but it does make the salad look even more tempting.

2 tablespoons light olive oil
1 clove garlic, peeled and crushed
2 cups orzo
3 cups vegetable broth
½ cup sliced black olives
3 scallions, thinly sliced
1 medium Roma tomato, seeded and diced
1 medium red bell pepper, seeded and diced
¼ cup crumbled feta cheese
1 tablespoon extra-virgin olive oil
1 tablespoon red wine vinegar
½ teaspoon ground black pepper
¼ teaspoon salt

1 Press the Sauté button on the Instant Pot® and heat light olive oil. Add garlic and orzo and cook, stirring frequently, until orzo is light golden brown, about 5 minutes. Press the Cancel button.

2 Add broth and stir. Close lid, set steam release to Sealing, press the Manual button, and set time to 3 minutes. When the timer beeps, let pressure release naturally for 5 minutes, then quick-release the remaining pressure until the float valve drops and open lid.

3 Transfer orzo to a medium bowl, then set aside to cool to room temperature, about 30 minutes. Add olives, scallions, tomato, bell pepper, feta, extra-virgin olive oil, vinegar, black pepper, and salt, and stir until combined. Serve at room temperature or refrigerate for at least 2 hours.

Orzo-Stuffed Tomatoes

Any type of larger tomato will work for this recipe. Use what is in season and available at a store near you.

½ cup orzo
4 large beefsteak tomatoes
1 cup shredded mozzarella cheese
2 cloves garlic, peeled and minced
2 tablespoons minced fresh basil
2 tablespoons minced fresh parsley
½ teaspoon salt
¼ teaspoon ground black pepper
2 tablespoons extra-virgin olive oil

SERVES 4	
Per Serving:	
Calories	322
Fat	16g
Protein	18g
Sodium	659mg
Fiber	2g
Carbohydrates	23g
Sugar	0g

1 Preheat oven to 350°F.

2 Place orzo in the Instant Pot® and add water just to cover. Close lid, set steam release to Sealing, press the Manual button, and set time to 3 minutes. When the timer beeps, quick-release the pressure until the float valve drops and open the lid. Drain orzo and set aside.

3 Cut tops off tomatoes and scoop out seeds and pulp. Place pulp in a medium bowl. Add orzo, cheese, garlic, basil, parsley, salt, and pepper.

4 Stuff tomatoes with orzo mixture and place on a baking sheet. Drizzle oil over tomatoes and bake for 15–20 minutes. Serve hot.

Pasta with Marinated Artichokes and Spinach

You don't have to use spaghetti here. Any long pasta or even a tube-shaped pasta, like penne or rigatoni, will do. If you do use a tube-shaped pasta, decrease the cooking time to 4 minutes.

1 pound whole-wheat spaghetti, broken in half
3½ cups water
4 tablespoons extra-virgin olive oil, divided
¼ teaspoon salt
2 cups baby spinach
1 cup drained marinated artichoke hearts
2 tablespoons chopped fresh oregano
2 tablespoons chopped fresh flat-leaf parsley
1 teaspoon ground black pepper
½ cup grated Parmesan cheese

SERVES 6	
Per Serving:	
Calories	414
Fat	16g
Protein	16g
Sodium	467mg
Fiber	9g
Carbohydrates	56g
Sugar	3g

1 Add pasta, water, 2 tablespoons oil, and salt to the Instant Pot®. Close lid, set steam release to Sealing, press the Manual button, and set time to 5 minutes.

2 When the timer beeps, quick-release the pressure until the float valve drops and open lid. Drain off any excess liquid. Stir in remaining 2 tablespoons oil and spinach. Toss until spinach is wilted. Stir in artichokes, oregano, and parsley until well mixed. Sprinkle with pepper and cheese, and serve immediately.

Couscous with Tomatoes and Olives

Many grocery stores have an olive bar that offers a variety of olives so you can make a custom olive mix that suits your taste. If your market does not offer an olive bar, buy jars of mixed olives in the salad dressings and condiments aisle.

1 tablespoon tomato paste
2 cups vegetable broth
1 cup couscous
1 cup halved cherry tomatoes
½ cup halved mixed olives
¼ cup minced fresh flat-leaf parsley
2 tablespoons minced fresh oregano
2 tablespoons minced fresh chives
1 tablespoon extra-virgin olive oil
1 tablespoon red wine vinegar
½ teaspoon ground black pepper

1 Pour tomato paste and broth into the Instant Pot® and stir until completely dissolved. Stir in couscous. Close lid, set steam release to Sealing, press the Manual button, and set time to 3 minutes. When the timer beeps, let pressure release naturally for 10 minutes, then quick-release the remaining pressure and open lid.

2 Fluff couscous with a fork. Add tomatoes, olives, parsley, oregano, chives, oil, vinegar, and pepper, and stir until combined. Serve warm or at room temperature.

SERVES 4	
Per Serving:	
Calories	232
Fat	5g
Protein	7g
Sodium	513mg
Fiber	2g
Carbohydrates	37g
Sugar	8g

WHAT IS COUSCOUS?

Couscous, from an Arabic word that means "to pound small," is a form of pasta made up of small balls of durum wheat. Couscous can be steamed or boiled, and you can even purchase a special couscous pot, or *couscoussier*, that is designed to steam couscous perfectly. Couscous is most commonly associated with the cuisines of the Mediterranean and North Africa, but the popularity of couscous has spread around the globe. It is served warm as a main or side dish or chilled in salads.

Couscous with Crab and Lemon

SERVES 4	
Per Serving:	
Calories	360
Fat	15g
Protein	22g
Sodium	388mg
Fiber	2g
Carbohydrates	34g
Sugar	0g

Low in fat, high in protein, and rich in omega-3 fatty acids and selenium, crab can easily be a part of a healthy diet when eaten in moderation.

1 cup couscous
1 clove garlic, peeled and minced
2 cups water
3 tablespoons extra-virgin olive oil, divided
¼ cup minced fresh flat-leaf parsley
1 tablespoon minced fresh dill
8 ounces jumbo lump crabmeat
3 tablespoons lemon juice
½ teaspoon ground black pepper
¼ cup grated Parmesan cheese

1 Place couscous, garlic, water, and 1 tablespoon oil in the Instant Pot® and stir well. Close lid, set steam release to Sealing, press the Manual button, and set time to 7 minutes. When the timer beeps, let pressure release naturally for 10 minutes, then quick-release the remaining pressure and open lid.

2 Fluff couscous with a fork. Add parsley, dill, crabmeat, lemon juice, pepper, and remaining 2 tablespoons oil, and stir until combined. Top with cheese and serve immediately.

Olive and Pepper Couscous Salad

SERVES 4	
Per Serving:	
Calories	192
Fat	2g
Protein	6g
Sodium	355mg
Fiber	3g
Carbohydrates	36g
Sugar	1g

Kalamata olives add a deep, savory flavor to this salad. For a similar flavor with a bit less olive in every bite, try the larger-pitted Niçoise olive.

1 cup couscous
2 cups water
½ cup chopped Kalamata olives
1 medium red bell pepper, seeded and diced
1 clove garlic, peeled and minced
1 teaspoon olive oil
1 teaspoon red wine vinegar
½ teaspoon salt

1 Stir couscous and water together in the Instant Pot®. Close lid, set steam release to Sealing, press the Manual button, and set time to 7 minutes.

2 When the timer beeps, let pressure release naturally for 10 minutes, then quick-release the remaining pressure. Open lid and fluff couscous with a fork. Stir in olives, bell pepper, garlic, oil, vinegar, and salt. Cover and refrigerate for 2 hours before serving.

Pasta Primavera

This light pasta dish is perfect for a mild spring day, or anytime you want something light and refreshing for lunch or dinner.

1 pound bowtie pasta
4 cups water
2 tablespoons olive oil, divided
1½ cups chopped summer squash
1½ cups chopped zucchini
3 cups chopped broccoli
½ cup sun-dried tomatoes
2 cloves garlic, peeled and chopped
1 cup white wine
2 tablespoons cold unsalted butter
½ teaspoon salt
¾ teaspoon ground black pepper
¼ cup chopped fresh basil

1 Place pasta, water, and 1 tablespoon oil in the Instant Pot®. Close lid, set steam release to Sealing, press the Manual button, and set time to 4 minutes. When the timer beeps, quick-release the pressure until the float valve drops and open the lid. Press the Cancel button. Drain pasta and set aside.

2 Clean and dry pot, and return to machine. Press the Sauté button and heat remaining 1 tablespoon oil. Add squash, zucchini, broccoli, and sun-dried tomatoes, and cook until very tender, about 10 minutes. Add garlic and wine. Allow wine to reduce for about 2–3 minutes.

3 Add butter to pot, stirring constantly to create an emulsion. Season with salt and pepper.

4 Pour sauce and vegetables over pasta, and stir to coat. Top with basil.

SERVES 8	
Per Serving:	
Calories	242
Fat	13g
Protein	6g
Sodium	170mg
Fiber	3g
Carbohydrates	24g
Sugar	3g

PASTA PRIMAVERA

You may think pasta primavera is an Italian invention, but you would be wrong. The dish actually originates in the United States and Canada, and was first served in the mid-1970s in New York. Its exact origins are murky, with multiple people laying claim to inventing the dish, but it exploded in popularity after the recipe was printed in *The New York Times.* If you are looking to enjoy more plant-based meals, this recipe is sure to become a favorite.

Rotini with Red Wine Marinara

SERVES 6	
Per Serving:	
Calories	320
Fat	4g
Protein	10g
Sodium	215mg
Fiber	4g
Carbohydrates	59g
Sugar	6g

When cooking with wine, use a wine that you like drinking. Cooking concentrates the flavors of the wine, so any flavors you do not enjoy are enhanced.

1 pound rotini

4 cups water

1 tablespoon olive oil

½ medium yellow onion, peeled and diced

3 cloves garlic, peeled and minced

1 (15-ounce) can crushed tomatoes

½ cup red wine

1 teaspoon sugar

2 tablespoons chopped fresh basil

½ teaspoon salt

¼ teaspoon ground black pepper

1 Add pasta and water to the Instant Pot®. Close lid, set steam release to Sealing, press the Manual button, and set time to 4 minutes. When the timer beeps, quick-release the pressure until the float valve drops and open the lid. Press the Cancel button. Drain pasta and set aside.

2 Clean pot and return to machine. Press the Sauté button and heat oil. Add onion and cook until it begins to caramelize, about 10 minutes. Add garlic and cook 30 seconds. Add tomatoes, red wine, and sugar, and simmer for 10 minutes. Add basil, salt, pepper, and pasta. Serve immediately.

Couscous with Tomato and Olives

SERVES 4	
Per Serving:	
Calories	228
Fat	4g
Protein	6g
Sodium	407mg
Fiber	2g
Carbohydrates	36g
Sugar	3g

This simple salad comes together in minutes, and is perfect for a quick yet elegant lunch or dinner. To bump up the protein in this dish, add some flaked cooked salmon or sliced grilled chicken.

1 tablespoon tomato paste

2 cups vegetable broth

1 cup couscous

1 cup sliced cherry tomatoes

½ large English cucumber, chopped

½ cup pitted and chopped mixed olives

¼ cup minced fresh flat-leaf parsley

2 tablespoons minced fresh oregano

2 tablespoons minced fresh chives

1 tablespoon extra-virgin olive oil

1 tablespoon red wine vinegar

½ teaspoon ground black pepper

1 Stir together tomato paste and broth until completely dissolved. Add to the Instant Pot® with couscous and stir well. Close lid, set steam release to Sealing, press the Manual button, and set time to 7 minutes. When the timer beeps, let pressure release naturally for 10 minutes, then quick-release the remaining pressure and open lid.

2 Fluff couscous with a fork. Add all remaining ingredients and stir until combined. Serve warm or at room temperature.

Bowtie Pesto Pasta Salad

Don't forget to add a little fat when cooking starchy foods, like pasta, in the Instant Pot®—it reduces the starchy foam that is created during cooking.

1 pound whole-wheat bowtie pasta
4 cups water
1 tablespoon extra-virgin olive oil
2 cups halved cherry tomatoes
2 cups baby spinach

½ cup chopped fresh basil
½ cup prepared pesto
½ teaspoon ground black pepper
½ cup grated Parmesan cheese

SERVES 8	
Per Serving:	
Calories	360
Fat	13g
Protein	16g
Sodium	372mg
Fiber	7g
Carbohydrates	44g
Sugar	3g

1 Add pasta, water, and olive oil to the Instant Pot®. Close lid, set steam release to Sealing, press the Manual button, and set time to 4 minutes.

2 When the timer beeps, quick-release the pressure until the float valve drops and open lid. Drain off any excess liquid. Allow pasta to cool to room temperature, about 30 minutes. Stir in tomatoes, spinach, basil, pesto, pepper, and cheese. Refrigerate for 2 hours. Stir well before serving.

Israeli Pasta Salad

This is a great light salad to enjoy during the summer and pairs well with grilled chicken or fish.

½ pound whole-wheat penne pasta
4 cups water
1 tablespoon plus ¼ cup extra-virgin olive oil, divided
1 cup quartered cherry tomatoes
½ English cucumber, chopped
½ medium orange bell pepper, seeded and chopped

½ medium red onion, peeled and chopped
½ cup crumbled feta cheese
1 teaspoon fresh thyme leaves
1 teaspoon chopped fresh oregano
½ teaspoon ground black pepper
¼ cup lemon juice

SERVES 6	
Per Serving:	
Calories	243
Fat	16g
Protein	7g
Sodium	180mg
Fiber	3g
Carbohydrates	20g
Sugar	3g

1 Add pasta, water, and 1 tablespoon oil to the Instant Pot®. Close lid, set steam release to Sealing, press the Manual button, and set time to 4 minutes.

2 When the timer beeps, quick-release the pressure until the float valve drops and open lid. Drain and set aside to cool for 30 minutes. Stir in tomatoes, cucumber, bell pepper, onion, feta, thyme, oregano, black pepper, lemon juice, and remaining ¼ cup oil. Refrigerate for 2 hours.

Rotini with Walnut Pesto, Peas, and Cherry Tomatoes

When most people think of pesto, they think of pine nuts, but those can be expensive. Walnuts, which are far less costly, are an excellent and nutritious substitute.

1 cup packed fresh basil leaves

⅓ cup chopped walnuts

¼ cup grated Parmesan cheese

¼ cup plus 1 tablespoon extra-virgin olive oil, divided

1 clove garlic, peeled

1 tablespoon lemon juice

¼ teaspoon salt

1 pound whole-wheat rotini pasta

4 cups water

1 pint cherry tomatoes

1 cup fresh or frozen green peas

½ teaspoon ground black pepper

1 In a food processor, add basil and walnuts. Pulse until finely chopped, about 12 pulses. Add cheese, ¼ cup oil, garlic, lemon juice, and salt, and pulse until a rough paste forms, about 10 pulses. Refrigerate until ready to use.

2 Add pasta, water, and remaining 1 tablespoon oil to the Instant Pot®. Close lid, set steam release to Sealing, press the Manual button, and set time to 4 minutes.

3 When the timer beeps, quick-release the pressure until the float valve drops and open lid. Drain off any excess liquid. Allow pasta to cool to room temperature, about 30 minutes. Stir in basil mixture until pasta is well coated. Add tomatoes, peas, and pepper and toss to coat. Refrigerate for 2 hours. Stir well before serving.

Pasta Salad with Tomato, Arugula, and Feta

Serve this pasta salad at room temperature or after chilling in the refrigerator for at least 2 hours.

1 pound rotini
4 cups water
3 tablespoons extra-virgin olive oil, divided
2 medium Roma tomatoes, diced
2 cloves garlic, peeled and minced
1 medium red bell pepper, seeded and diced

2 tablespoons white wine vinegar
5 ounces baby arugula
1 cup crumbled feta cheese
½ teaspoon salt
½ teaspoon ground black pepper

SERVES 8	
Per Serving:	
Calories	332
Fat	12g
Protein	12g
Sodium	480mg
Fiber	3g
Carbohydrates	44g
Sugar	3g

1   Add pasta, water, and 1 tablespoon oil to the Instant Pot®. Close lid, set steam release to Sealing, press the Manual button, and set time to 4 minutes. When the timer beeps, quick-release the pressure until the float valve drops, open lid, drain pasta, then rinse with cold water. Set aside.

2   In a large bowl, mix remaining 2 tablespoons oil, tomatoes, garlic, bell pepper, vinegar, arugula, and cheese. Stir in pasta and season with salt and pepper. Cover and refrigerate for 2 hours before serving.

Mixed Vegetable Couscous

You can grill the vegetables instead of sautéing them. Cut them into quarters, brush lightly with olive oil, and grill until just tender, about 1 minute per side. Cool, then chop.

1 tablespoon light olive oil
1 medium zucchini, trimmed and chopped
1 medium yellow squash, chopped
1 large red bell pepper, seeded and chopped
1 large orange bell pepper, seeded and chopped
2 tablespoons chopped fresh oregano

2 cups Israeli couscous
3 cups vegetable broth
½ cup crumbled feta cheese
¼ cup red wine vinegar
¼ cup extra-virgin olive oil
½ teaspoon ground black pepper
¼ cup chopped fresh basil

SERVES 8	
Per Serving:	
Calories	355
Fat	9g
Protein	14g
Sodium	588mg
Fiber	7g
Carbohydrates	61g
Sugar	9g

1   Press the Sauté button on the Instant Pot® and heat light olive oil. Add zucchini, squash, bell peppers, and oregano, and sauté 8 minutes. Press the Cancel button. Transfer to a serving bowl and set aside to cool.

2   Add couscous and broth to the Instant Pot® and stir well. Close lid, set steam release to Sealing, press the Manual button, and set time to 2 minutes. When the timer beeps, let pressure release naturally for 5 minutes, then quick-release the remaining pressure and open lid.

3   Fluff with a fork and stir in cooked vegetables, cheese, vinegar, extra-virgin olive oil, black pepper, and basil. Serve warm.

Toasted Couscous with Feta, Cucumber, and Tomato

Israeli couscous, also called pearl couscous or Jerusalem couscous, is a type of round pasta similar to but much larger than traditional couscous. It can be served hot or cold. This pasta does not get sticky or clumpy, even when it's chilled, making it perfect for salads.

1 tablespoon plus ¼ cup light olive oil, divided
2 cups Israeli couscous
3 cups vegetable broth
2 large tomatoes, seeded and diced
1 large English cucumber, diced
1 medium red onion, peeled and chopped
½ cup crumbled feta cheese
¼ cup red wine vinegar
½ teaspoon ground black pepper
¼ cup chopped flat-leaf parsley
¼ cup chopped fresh basil

1 Press the Sauté button on the Instant Pot® and heat 1 tablespoon oil. Add couscous and cook, stirring frequently, until couscous is light golden brown, about 7 minutes. Press the Cancel button.

2 Add broth and stir. Close lid, set steam release to Sealing, press the Manual button, and set time to 2 minutes. When the timer beeps, let pressure release naturally for 5 minutes, then quick-release the remaining pressure until the float valve drops and open lid.

3 Fluff couscous with a fork, then transfer to a medium bowl and set aside to cool to room temperature, about 30 minutes. Add remaining ¼ cup oil, tomatoes, cucumber, onion, feta, vinegar, pepper, parsley, and basil, and stir until combined. Serve at room temperature or refrigerate for at least 2 hours.

Pasta with Chickpeas and Cabbage

Chickpeas are found all over the world and are the primary ingredient in various Middle Eastern, African, Mexican, and Indian dishes.

1 pound rotini pasta

8 cups water, divided

2 tablespoons olive oil, divided

1 stalk celery, thinly sliced

1 medium red onion, peeled and sliced

1 small head savoy cabbage, cored and shredded

⅔ cup dried chickpeas, soaked overnight and drained

8 ounces button mushrooms, sliced

½ teaspoon salt

¾ teaspoon ground black pepper

½ cup grated Pecorino Romano cheese

SERVES 8	
Per Serving:	
Calories	301
Fat	5g
Protein	9g
Sodium	207mg
Fiber	3g
Carbohydrates	49g
Sugar	4g

1 Add pasta, 4 cups water, and 1 tablespoon oil to the Instant Pot®. Close lid, set steam release to Sealing, press the Manual button, and set time to 4 minutes. When the timer beeps, quick-release the pressure until the float valve drops, open lid, and drain pasta. Press the Cancel button. Set aside.

2 Press the Sauté button and heat remaining 1 tablespoon oil. Add celery and onion, and cook until just tender, about 4 minutes. Stir in cabbage and cook until wilted, about 2 minutes. Add chickpeas, mushrooms, and remaining 4 cups water. Stir well, then press the Cancel button.

3 Close lid, set steam release to Sealing, press the Manual button, and set time to 20 minutes. When the timer beeps, let pressure release naturally, about 25 minutes.

4 Open lid and stir well. Season with salt and pepper. Use a fork to mash some of the chickpeas to thicken sauce. Pour sauce over pasta and top with cheese. Serve hot.

Yogurt and Dill Pasta Salad

This is a healthier take on the classic macaroni salad you see at barbecues and picnics. This version swaps mayonnaise for tangy yogurt flavored with fresh dill. Remember this salad for your next potluck party.

APPLE CIDER VINEGAR

Apple cider vinegar is made from fermented apple juice. It's said to have many health benefits, from blood sugar control and reduced cholesterol to weight loss and better digestive health. Vinegar also contains antioxidants that can curb cell damage caused by free radicals that can lead to other diseases such as cancer. Consuming a tablespoon or two of apple cider vinegar daily may improve your health, and it will certainly add a lot of flavor to your diet!

½ cup low-fat plain Greek yogurt
1 tablespoon apple cider vinegar
2 tablespoons chopped fresh dill
1 teaspoon honey
1 pound whole-wheat elbow macaroni
4 cups water
1 tablespoon extra-virgin olive oil
1 medium red bell pepper, seeded and chopped
1 medium sweet onion, peeled and diced
1 stalk celery, diced
½ teaspoon ground black pepper

1 In a small bowl, combine yogurt and vinegar. Add dill and honey, and mix well. Refrigerate until ready to use.

2 Place pasta, water, and olive oil to the Instant Pot®. Close lid, set steam release to Sealing, press the Manual button, and set time to 4 minutes.

3 When the timer beeps, quick-release the pressure until the float valve drops and open lid. Drain off any excess liquid. Cool pasta to room temperature, about 30 minutes. Add prepared dressing and toss until pasta is well coated. Add bell pepper, onion, celery, and black pepper, and toss to coat. Refrigerate for 2 hours. Stir well before serving.

Angel Hair Pasta with Fresh Spinach and White Wine

This light pasta dish can be made alcohol-free by substituting vegetable stock and 1 teaspoon of vinegar for the white wine.

SERVES 6

Per Serving:

Calories	367
Fat	24g
Protein	11g
Sodium	218mg
Fiber	4g
Carbohydrates	56g
Sugar	3g

1 pound angel hair pasta
4¼ cups water, divided
2 tablespoons olive oil, divided
¼ medium yellow onion, peeled and diced
2 cloves garlic, peeled and minced
½ cup white wine
1 tablespoon unsalted butter
1 tablespoon all-purpose flour
½ teaspoon salt
¼ teaspoon ground black pepper
1 cup steamed spinach

1 Place pasta, 4 cups water, and 1 tablespoon oil in the Instant Pot®. Close lid, set steam release to Sealing, press the Manual button, and set time to 4 minutes. When the timer beeps, quick-release the pressure until the float valve drops and open lid. Press the Cancel button. Drain pasta and set aside.

2 Press the Sauté button and heat remaining 1 tablespoon oil. Add onion and garlic. Cook until onion is soft, about 5 minutes. Add white wine and remaining ¼ cup water, then bring to a low simmer. Continue simmering for about 10 minutes.

3 Add butter and flour, stirring until completely combined and sauce begins to thicken. If the sauce becomes too thick, add more water until you reach the desired consistency. Season with salt and pepper.

4 In a large mixing bowl, combine spinach, pasta, and white wine sauce, then toss until the pasta is completely coated. Serve immediately.

Tahini Soup

Tahini is a ground sesame paste that has been used in cooking through-out the Eastern Mediterranean for many centuries. Most well-stocked supermarkets carry at least one brand of tahini.

2 cups orzo

8 cups water

1 tablespoon olive oil

1 teaspoon salt

½ teaspoon ground black pepper

½ cup tahini

¼ cup lemon juice

SERVES 6	
Per Serving:	
Calories	338
Fat	13g
Protein	12g
Sodium	389mg
Fiber	5g
Carbohydrates	49g
Sugar	1g

1 Add pasta, water, oil, salt, and pepper to the Instant Pot®. Close lid, set steam release to Sealing, press the Manual button, and set time to 4 minutes. When the timer beeps, quick-release the pressure until the float valve drops, and open lid. Set aside.

2 Add tahini to a small mixing bowl and slowly add lemon juice while whisking constantly. Once lemon juice has been incorporated, take about ½ cup hot broth from the pot and slowly add to tahini mixture while whisking, until creamy smooth.

3 Pour mixture into the soup and mix well. Serve immediately.

Pasta e Fagioli

This Italian dish is often served as a soup, but this less brothy version can be served as a main course pasta dish too.

1 pound spaghetti

4 cups water

1 tablespoon olive oil

4 cups cooked pinto beans

4 cups marinara sauce

1 cup shredded mozzarella cheese

2 tablespoons chopped fresh basil

SERVES 8	
Per Serving:	
Calories	498
Fat	12g
Protein	24g
Sodium	453mg
Fiber	12g
Carbohydrates	78g
Sugar	12g

1 Add pasta, water, and olive oil to the Instant Pot®. Close lid, set steam release to Sealing, press the Manual button, and set time to 4 minutes. When the timer beeps, quick-release the pressure until the float valve drops and open lid. Add beans and marinara sauce, and stir well.

2 Top with cheese and basil and serve hot.

Greek Spaghetti with Meat Sauce

<table>
<tr><td colspan="2">SERVES 6</td></tr>
<tr><td colspan="2">Per Serving:</td></tr>
<tr><td>Calories</td><td>447</td></tr>
<tr><td>Fat</td><td>15g</td></tr>
<tr><td>Protein</td><td>18g</td></tr>
<tr><td>Sodium</td><td>394mg</td></tr>
<tr><td>Fiber</td><td>4g</td></tr>
<tr><td>Carbohydrates</td><td>60g</td></tr>
<tr><td>Sugar</td><td>5g</td></tr>
</table>

BAY LEAVES

Bay leaves are a favorite Mediterranean aromatic for cooking. The leaves come from a tree that grows throughout the Mediterranean, and they add a savory note in soups, roasts, and sauces. Fresh bay leaves are more aromatic, but dried bay leaves are just as good.

Well-stocked cheese shops should carry Greek myzithra cheese. If you can find it, use it for an authentic flavor. If you can't find it, Parmesan cheese is a good substitute.

1 pound spaghetti
4 cups water
3 tablespoons olive oil, divided
1 medium white onion, peeled and diced
½ pound lean ground veal
½ teaspoon salt
¼ teaspoon ground black pepper
¼ cup white wine
½ cup tomato sauce
1 (3") cinnamon stick
2 bay leaves
1 clove garlic, peeled
¼ cup grated aged myzithra or Parmesan cheese

1 Add pasta, water, and 1 tablespoon oil to the Instant Pot®. Close lid, set steam release to Sealing, press the Manual button, and set time to 4 minutes. When the timer beeps, quick-release the pressure until the float valve drops, open lid, and drain. Press the Cancel button. Set aside.

2 Press the Sauté button and heat remaining 2 tablespoons oil. Add onion and cook until soft, about 3 minutes. Add veal and crumble well. Keep stirring until meat is browned, about 5 minutes. Add salt, pepper, wine, and tomato sauce, and mix well.

3 Stir in cinnamon stick, bay leaves, and garlic. Press the Cancel button. Close lid, set steam release to Sealing, press the Manual button, and set time to 5 minutes. When the timer beeps, quick-release the pressure until the float valve drops and open lid. Remove and discard cinnamon stick and bay leaves.

4 Place pasta in a large bowl. Sprinkle with cheese and spoon meat sauce over top. Serve immediately.

Avgolemono

This lemon chicken soup can be made with rice, but here it is made with orzo for a variation that is a little more filling.

6 cups chicken stock
½ cup orzo
1 tablespoon olive oil
12 ounces cooked chicken breast, shredded
½ teaspoon salt

½ teaspoon ground black pepper
¼ cup lemon juice
2 large eggs
2 tablespoons chopped fresh dill
1 tablespoon chopped fresh flat-leaf parsley

1. Add stock, orzo, and olive oil to the Instant Pot®. Close lid, set steam release to Sealing, press the Manual button, and set time to 3 minutes. When the timer beeps, quick-release the pressure until the float valve drops. Open lid and stir in chicken, salt, and pepper.

2. In a medium bowl, combine lemon juice and eggs, then slowly whisk in hot cooking liquid from the pot, ¼ cup at a time, until 1 cup of liquid has been added. Immediately add egg mixture to soup and stir well. Let stand on the Keep Warm setting, stirring occasionally, for 10 minutes. Add dill and parsley. Serve immediately.

SERVES 6	
Per Serving:	
Calories	193
Fat	5g
Protein	21g
Sodium	552mg
Fiber	1g
Carbohydrates	15g
Sugar	1g

Easy Couscous

Couscous, the national dish of Morocco, is small granules of pasta made from semolina flour. Traditionally, they are rolled out by hand and then set out to dry. Serve this recipe as a side dish, or add some meat and vegetables during the cooking process for a more complete meal.

2 cups couscous
2½ cups water
1 cup low-sodium chicken broth
1 teaspoon salt
1 tablespoon unsalted butter
1 teaspoon grated lemon zest

1. Place all ingredients in the Instant Pot® and stir to combine.

2. Close lid, set steam release to Sealing, press the Manual button, and set time to 4 minutes. When the timer beeps, quick-release the pressure until the float valve drops, open lid, and stir well. Serve immediately.

SERVES 6	
Per Serving:	
Calories	272
Fat	6g
Protein	8g
Sodium	417mg
Fiber	3g
Carbohydrates	45g
Sugar	0g

Chilled Pearl Couscous Salad

SERVES 6

Per Serving:	
Calories	177
Fat	11g
Protein	5g
Sodium	319mg
Fiber	1g
Carbohydrates	12g
Sugar	2g

Also known as Israeli couscous, large-grained pearl couscous is perfect to use for this refreshing side salad because it adds more substance than its smaller counterpart. The acidity and sweetness of the orange juice combined with the freshness of the cucumber, pepper, and tomatoes will keep you coming back for more.

3 tablespoons olive oil, divided
1 cup pearl couscous
1 cup water
1 cup orange juice
1 small cucumber, seeded and diced
1 small yellow bell pepper, seeded and diced
2 small Roma tomatoes, seeded and diced
¼ cup slivered almonds
¼ cup chopped fresh mint leaves
2 tablespoons lemon juice
1 teaspoon grated lemon zest
¼ cup crumbled feta cheese
¼ teaspoon fine sea salt
1 teaspoon smoked paprika
1 teaspoon garlic powder

1 Press the Sauté button and heat 1 tablespoon oil. Add couscous and cook for 2–4 minutes until couscous is slightly browned. Add water and orange juice. Press the Cancel button.

2 Close lid, set steam release to Sealing, press the Manual button, and set time to 5 minutes. When the timer beeps, let pressure release naturally for 5 minutes. Quick-release any remaining pressure until the float valve drops and open lid. Drain any liquid and set aside to cool for 20 minutes.

3 Combine remaining 2 tablespoons oil, cucumber, bell pepper, tomatoes, almonds, mint, lemon juice, lemon zest, cheese, salt, paprika, and garlic powder in a medium bowl. Add couscous and toss ingredients together. Cover and refrigerate overnight before serving.

CHAPTER 7

Beans

Green Beans with Chickpeas, Herbs, and Mushrooms

This green bean salad is perfect for vegetable lovers who are looking for a light, crisp, and filling salad. Pack this for a lunch that won't weigh you down, or enjoy it for dinner along with grilled or baked salmon or white fish.

PARMESAN CHEESE

Parmesan cheese makes an excellent garnish to soups, salads, and savory dishes. It has a strong aroma and a salty flavor with a hint of nuttiness, and it adds just a hint of richness. Keep a small bowl of extra Parmesan cheese on the table so your lunch or dinner guests can add more cheese if they desire. Parmesan also makes a lovely snack or appetizer when shaved or cut into pieces. It goes great with a glass of red wine.

- 2 cups dried chickpeas, soaked overnight and drained
- ½ teaspoon salt
- 9 cups water, divided
- ½ pound fresh green beans, trimmed and cut into 1" pieces
- 4 ounces sliced button mushrooms
- ½ red bell pepper, seeded, thinly sliced, and cut into 1" pieces
- ½ medium red onion, peeled and diced
- ¼ cup chopped fresh flat-leaf parsley
- 2 tablespoons chopped fresh chives
- 2 tablespoons chopped fresh tarragon
- ¼ cup extra-virgin olive oil
- 2 tablespoons red wine vinegar
- 1 teaspoon Dijon mustard
- 1 teaspoon honey
- ½ teaspoon ground black pepper
- ¼ teaspoon salt
- ¼ cup grated Parmesan cheese

1 Add chickpeas, salt, and 8 cups water to the Instant Pot®. Close lid, set steam release to Sealing, press the Manual button, and set time to 40 minutes.

2 When the timer beeps, let pressure release naturally for 10 minutes, then quick-release the remaining pressure. Press the Cancel button. Open lid and drain chickpeas. Transfer to a large bowl and cool to room temperature.

3 Add remaining 1 cup water to the Instant Pot®. Add rack to pot, top with steamer basket, and add green beans. Close lid, set steam release to Sealing, press the Manual button, and set time to 0 minutes. When the timer beeps, open lid, remove steamer basket, and rinse green beans with cool water. Add to bowl with chickpeas.

4 Add to the bowl mushrooms, bell pepper, red onion, parsley, chives, and tarragon. Toss to mix. In a small bowl, combine olive oil, vinegar, mustard, honey, black pepper, and salt. Whisk to combine, then pour over chickpea and green bean mixture, and toss to coat. Top with cheese and serve immediately.

Warm Chickpea Salad

If you prefer, you can transfer the chickpeas with dressing to a medium baking dish, top it with cheese, and bake at 375°F for 10 minutes, or until the cheese is melted. You can also chill the salad overnight and serve it cold.

1 pound dried chickpeas
1½ tablespoons plus ¼ cup olive oil, divided
4 cups water
¾ teaspoon salt
4 scallions, sliced
1 medium red onion, peeled and diced
1 small green bell pepper, seeded and diced
1 small red bell pepper, seeded and diced
½ cup minced fresh parsley
1 large carrot, peeled and grated
2 teaspoons lemon juice
2 teaspoons white wine vinegar
1 tablespoon olive oil mayonnaise
1 clove garlic, peeled and minced
⅛ teaspoon ground white pepper
½ teaspoon dried oregano
¼ cup grated Parmesan cheese

SERVES 12	
Per Serving:	
Calories	241
Fat	10g
Protein	10g
Sodium	249mg
Fiber	5g
Carbohydrates	28g
Sugar	7g

1 Place chickpeas in the Instant Pot® along with 1½ tablespoons oil, 4 cups water, and salt. Close lid, set steam release to Sealing, press the Manual button, and set time to 20 minutes. When the timer beeps, let pressure release naturally, about 25 minutes. Open lid, drain chickpeas, and return to pot.

2 Add scallions, onion, bell peppers, parsley, and carrot to chickpeas and toss to combine.

3 In a small bowl, combine remaining ¼ cup oil, lemon juice, vinegar, mayonnaise, garlic, white pepper, and oregano, and whisk to mix. Pour dressing over chickpea mixture and stir to combine. Sprinkle cheese on top. Close lid and allow to stand on the Keep Warm setting for 10 minutes before serving.

Three-Bean Salad

SERVES 8

Per Serving:

Calories	208
Fat	8g
Protein	8g
Sodium	162mg
Fiber	6g
Carbohydrates	26g
Sugar	3g

BEAN SALADS

Cooked bean salads are popular the world over, and date back to ancient times. Today, warm or cold bean salads are often served at potlucks and picnics. Beans provide plant-based protein in a usually meat- and dairy-free dish. Additional vegetables make bean salads tasty, hearty, and good for you!

Three-bean salads are staples of the summer grilling season and potluck parties. You can use any combination of beans you like, but this easy-to-make version features three heart-healthy beans loaded with filling fiber and protein.

¼ pound dried pinto beans, soaked overnight and drained
¼ pound dried black beans, soaked overnight and drained
¼ pound dried red beans, soaked overnight and drained
8 cups water
1 tablespoon light olive oil
1 stalk celery, chopped
½ medium red onion, peeled and chopped
½ medium green bell pepper, seeded and chopped
¼ cup minced fresh cilantro
¼ cup minced fresh flat-leaf parsley
3 tablespoons extra-virgin olive oil
3 tablespoons red wine vinegar
1 tablespoon honey
½ teaspoon ground black pepper
½ teaspoon sea salt

1 Place beans, water, and light olive oil in the Instant Pot®. Close lid, set steam release to Sealing, and press the Bean button and cook for the default time of 30 minutes. When the timer beeps, let pressure release naturally, about 20 minutes. Open lid and drain beans. Cool to room temperature.

2 Transfer cooled beans to a large bowl. Add celery, onion, bell pepper, cilantro, and parsley. Mix well. In a small bowl, whisk together extra-virgin olive oil, vinegar, honey, black pepper, and salt. Pour dressing over bean mixture and toss to coat. Refrigerate for 4 hours before serving.

White Beans with Garlic and Tomatoes

SERVES 6	
Per Serving:	
Calories	128
Fat	2g
Protein	7g
Sodium	809mg
Fiber	4g
Carbohydrates	20g
Sugar	2g

Hearty tomatoes, like cherry or Roma, work best for this recipe, but in a pinch, any variety will do.

1 cup dried cannellini beans, soaked overnight and drained

4 cups water

4 cups vegetable stock

1 tablespoon olive oil

1 teaspoon salt

2 cloves garlic, peeled and minced

½ cup diced tomato

½ teaspoon dried sage

½ teaspoon ground black pepper

1 Add beans and water to the Instant Pot®. Close lid, set steam release to Sealing, press the Bean button, and cook for default time of 30 minutes. When timer beeps, quick-release the pressure until the float valve drops.

2 Press the Cancel button, open lid, drain and rinse beans, and return to pot along with stock. Soak for 1 hour.

3 Add olive oil, salt, garlic, tomato, sage, and pepper to beans. Close lid, set steam release to Sealing, press the Manual button, and set time to 10 minutes. When the timer beeps, quick-release the pressure until the float valve drops and open lid. Serve hot.

Sea Salt Soybeans

SERVES 4	
Per Serving:	
Calories	76
Fat	5g
Protein	4g
Sodium	768mg
Fiber	2g
Carbohydrates	5g
Sugar	1g

Baby soybeans, or edamame, are often enjoyed as an appetizer or in salads. They make a great snack and plant-based protein source for people concerned with their blood sugar as they do not cause a blood glucose spike.

1 cup shelled edamame

8 cups water, divided

1 tablespoon vegetable oil

1 teaspoon coarse sea salt

2 tablespoons soy sauce

1 Add edamame and 4 cups water to the Instant Pot®. Close lid, set steam release to Sealing, and set time to 1 minute. When the timer beeps, quick-release the pressure until the float valve drops. Press the Cancel button.

2 Open lid, drain and rinse edamame, and return to pot with the remaining 4 cups water. Soak for 1 hour.

3 Add oil. Close lid, set steam release to Sealing, press the Manual button, and set time to 11 minutes. When the timer beeps, let pressure release naturally, about 25 minutes, then open lid.

4 Drain edamame and transfer to a serving bowl. Sprinkle with salt and serve with soy sauce on the side for dipping.

Greek-Style Black-Eyed Pea Soup

Don't drain the tomatoes before adding to the soup. The liquid in the can adds a tremendous amount of tomato flavor to the broth.

2 tablespoons light olive oil

2 stalks celery, chopped

1 medium white onion, peeled and chopped

2 cloves garlic, peeled and minced

2 tablespoons chopped fresh oregano

1 teaspoon fresh thyme leaves

1 pound dried black-eyed peas, soaked overnight and drained

¼ teaspoon salt

1 teaspoon ground black pepper

4 cups water

1 (15-ounce) can diced tomatoes

SERVES 8	
Per Serving:	
Calories	153
Fat	3g
Protein	8g
Sodium	189mg
Fiber	5g
Carbohydrates	25g
Sugar	6g

1 Press the Sauté button on the Instant Pot® and heat oil. Add celery and onion, and cook until just tender, about 5 minutes. Add garlic, oregano, and thyme, and cook until fragrant, about 30 seconds. Press the Cancel button.

2 Add black-eyed peas, salt, pepper, water, and tomatoes to the Instant Pot® and stir well. Close lid, set steam release to Sealing, press the Manual button, and set time to 20 minutes. When the timer beeps, let pressure release naturally, about 20 minutes.

3 Open lid and stir well. Serve hot.

Black-Eyed Peas with Olive Oil and Herbs

To make it easier to remove the herb stems from the black-eyed pea cooking liquid, tie them with butcher's twine into a bundle, also called a bouquet garni, *or garnished bouquet.*

¼ cup extra-virgin olive oil

4 sprigs oregano, leaves minced and stems reserved

2 sprigs thyme, leaves stripped and stems reserved

4 sprigs dill, fronds chopped and stems reserved

1 pound dried black-eyed peas, soaked overnight and drained

¼ teaspoon salt

1 teaspoon ground black pepper

4 cups water

SERVES 8	
Per Serving:	
Calories	119
Fat	7g
Protein	6g
Sodium	76mg
Fiber	3g
Carbohydrates	9g
Sugar	2g

1 In a small bowl, combine oil, oregano leaves, thyme leaves, and dill fronds, and mix to combine. Cover and set aside.

2 Tie herb stems together with butcher's twine. Add to the Instant Pot® along with black-eyed peas, salt, pepper, and water. Close lid, set steam release to Sealing, press the Manual button, and set time to 20 minutes. When the timer beeps, let pressure release naturally, about 20 minutes.

3 Open lid, remove and discard herb stem bundle, and drain off any excess liquid. Stir in olive oil mixture. Serve hot.

Black Bean Sliders

ADD A SPICY SPREAD

If you want to spice up your sliders, just add a dollop of this quick chipotle mayonnaise. In a food processor, pulse together 1 cup mayonnaise, 1/4 cup sour cream, 2 chipotles in adobo sauce, 1 tablespoon lime juice, and 1/8 teaspoon salt. Refrigerate overnight until ready to serve.

Top these spiced sliders with fresh slices of avocado, tomato, and red onion. Then add a little kick with some chipotle mayonnaise. Whatever you want to add, do it! Your mouth will thank you.

1 tablespoon olive oil
1 slice bacon
1 small red bell pepper, seeded and diced
2 cups vegetable broth
1 cup dried black beans, soaked overnight and drained
1/2 teaspoon garlic powder
1/4 teaspoon coriander
1/2 teaspoon chili powder
1/2 teaspoon ground cumin
1/2 teaspoon sea salt
1/4 cup chopped fresh cilantro
1 large egg
1 cup panko bread crumbs
16 slider buns

1 Press the Sauté button on the Instant Pot® and heat oil. Add bacon and bell pepper. Cook until bacon is cooked through, about 5 minutes. Add broth and scrape bottom of pot to release browned bits.

2 Add beans, garlic powder, coriander, chili powder, cumin, salt, and cilantro. Stir well, then press the Cancel button.

3 Close lid, set steam release to Sealing, press the Bean button, and cook for the default time of 30 minutes. When the timer beeps, let pressure release naturally for 10 minutes. Quick-release any remaining pressure until the float valve drops and open lid. Press the Cancel button.

4 Remove and discard bacon. Press the Sauté button, press the Adjust button to change the heat to Less, and simmer bean mixture, uncovered, for 10 minutes to thicken. Transfer mixture to a large bowl. Once cool enough to handle, quickly mix in egg and bread crumbs.

5 Form into 16 equal-sized small patties. Cook on stovetop in a skillet over medium heat for approximately 2–3 minutes per side until browned. Remove from heat and add each patty to a bun. Serve warm.

Giant Beans with Tomato and Parsley

Giant beans, also sold as gigante beans, can be found online, in Mediterranean markets, and in some natural food markets. If you are unable to locate them, substitute with Great Northern beans; just reduce the cooking time to 30 minutes.

2 tablespoons light olive oil

1 medium white onion, peeled and chopped

2 cloves garlic, peeled and minced

1 pound dried giant beans, soaked overnight and drained

2 thyme sprigs

1 bay leaf

5 cups water

1 (15-ounce) can diced tomatoes, drained

1 (8-ounce) can tomato sauce

¼ cup chopped fresh flat-leaf parsley

2 tablespoons chopped fresh oregano

1 tablespoon chopped fresh dill

½ cup crumbled feta cheese

1 small lemon, cut into 8 wedges

1 Press the Sauté button on the Instant Pot® and heat oil. Add onion and cook until tender, about 3 minutes. Add garlic and cook until fragrant, about 30 seconds. Press the Cancel button.

2 Add beans, thyme, bay leaf, and water to the Instant Pot®. Close lid, set steam release to Sealing, press the Manual button, and set time to 50 minutes. When the timer beeps, quick-release the pressure until the float valve drops. Open lid and check that beans are soft. If they are not tender, close lid and cook under pressure for 10 minutes more.

3 Add diced tomatoes and tomato sauce. Close lid and let stand on the Keep Warm setting for 10 minutes to heat through. Remove and discard bay leaf. Stir in herbs and ladle into soup bowls. Garnish with feta and lemon slices, and serve hot.

SERVES 8	
Per Serving:	
Calories	241
Fat	6g
Protein	14g
Sodium	458mg
Fiber	10g
Carbohydrates	33g
Sugar	5g

ADDING SOME ACID

Have you ever had a soup, pasta dish, or even a stew that tasted dull? Something about the flavors just didn't pop? The solution might be a spritz of lemon. Adding a little acid to a dull-tasting dish can help brighten the flavor and cut some of the heaviness that is weighing the flavors down.

Black Beans with Corn and Tomato Relish

You can serve this hearty bean salad at room temperature or chilled. It tastes better if it's allowed to sit overnight so the flavors can develop, but if you are short on time, you can eat it right away and it will still taste amazing.

½ pound dried black beans, soaked overnight and drained
1 medium white onion, peeled and sliced in half
2 cloves garlic, peeled and lightly crushed
8 cups water
1 cup corn kernels
1 large tomato, seeded and chopped
½ medium red onion, peeled and chopped
¼ cup minced fresh cilantro
½ teaspoon ground cumin
¼ teaspoon smoked paprika
¼ teaspoon ground black pepper
¼ teaspoon salt
3 tablespoons extra-virgin olive oil
3 tablespoons lime juice

1 Add beans, white onion, garlic, and water to the Instant Pot®. Close lid, set steam release to Sealing, press the Bean button, and cook for the default time of 30 minutes. When the timer beeps, let pressure release naturally, about 20 minutes.

2 Open lid and remove and discard onion and garlic. Drain beans well and transfer to a medium bowl. Cool to room temperature, about 30 minutes.

3 In a separate small bowl, combine corn, tomato, red onion, cilantro, cumin, paprika, pepper, and salt. Toss to combine. Add to black beans and gently fold to mix. Whisk together olive oil and lime juice in a small bowl and pour over black bean mixture. Gently toss to coat. Serve at room temperature or refrigerate for at least 2 hours.

SERVES 6	
Per Serving:	
Calories	216
Fat	7g
Protein	8g
Sodium	192mg
Fiber	6g
Carbohydrates	28g
Sugar	4g

BLACK BEANS FOR HEALTH

With a dense interior and meaty texture, black beans make a satisfying substitute for meat in things like burgers, chilis, and soups. Black beans are an excellent source of protein and fiber. A 100g serving contains 21 percent of the recommended daily value (DV) of thiamine, 37 percent of the DV for folate, and 20 percent of both magnesium and phosphorus. Eating heart-healthy black beans regularly may also help reduce your cholesterol level. And they're delicious!

Fasolada (White Bean Soup)

SERVES 8

Per Serving:

Calories	276
Fat	8g
Protein	11g
Sodium	539mg
Fiber	13g
Carbohydrates	39g
Sugar	5g

Fasolada, a white bean soup, is considered one of the national dishes of Greece and has been a staple food in that country for centuries.

4 cups water

1 pound dried white kidney beans, soaked overnight and drained

2 medium carrots, peeled and sliced

2 medium onions, peeled and diced

2 stalks celery, thinly sliced

1 medium parsnip, peeled and thinly sliced

1 cup tomato sauce

1 tablespoon dried rosemary

1 tablespoon dried thyme

3 bay leaves

4 tablespoons minced fresh parsley

¼ cup olive oil

4 cloves garlic, peeled

¾ teaspoon salt

½ teaspoon ground black pepper

1 Place water, beans, carrots, onions, celery, parsnip, tomato sauce, rosemary, thyme, bay leaves, parsley, oil, and garlic in the Instant Pot®.

2 Close lid, set steam release to Sealing, press the Bean button, and cook for the default time of 30 minutes. When the timer beeps, let pressure release naturally, about 20 minutes. Open lid, remove and discard bay leaves, and season with salt and pepper. Serve hot.

Creamy White Bean Soup

SERVES 6

Per Serving:

Calories	75
Fat	2g
Protein	3g
Sodium	577mg
Fiber	5g
Carbohydrates	14g
Sugar	4g

The easiest way to add a creamy texture to bean soups is to mash some of the beans and stir them back in.

1 tablespoon olive oil

1 medium white onion, peeled and chopped

1 medium carrot, peeled and chopped

1 stalk celery, chopped

2 cloves garlic, peeled and minced

1 cup dried cannellini beans, soaked overnight and drained

4 cups vegetable broth

1 (15-ounce) can diced tomatoes

1 teaspoon minced fresh sage

½ teaspoon ground black pepper

½ teaspoon sea salt

1 Press the Sauté button on the Instant Pot® and heat oil. Add onion, carrot, and celery and sauté 5 minutes. Add garlic and cook 30 seconds. Stir in beans. Press the Cancel button.

2 Add broth, tomatoes, sage, pepper, and salt and stir. Close lid, set steam release to Sealing, press the Manual button, and set time to 20 minutes. When the timer beeps, quick-release the pressure until the float valve drops, then open lid and stir. Press the Cancel button.

3 Remove 1 cup beans and mash until smooth. Stir back into pot. Serve hot.

Herbed Lima Beans

Baby lima beans have a pale green color and are most often sold frozen in your grocery store. Regular lima beans are a pale brown color and are sold dry. For this recipe, use the tender baby lima beans for the best flavor.

1 pound frozen baby lima beans, thawed
2 cloves garlic, peeled and minced
2 thyme sprigs
1 bay leaf
2 tablespoons extra-virgin olive oil

3 cups water
1 tablespoon chopped fresh dill
1 tablespoon chopped fresh tarragon
1 tablespoon chopped fresh mint

SERVES 6	
Per Serving:	
Calories	134
Fat	5g
Protein	5g
Sodium	206mg
Fiber	4g
Carbohydrates	17g
Sugar	2g

1 Add lima beans, garlic, thyme, bay leaf, oil, and water to the Instant Pot®. Close lid, set steam release to Sealing, press the Manual button, and set time to 6 minutes. When the timer beeps, quick-release the pressure until the float valve drops. Open lid, remove and discard thyme and bay leaf, and stir well.

2 Stir in dill, tarragon, and mint, and let stand for 10 minutes on the Keep Warm setting before serving.

Greek Navy Bean Soup

This is a hearty vegetarian soup. Using an Instant Pot® cuts the cooking time in half! You'll have to start this soup the night before to soak the beans.

1 cup small dried navy beans, soaked overnight and drained
1 large stalk celery, halved lengthwise and sliced into ½" pieces
1 large carrot, peeled, halved, and sliced into ½" pieces
2 medium onions, peeled and chopped
½ cup tomato purée

½ cup olive oil
2 bay leaves
1 medium chili pepper, stemmed and minced
2 teaspoons smoked paprika
8 cups water
½ teaspoon salt

SERVES 8	
Per Serving:	
Calories	180
Fat	14g
Protein	5g
Sodium	170mg
Fiber	7g
Carbohydrates	16g
Sugar	4g

1 Add beans, celery, carrot, onions, tomato purée, oil, bay leaves, chili pepper, paprika, and water to the Instant Pot®. Close lid, set steam release to Sealing, press the Bean button, and cook for default time of 30 minutes.

2 When the timer beeps, let pressure release naturally, about 25 minutes. Open lid and season with salt. Remove and discard bay leaves. Serve hot.

Three-Bean Vegan Chili

SERVES 12

Per Serving:

Calories	195
Fat	1g
Protein	10g
Sodium	521mg
Fiber	10g
Carbohydrates	35g
Sugar	5g

QUICK SOAKED BEANS

You can speed-soak beans in your Instant Pot®. Just rinse them, put them in the pot, and add 4 cups of water for every 1 cup of dried beans. Press the Sauté button and bring beans to a boil, then press the Cancel button and close the lid. Set steam release to Sealing, press the Manual button, and set time to 2 minutes. When the timer beeps, let pressure release naturally, about 20 minutes, then drain and proceed with your recipe.

This chili is great for vegans, but it will also satisfy any meat eaters in your group. Try it on tortilla chips with vegan cheese sauce for stadium-style nachos or pour it over a crisp baked potato for a filling lunch or dinner.

1 cup dried pinto beans, soaked overnight and drained
1 cup dried red beans, soaked overnight and drained
1 cup dried black beans, soaked overnight and drained
2 medium white onions, peeled and chopped
2 medium red bell peppers, seeded and chopped
2 stalks celery, chopped
1 (28-ounce) can diced tomatoes
1 (15-ounce) can tomato sauce
¼ cup chili powder
2 tablespoons smoked paprika
1 teaspoon ground cumin
1 teaspoon ground coriander
½ teaspoon salt
½ teaspoon ground black pepper
3 cups vegetable broth
1 cup water

1 Place all ingredients in the Instant Pot® and stir to combine. Close lid, set steam release to Sealing, press the Chili button, and cook for the default time of 30 minutes.

2 When the timer beeps, quick-release the pressure until the float valve drops, then open lid and stir well. If chili is too thin, press the Cancel button and then press the Sauté button and let chili simmer, uncovered, until desired thickness is reached. Serve warm.

White Bean and Barley Soup

You can add any fresh or canned vegetables you like to this soup. If you do include fresh vegetables, sauté them at the start with the onion, celery, and carrot. If you are using canned vegetables, add them at the end with the beans.

2 tablespoons light olive oil

½ medium onion, peeled and chopped

1 medium carrot, peeled and chopped

1 stalk celery, chopped

2 cloves garlic, peeled and minced

2 sprigs fresh thyme

1 bay leaf

½ teaspoon ground black pepper

1 (14-ounce) can fire-roasted diced tomatoes, undrained

½ cup medium pearl barley, rinsed and drained

4 cups vegetable broth

2 cups water

2 (15-ounce) cans Great Northern beans, drained and rinsed

½ teaspoon salt

1 Press the Sauté button on the Instant Pot® and heat oil. Add onion, carrot, and celery. Cook until just tender, about 5 minutes. Add garlic, thyme, bay leaf, and pepper, and cook until fragrant, about 30 seconds. Press the Cancel button.

2 Add the tomatoes, barley, broth, and water. Close lid, set steam release to Sealing, press the Soup button, and cook for default time of 20 minutes.

3 When the timer beeps, let pressure release naturally, about 20 minutes. Open lid, stir soup, then add beans and salt. Close lid and let stand on the Keep Warm setting for 10 minutes. Remove and discard bay leaf. Serve hot.

SERVES 8	
Per Serving:	
Calories	129
Fat	4g
Protein	5g
Sodium	636mg
Fiber	5g
Carbohydrates	20g
Sugar	3g

BEAN BENEFITS

If you want to lower your cholesterol and increase the amount of low-fat, plant-based protein in your diet, beans should be a staple. They are rich in soluble and insoluble fiber, prevent heart disease, and lower cholesterol when eaten as a regular part of your diet. Fiber-rich beans are also a good option if you're watching your blood sugar as they do not cause a blood sugar spike.

Black Bean and Lentil Chili

BENEFITS OF CANNED TOMATOES

While it is a general rule that fresh fruit and vegetables are best in terms of nutritional benefit, there are a few exceptions, one of which is tomatoes. When tomatoes go through the canning process, the lycopene in the tomatoes becomes more nutritionally available. Lycopene is an antioxidant that is linked to heart health and the prevention of some types of cancer.

If you prefer hotter chili, substitute scotch bonnet pepper or serrano pepper for the jalapeño. You can also use hot instead of mild chili powder, or substitute Mrs. Dash Extra Spicy Seasoning Blend for some of the chili powder. Serve with corn bread.

2 tablespoons vegetable oil
1 large Spanish onion, peeled and diced
1 small jalapeño pepper, seeded and minced
1 clove garlic, peeled and minced
1 cup dried brown or green lentils, rinsed and drained
1 (15-ounce) can black beans, drained and rinsed
1 cup pearl barley, rinsed and drained
3 tablespoons chili powder
1 tablespoon sweet paprika
1 teaspoon dried oregano
1 teaspoon ground cumin
1 (28-ounce) can diced tomatoes
1 chipotle pepper in adobo sauce, minced
6 cups vegetable broth
½ teaspoon salt
¼ teaspoon ground black pepper

1 Press the Sauté button on the Instant Pot® and heat oil. Add onion and cook until just tender, about 3 minutes. Stir in jalapeño and cook for 1 minute.

2 Add garlic and cook until fragrant, about 30 seconds. Stir in lentils, black beans, barley, chili powder, paprika, oregano, cumin, tomatoes, chipotle pepper, and vegetable broth. Press the Cancel button.

3 Close lid, set steam release to Sealing, press the Manual button, and set time to 10 minutes. When the timer beeps, let pressure release naturally for 10 minutes. Quick-release any remaining pressure until the float valve drops.

4 Open the lid, press the Cancel button, then press the Sauté button. Bring to a simmer. Season with salt and black pepper, and simmer until slightly thickened, about 10 minutes. Serve immediately.

Chili-Spiced Beans

These beans can be used as a topping for a baked potato, served with grilled chicken, or mashed for a hearty dip with toasted pita or baked corn chips.

1 pound dried pinto beans, soaked overnight and drained

1 medium onion, peeled and chopped

¼ cup chopped fresh cilantro

1 (15-ounce) can tomato sauce

¼ cup chili powder

2 tablespoons smoked paprika

1 teaspoon ground cumin

1 teaspoon ground coriander

½ teaspoon ground black pepper

2 cups vegetable broth

1 cup water

SERVES 8	
Per Serving:	
Calories	86
Fat	0g
Protein	5g
Sodium	323mg
Fiber	4g
Carbohydrates	17g
Sugar	4g

1 Place all ingredients in the Instant Pot® and stir to combine.

2 Close lid, set steam release to Sealing, press the Chili button, and cook for the default time of 30 minutes. When the timer beeps, quick-release the pressure until the float valve drops, open lid, and stir well. If beans are too thin, press the Cancel button, then press the Sauté button and let beans simmer, uncovered, until desired thickness is reached. Serve warm.

Creamy Lima Bean Soup

Be very careful when blending hot soups. Do not overfill the blender, and be sure to use a kitchen towel to hold the lid in place during blending. The easiest way to blend hot soups is with an immersion blender. It saves on cleanup too.

1 tablespoon olive oil

1 small onion, peeled and diced

1 clove garlic, peeled and minced

2 cups vegetable stock

½ cup water

2 cups dried lima beans, soaked overnight and drained

½ teaspoon salt

½ teaspoon ground black pepper

2 tablespoons thinly sliced chives

SERVES 6	
Per Serving:	
Calories	67
Fat	2g
Protein	2g
Sodium	394mg
Fiber	2g
Carbohydrates	9g
Sugar	2g

1 Press the Sauté button on the Instant Pot® and heat oil. Add onion and cook until golden brown, about 10 minutes. Add garlic and cook until fragrant, about 30 seconds. Press the Cancel button.

2 Add stock, water, and lima beans. Close lid, set steam release to Sealing, press the Manual button, and set time to 6 minutes. When the timer beeps, let pressure release naturally, about 20 minutes.

3 Open lid and purée soup with an immersion blender or in batches in a blender. Season with salt and pepper, then sprinkle with chives before serving.

Vegetarian Dinner Loaf

<table>
<tr><td colspan="2">SERVES 6</td></tr>
<tr><td colspan="2">Per Serving:</td></tr>
<tr><td>Calories</td><td>278</td></tr>
<tr><td>Fat</td><td>17g</td></tr>
<tr><td>Protein</td><td>9g</td></tr>
<tr><td>Sodium</td><td>477mg</td></tr>
<tr><td>Fiber</td><td>6g</td></tr>
<tr><td>Carbohydrates</td><td>27g</td></tr>
<tr><td>Sugar</td><td>8g</td></tr>
</table>

MOCK MEATLOAF

There are many ingredients you can use to turn regular meatloaf into a meatless version. For the easiest option, use vegetarian ground beef, such as Gimme Lean Ground Beef, instead of real meat in your favorite recipe.

You won't be missing the meatloaf on your dinner table when you try this dinner loaf instead. To make a vegan version, replace the egg with 1 teaspoon cornstarch combined with 1 tablespoon water.

1 cup dried pinto beans, soaked overnight and drained
8 cups water, divided
1 tablespoon vegetable oil
1 teaspoon salt
1 cup diced onion
1 cup chopped walnuts
½ cup rolled oats
1 large egg, beaten
¾ cup ketchup
1 teaspoon garlic powder
1 teaspoon dried basil
1 teaspoon dried parsley
½ teaspoon salt
½ teaspoon ground black pepper

1 Add beans and 4 cups water to the Instant Pot®. Close lid, set steam release to Sealing, press the Manual button, and set time to 1 minute. When the timer beeps, quick-release the pressure until the float valve drops. Press the Cancel button.

2 Open lid, then drain and rinse beans and return to the pot with remaining 4 cups water. Soak for 1 hour.

3 Preheat oven to 350°F.

4 Add the oil and salt to pot. Close lid, set steam release to Sealing, press the Manual button, and set time to 11 minutes. When the timer beeps, let pressure release naturally, about 25 minutes, and open lid. Drain beans and pour into a large mixing bowl.

5 Stir in onion, walnuts, oats, egg, ketchup, garlic powder, basil, parsley, salt, and pepper. Spread the mixture into a loaf pan and bake for 30–35 minutes. Cool for 20 minutes in pan before slicing and serving.

Revithosoupa (Chickpea Soup)

Canned chickpeas can be used for this recipe, but you will need to reduce the cook time. So, instead of using the Bean function, use the Soup function and cook for the default time.

SERVES 8	
Per Serving:	
Calories	464
Fat	30g
Protein	12g
Sodium	236mg
Fiber	10g
Carbohydrates	38g
Sugar	8g

1 pound dried chickpeas

4 cups water

¾ teaspoon salt

½ teaspoon ground black pepper

10 strands saffron

2 medium onions, peeled and diced

1 cup extra-virgin olive oil

1 teaspoon dried oregano

3 tablespoons lemon juice

2 tablespoons chopped fresh parsley

1 Add chickpeas, water, salt, pepper, saffron, onions, oil, and oregano to the Instant Pot® and stir well. Close lid, set steam release to Sealing, press the Bean button, and cook for the default time of 30 minutes.

2 When the timer beeps, let pressure release naturally, about 25 minutes. Open lid. Serve hot or cold, sprinkled with lemon juice. Garnish with chopped parsley.

White Bean Soup with Kale and Lemon

If you are running short on time, you can buy kale that is already chopped, which you can find in most well-stocked produce departments.

SERVES 8	
Per Serving:	
Calories	129
Fat	3g
Protein	7g
Sodium	501mg
Fiber	6g
Carbohydrates	22g
Sugar	4g

1 tablespoon light olive oil

2 stalks celery, chopped

1 medium yellow onion, peeled and chopped

2 cloves garlic, peeled and minced

1 tablespoon chopped fresh oregano

4 cups chopped kale

1 pound dried Great Northern beans, soaked overnight and drained

8 cups vegetable broth

¼ cup lemon juice

1 tablespoon extra-virgin olive oil

1 teaspoon ground black pepper

1 Press the Sauté button on the Instant Pot® and heat light olive oil. Add celery and onion and cook 5 minutes. Add garlic and oregano and sauté 30 seconds. Add kale and turn to coat, then cook until just starting to wilt, about 1 minute. Press the Cancel button.

2 Add beans, broth, lemon juice, extra-virgin olive oil, and pepper to the Instant Pot® and stir well. Close lid, set steam release to Sealing, press the Manual button, and set time to 20 minutes. When the timer beeps, let pressure release naturally, about 20 minutes. Open lid and stir well. Serve hot.

White Bean Cassoulet

This hearty recipe, traditionally cooked in a dish called a cassole, *originated in the south of France and involved slow-cooking meat of some sort. This Instant Pot® dish foregoes the meat and is made with beans and vegetables instead. It is delicious served with some crusty artisanal bread to sop up all of the goodness.*

SERVES 8

Per Serving:	
Calories	128
Fat	2g
Protein	6g
Sodium	387mg
Fiber	5g
Carbohydrates	21g
Sugar	4g

WHEN IN ROME

In Mediterranean countries, having a meal means sitting at a proper table with family or friends, not eating a sandwich at your desk in front of your computer. Take the time to enjoy your food at a leisurely pace and to really connect with your friends and family.

1 tablespoon olive oil
1 medium onion, peeled and diced
2 cups dried cannellini beans, soaked overnight and drained
1 medium parsnip, peeled and diced
2 medium carrots, peeled and diced
2 stalks celery, diced
1 medium zucchini, trimmed and chopped
½ teaspoon fennel seed
¼ teaspoon ground nutmeg
½ teaspoon garlic powder
1 teaspoon sea salt
½ teaspoon ground black pepper
2 cups vegetable broth
1 (14.5-ounce) can diced tomatoes, including juice
2 sprigs rosemary

1 Press the Sauté button on the Instant Pot® and heat oil. Add onion and cook until translucent, about 5 minutes. Add beans and toss.

2 Add a layer of parsnip, then a layer of carrots, and next a layer of celery. Finally, add a layer of zucchini. Sprinkle in fennel seed, nutmeg, garlic powder, salt, and pepper. Press the Cancel button.

3 Gently pour in broth and canned tomatoes. Top with rosemary.

4 Close lid, set steam release to Sealing, press the Bean button, and cook for the default time of 30 minutes. When the timer beeps, let pressure release naturally for 10 minutes. Quick-release any remaining pressure until the float valve drops and open lid. Press the Cancel button.

5 Press the Sauté button, then press the Adjust button to change the temperature to Less, and simmer bean mixture uncovered for 10 minutes to thicken. Transfer to a serving bowl and carefully toss. Remove and discard rosemary and serve.

CHAPTER 8

Lentils

Dhal

Dhal, derived from the Sanskrit for "to split," is an Indian-style spread made of split pulses such as lentils or split peas. Serve it on toasted pita bread or as a dip for fresh vegetables, like carrot sticks, cucumber slices, or bell pepper strips.

MAKES 2 CUPS

Per Serving (¼ cup):

Calories	91
Fat	3g
Protein	6g
Sodium	17mg
Fiber	6g
Carbohydrates	15g
Sugar	2g

VEGGIE WRAPS

Spread dhal over a soft tortilla, pita, or other flatbread and top with grilled vegetables, such as zucchini and red onions. Add couscous or grated cheese. Roll up and serve. Whole-wheat low-carb tortillas have extra fiber, so look for those at your grocery store.

1 tablespoon olive oil
1 teaspoon unsalted butter
1 small onion, peeled and diced
2 teaspoons grated fresh ginger
1 small serrano chili pepper, seeded and minced
1 clove garlic, peeled and minced
½ teaspoon garam masala
¼ teaspoon ground turmeric
½ teaspoon dried mustard
1 cup dried yellow split peas, washed and drained
2 cups water
¼ cup plain low-fat yogurt
2 tablespoons minced fresh cilantro

1 Press the Sauté button on the Instant Pot® and heat oil and butter. Add onion, ginger, and chili pepper, and cook until soft, about 5 minutes. Add garlic, garam masala, turmeric, and mustard, and cook until fragrant, about 1 minute. Stir in split peas. Press the Cancel button.

2 Pour in water. Close lid, set steam release to Sealing, press the Manual button, and set time to 8 minutes. When the timer beeps, let pressure release naturally, about 20 minutes. Open lid, transfer cooked split pea mixture to a medium bowl, and stir until cooled.

3 Add yogurt and mix until smooth. Stir in cilantro. Serve warm or cold.

Santorini (Fava)

If you can find them, Santorini yellow split peas (known as favas to Greeks) are far superior for this dish than commonly available varieties of split peas.

1 pound dried yellow split peas, washed and drained

4 cups vegetable broth

1 medium onion, peeled and diced

3 tablespoons extra-virgin olive oil

3 tablespoons lemon juice

1 teaspoon dried oregano

½ teaspoon salt

SERVES 6	
Per Serving:	
Calories	316
Fat	8g
Protein	16g
Sodium	664mg
Fiber	21g
Carbohydrates	47g
Sugar	5g

1 Add peas, broth, onion, olive oil, lemon juice, oregano, and salt to the Instant Pot® and stir to combine. Close lid, set steam release to Sealing, press the Bean button, and cook for default time of 30 minutes.

2 When the timer beeps, quick-release the pressure until the float valve drops and open lid. With an immersion blender, or in batches in a blender, purée until smooth.

3 Refrigerate for 4 hours before serving.

Creamy Yellow Lentil Soup

This creamy soup has no butter or cream. Instead, the soup becomes creamy when you purée the lentils after cooking. If you prefer, you can skip blending and serve it as a chunky soup.

2 tablespoons olive oil

1 medium yellow onion, peeled and chopped

1 medium carrot, peeled and chopped

2 cloves garlic, peeled and minced

1 teaspoon ground cumin

½ teaspoon ground black pepper

¼ teaspoon salt

2 cups dried yellow lentils, rinsed and drained

6 cups water

SERVES 6	
Per Serving:	
Calories	248
Fat	5g
Protein	15g
Sodium	118mg
Fiber	8g
Carbohydrates	35g
Sugar	4g

1 Press the Sauté button on the Instant Pot® and heat oil. Add onion and carrot and cook until just tender, about 3 minutes. Add garlic, cumin, pepper, and salt and cook until fragrant, about 30 seconds. Press the Cancel button.

2 Add lentils and water, close lid, set steam release to Sealing, press the Manual button, and set time to 15 minutes. When the timer beeps, let pressure release naturally, about 15 minutes. Open lid and purée with an immersion blender or in batches in a blender. Serve warm.

Lentil Chili

Traditional beef chili is made with fatty cuts of beef that are loaded with saturated fat. This version replaces beef with lentils, so you can enjoy a bowl of chili anytime a craving strikes.

2 tablespoons olive oil
1 medium yellow onion, peeled and chopped
1 large poblano pepper, seeded and chopped
¼ cup chopped fresh cilantro
2 cloves garlic, peeled and minced
1 tablespoon chili powder
½ teaspoon ground cumin
½ teaspoon ground black pepper
¼ teaspoon salt
2 cups dried red lentils, rinsed and drained
6 cups vegetable broth
1 (10-ounce) can tomatoes with green chilies, drained
1 (15-ounce) can kidney beans, drained and rinsed
1 tablespoon lime juice

1 Press the Sauté button on the Instant Pot® and heat oil. Add onion and poblano pepper, and cook until just tender, about 3 minutes. Add cilantro, garlic, chili powder, cumin, black pepper, and salt, and cook until fragrant, about 30 seconds. Press the Cancel button.

2 Add lentils and broth, close lid, set steam release to Sealing, press the Manual button, and set time to 25 minutes. When the timer beeps, let pressure release naturally, about 15 minutes.

3 Open lid and stir in tomatoes, beans, and lime juice. Let stand uncovered on the Keep Warm setting for 10 minutes. Serve warm.

Lentils with Cilantro and Lime

This lentil dish is a perfect companion to grilled fish, chicken, or tofu. It also makes an interesting change from the typical side dishes of rice or beans.

2 tablespoons olive oil

1 medium yellow onion, peeled and chopped

1 medium carrot, peeled and chopped

1/4 cup chopped fresh cilantro

1/2 teaspoon ground cumin

1/2 teaspoon salt

2 cups dried green lentils, rinsed and drained

4 cups low-sodium chicken broth

2 tablespoons lime juice

SERVES 6	
Per Serving:	
Calories	316
Fat	5g
Protein	20g
Sodium	349mg
Fiber	21g
Carbohydrates	44g
Sugar	4g

1 Press the Sauté button on the Instant Pot® and heat oil. Add onion and carrot, and cook until just tender, about 3 minutes. Add cilantro, cumin, and salt, and cook until fragrant, about 30 seconds. Press the Cancel button.

2 Add lentils and broth to pot. Close lid, set steam release to Sealing, press the Manual button, and set time to 15 minutes.

3 When the timer beeps, let pressure release naturally, about 25 minutes. Open lid and stir in lime juice. Serve warm.

Lentils with Spinach

This dish is simple, hearty, and packed with healthful ingredients. If you prefer a milder spinach flavor, use baby spinach in place of regular spinach.

1 cup dried yellow lentils, rinsed and drained

4 cups water

1 tablespoon olive oil

1/2 medium yellow onion, peeled and chopped

1 clove garlic, peeled and minced

1/2 teaspoon smoked paprika

1/2 teaspoon ground black pepper

1 (15-ounce) can diced tomatoes, drained

10 ounces baby spinach leaves

1/2 cup crumbled feta cheese

SERVES 4	
Per Serving:	
Calories	289
Fat	8g
Protein	21g
Sodium	623mg
Fiber	10g
Carbohydrates	31g
Sugar	6g

1 Add lentils and water to the Instant Pot®. Close lid, set steam release to Sealing, press the Manual button, and set time to 6 minutes. When the timer beeps, quick-release the pressure. Press the Cancel button and open lid. Drain lentils and set aside. Clean pot.

2 Press the Sauté button and heat oil. Add onion and cook until just tender, about 3 minutes. Add garlic, smoked paprika, and pepper, and cook for an additional 30 seconds. Stir in tomatoes, spinach, and lentils. Simmer for 10 minutes. Top with feta and serve.

Greek-Style Lentils

Black lentils are a little more expensive than green, red, or yellow lentils. Sometimes labeled as "beluga" or "caviar lentils," they hold their shape better than traditional lentils when cooked, and serve as a great base for salads.

SERVES 6	
Per Serving:	
Calories	200
Fat	14g
Protein	5g
Sodium	250mg
Fiber	2g
Carbohydrates	15g
Sugar	2g

1 cup dried black lentils, rinsed and drained
2 cups water
½ medium red onion, peeled and diced
¼ cup chopped sun-dried tomatoes
¼ cup chopped Kalamata olives
2 tablespoons chopped fresh basil
2 tablespoons chopped fresh flat-leaf parsley
¼ cup extra-virgin olive oil
¼ cup lemon juice
2 tablespoons red wine vinegar
1 tablespoon tahini
1 clove garlic, peeled and minced
¼ teaspoon salt
¼ teaspoon ground black pepper

1 Add lentils and water to the Instant Pot®. Close lid, set steam release to Sealing, press the Manual button, and set time to 6 minutes. When the timer beeps, let pressure release naturally for 15 minutes, then quick-release any remaining pressure until the float valve drops. Open lid and drain off any excess liquid.

2 Transfer lentils to a large bowl. Stir in onion, sun-dried tomatoes, olives, basil, and parsley. In a small bowl, combine oil, lemon juice, vinegar, tahini, garlic, salt, and pepper, and whisk to mix. Pour dressing over lentil mixture and toss to coat. Serve warm or at room temperature.

Lebanese Lentil Salad

You can use any lentils you like here, but green lentils are the most traditional. The salad can be served warm or at room temperature, so if you make it ahead of time, be sure to let it come to room temperature before serving.

1 cup dried green, red, or brown lentils, rinsed and drained
½ teaspoon salt
2 cups water
½ medium red onion, peeled and diced
½ medium red bell pepper, seeded and diced
2 tablespoons chopped fresh mint
2 tablespoons chopped fresh flat-leaf parsley
¼ cup extra-virgin olive oil
¼ cup lemon juice
½ teaspoon ground cumin
¼ teaspoon ground allspice
¼ teaspoon ground black pepper
1 clove garlic, peeled and minced
½ cup crumbled feta cheese

SERVES 6	
Per Serving:	
Calories	181
Fat	12g
Protein	10g
Sodium	438mg
Fiber	10g
Carbohydrates	18g
Sugar	3g

1 Add lentils, salt, and water to the Instant Pot®. Close lid, set steam release to Sealing, press the Manual button, and set time to 15 minutes. When the timer beeps, let pressure release naturally for 15 minutes, then quick-release any remaining pressure until the float valve drops. Open lid and drain off any excess liquid.

2 Add onion, bell pepper, mint, parsley, olive oil, lemon juice, cumin, allspice, black pepper, and garlic, and toss to mix. Transfer to a serving bowl and top with feta. Serve warm or at room temperature.

Red Lentils with Kale and Feta

Kale and lentils are combined to create a dish with a long list of nutritional benefits. Kale is packed with vitamin C, vitamin K, and antioxidants; and lentils are rich in folate, manganese, polyphenols, protein, and fiber.

TYPES OF LENTILS

Lentils can be classified by size, by color, or by whether or not the legumes are whole or split. Brown lentils are the most commonly available variety. They take longer to cook than red or yellow lentils, so be sure to add about 10 minutes to your cooking time if you are substituting brown lentils for red or yellow varieties. It's not a good idea to substitute canned lentils for dried lentils in most recipes—the boiling required to cook dried lentils will turn the canned ones into mush.

1 tablespoon olive oil
1 medium yellow onion, peeled and chopped
1 clove garlic, peeled and minced
3 cups chopped kale
1 cup dried red lentils, rinsed and drained
2 cups water
3 tablespoons chopped fresh mint
2 tablespoons chopped fresh flat-leaf parsley
1 tablespoon lemon juice
¼ teaspoon ground allspice
¼ teaspoon salt
¼ teaspoon ground black pepper
½ cup crumbled feta cheese

1   Press the Sauté button on the Instant Pot® and heat oil. Add onion and cook until just tender, about 3 minutes. Add garlic and cook until fragrant, about 30 seconds. Add kale and toss to coat in onion mixture. Cook until starting to wilt, about 1 minute. Press the Cancel button.

2   Add lentils and water to pot. Close lid, set steam release to Sealing, press the Manual button, and set time to 5 minutes. When the timer beeps, let pressure release naturally for 5 minutes, then quick-release any remaining pressure until the float valve drops. Open lid and drain off any excess liquid.

3   Add mint, parsley, lemon juice, allspice, salt, and pepper, and toss to mix. Transfer to a serving bowl and top with feta. Serve warm or at room temperature.

Lentil and Spinach Curry

SERVES 4

Per Serving:

Calories	195
Fat	4g
Protein	13g
Sodium	111mg
Fiber	8g
Carbohydrates	26g
Sugar	3g

There are so many reasons to cook this vegetarian dish. It's quick to make, full of nutrients, and fragrant with the mix of spices. Alter the recipe by replacing the spinach with chard, kale, collard greens, or even beet greens.

1 tablespoon olive oil
½ cup diced onion
1 clove garlic, peeled and minced
1 cup dried yellow lentils, rinsed and drained
4 cups water
½ teaspoon ground coriander
½ teaspoon ground turmeric
½ teaspoon curry powder
½ cup diced tomatoes
5 ounces baby spinach leaves

1 Press the Sauté button on the Instant Pot® and heat oil. Add onion and cook until translucent, about 5 minutes. Add garlic and cook for 30 seconds. Add lentils and toss to combine. Press the Cancel button.

2 Pour in water. Close lid, set steam release to Sealing, press the Manual button, and set time to 6 minutes. When the timer beeps, quick-release the pressure until the float valve drops and open lid. Press the Cancel button. Drain any residual liquid. Stir in coriander, turmeric, curry powder, tomatoes, and spinach.

3 Press the Sauté button, press the Adjust button to change the heat to Less, and simmer uncovered until tomatoes are heated through and spinach has wilted, about 5 minutes.

4 Transfer to a dish and serve.

Golden Lentil and Spinach Soup

Eating cooked spinach actually helps your body to absorb more calcium. Raw spinach contains oxalic acid, which binds to calcium and inhibits its absorption. Cooking the spinach releases that bond, freeing the calcium to be more readily absorbed into your body.

2 tablespoons olive oil

1 medium yellow onion, peeled and chopped

1 medium carrot, peeled and sliced

1 stalk celery, chopped

2 cloves garlic, peeled and minced

1 teaspoon fresh thyme leaves

½ teaspoon ground turmeric

½ teaspoon ground cumin

½ teaspoon ground black pepper

¼ teaspoon ground cinnamon

¼ teaspoon salt

2 cups dried yellow lentils, rinsed and drained

1 large sweet potato, peeled and chopped

4 cups baby spinach

6 cups water

SERVES 6	
Per Serving:	
Calories	285
Fat	6g
Protein	18g
Sodium	162mg
Fiber	10g
Carbohydrates	42g
Sugar	5g

1 Press the Sauté button on the Instant Pot® and heat oil. Add onion, carrot, and celery. Cook until just tender, about 3 minutes. Add garlic, thyme, turmeric, cumin, pepper, cinnamon, and salt, and cook until fragrant, about 30 seconds. Press the Cancel button.

2 Add lentils, sweet potato, spinach, and water, then close lid, set steam release to Sealing, press the Manual button, and set time to 12 minutes. When the timer beeps, quick-release the pressure until the float valve drops. Open lid and stir well. Serve warm.

Green Lentil Stew

SERVES 6	
Per Serving:	
Calories	348
Fat	5g
Protein	22g
Sodium	434mg
Fiber	19g
Carbohydrates	48g
Sugar	6g

When the weather is chilly and you need something to warm you up, this is the stew for you. You can use any hearty winter vegetables like butternut squash, acorn squash, or pumpkin here, so play around with the ingredients.

2 tablespoons olive oil
1 medium yellow onion, peeled and chopped
1 medium carrot, peeled and chopped
2 cloves garlic, peeled and minced
½ teaspoon salt

2 cups dried green lentils, rinsed and drained
1 medium sweet potato, peeled and diced
6 cups low-sodium chicken broth

1 Press the Sauté button on the Instant Pot® and heat oil. Add onion and carrot, and cook until just tender, about 3 minutes. Add garlic and salt, and cook until fragrant, about 30 seconds. Press the Cancel button.

2 Add lentils, sweet potato, and broth to the pot. Close lid, set steam release to Sealing, press the Manual button, and set time to 25 minutes.

3 When the timer beeps, let pressure release naturally, about 25 minutes. Open lid and stir. Serve warm.

Red Lentil and Carrot Soup

SERVES 6	
Per Serving:	
Calories	230
Fat	6g
Protein	13g
Sodium	135mg
Fiber	7g
Carbohydrates	34g
Sugar	6g

We are all familiar with the orange carrot, but did you know that carrots come in a variety of colors, such as white, purple, red, and yellow? If you can get your hands on any of these fancy carrots, use them to make this soup.

2 tablespoons olive oil
4 medium carrots, peeled and sliced
1 medium yellow onion, peeled and chopped
1 stalk celery, chopped
1 tablespoon grated fresh ginger
2 cloves garlic, peeled and minced

¼ teaspoon ground allspice
½ teaspoon ground black pepper
¼ teaspoon salt
2 cups dried red lentils, rinsed and drained
6 cups water

1 Press the Sauté button on the Instant Pot® and heat oil. Add carrots, onion, and celery. Sauté 5 minutes. Add ginger, garlic, allspice, pepper, and salt, and cook 30 seconds. Press the Cancel button.

2 Add lentils and water, stir, close lid, set steam release to Sealing, press the Manual button, and set time to 12 minutes. When the timer beeps, let pressure release naturally, about 15 minutes. Open lid and stir well. Serve warm.

Mediterranean Lentil Soup

This soup is ready in a matter of minutes. Turn this dish into a special treat by drizzling soup with peppery extra-virgin olive oil and serving it with a loaf of crusty whole-grain bread for dipping.

2 tablespoons olive oil

2 medium carrots, peeled and chopped

1 medium yellow onion, peeled and chopped

1 stalk celery, chopped

1 large orange bell pepper, seeded and chopped

4 cloves garlic, peeled and minced

1 tablespoon tomato paste

½ teaspoon ground cumin

½ teaspoon ground black pepper

¼ teaspoon salt

2 cups dried green lentils, rinsed and drained

1 large russet potato, peeled and chopped

6 cups water

½ cup chopped fresh flat-leaf parsley

SERVES 6	
Per Serving:	
Calories	323
Fat	5g
Protein	18g
Sodium	123mg
Fiber	21g
Carbohydrates	52g
Sugar	6g

1 Press the Sauté button on the Instant Pot® and heat oil. Add carrots, onion, celery, and bell pepper. Cook until just tender, about 5 minutes. Add garlic, tomato paste, cumin, black pepper, and salt, and cook until fragrant and tomato paste is slightly darker in color, about 1 minute. Press the Cancel button.

2 Add lentils, potato, and water, then close lid, set steam release to Sealing, press the Manual button, and set time to 12 minutes. When the timer beeps, let pressure release naturally, about 15 minutes. Open lid, stir well, and serve warm, topped with parsley.

Simple Tri-Color Lentil Salad

SERVES 6

Per Serving:

Calories	469
Fat	19g
Protein	14g
Sodium	730mg
Fiber	4g
Carbohydrates	62g
Sugar	5g

If you are unable to find a tri-color lentil mix in your local supermarket, head to the bulk food section of a natural food store. You can usually find green, red, and yellow or brown lentils available, making it easy to create your own blend.

2 cups tri-color dried lentils, rinsed and drained
½ teaspoon salt
4 cups water
1 medium red onion, peeled and diced
1 stalk celery, diced
1 cup sliced cherry tomatoes
½ medium yellow bell pepper, seeded and diced
¼ cup chopped fresh cilantro
¼ cup extra-virgin olive oil
¼ cup red wine vinegar
1 tablespoon chopped fresh oregano
1 teaspoon fresh thyme leaves
¼ teaspoon ground black pepper
½ cup crumbled feta cheese
½ cup halved Kalamata olives

1 Add lentils, salt, and water to the Instant Pot®. Close lid, set steam release to Sealing, press the Manual button, and set time to 12 minutes. When the timer beeps, quick-release the pressure until the float valve drops. Open lid and drain off any excess liquid. Let lentils cool to room temperature, about 30 minutes.

2 Add onion, celery, tomatoes, bell pepper, cilantro, oil, vinegar, oregano, thyme, and black pepper, and toss to mix. Transfer to a serving bowl and garnish with feta and olives. Serve at room temperature or refrigerate for at least 2 hours.

Lentils and Rice

This dish is a great base for other foods. Serve it topped with grilled shrimp or chicken, with a crisp salad, or as the base for a veggie burrito bowl.

3 cups water

2 cups dried lentils (red, green, yellow, or a mix), rinsed and drained

1 cup long-grain brown rice

1 clove garlic, peeled and minced

1 teaspoon ground fennel

1 teaspoon dried oregano

1 teaspoon onion powder

½ teaspoon ground turmeric

2 tablespoons extra-virgin olive oil

1 tablespoon red wine vinegar

¼ teaspoon salt

¼ teaspoon ground black pepper

2 tablespoons chopped fresh flat-leaf parsley

SERVES 8	
Per Serving:	
Calories	218
Fat	4g
Protein	6g
Sodium	74mg
Fiber	3g
Carbohydrates	39g
Sugar	1g

1 Add water, lentils, rice, garlic, fennel, oregano, onion powder, and turmeric to the Instant Pot®. Close lid, set steam release to Sealing, press the Manual button, and set time to 10 minutes. When the timer beeps, let pressure release naturally for 15 minutes, then quick-release any remaining pressure until the float valve drops.

2 Open lid and add oil, vinegar, salt, and pepper. Toss to combine. Transfer to a serving dish and garnish with parsley.

Puréed Red Lentil Soup

To brighten the flavor of this soup, add a teaspoon or two of fresh lemon juice or serve it with lemon wedges on the side.

2 tablespoons olive oil

1 medium yellow onion, peeled and chopped

1 medium carrot, peeled and chopped

1 medium red bell pepper, seeded and chopped

1 clove garlic, peeled and minced

1 bay leaf

½ teaspoon ground black pepper

¼ teaspoon salt

1 (15-ounce) can diced tomatoes, drained

2 cups dried red lentils, rinsed and drained

6 cups low-sodium chicken broth

SERVES 6	
Per Serving:	
Calories	289
Fat	6g
Protein	18g
Sodium	438mg
Fiber	8g
Carbohydrates	39g
Sugar	8g

1 Press the Sauté button on the Instant Pot® and heat oil. Add onion, carrot, and bell pepper. Cook until just tender, about 5 minutes. Add garlic, bay leaf, black pepper, and salt, and cook until fragrant, about 30 seconds. Press the Cancel button.

2 Add tomatoes, lentils, and broth, then close lid, set steam release to Sealing, press the Manual button, and set time to 15 minutes. When the timer beeps, let pressure release naturally, about 15 minutes. Open lid, remove and discard bay leaf, and purée with an immersion blender or in batches in a blender. Serve warm.

Lentils in Tomato Sauce

This may be the easiest lentil recipe you make because you can use a supermarket shortcut—jarred marinara sauce.

2 cups red, green, or brown dried lentils, rinsed and drained
½ teaspoon salt
4 cups water
1 (24-ounce) jar marinara sauce
1 tablespoon extra-virgin olive oil
1 tablespoon chopped fresh oregano
1 teaspoon ground fennel
¼ teaspoon ground black pepper
½ cup grated Parmesan cheese
½ cup minced fresh flat-leaf parsley

1　Add lentils, salt, and water to the Instant Pot®. Close lid, set steam release to Sealing, press the Manual button, and set time to 6 minutes. When the timer beeps, quick-release the pressure until the float valve drops. Press the Cancel button. Open lid and drain off any excess liquid.

2　Add sauce, oil, oregano, fennel, and pepper to pot and stir well. Close lid, set steam release to Sealing, press the Manual button, and set time to 5 minutes. When the timer beeps, let pressure release naturally for 10 minutes, then quick-release any remaining pressure until the float valve drops. Open lid and top with cheese and parsley.

Fakkes (Lentil Soup)

Garnish this soup with a few Kalamata olives and a splash of wine vinegar.

1 pound dried lentils, rinsed and drained
2 cups water
1 medium onion, peeled and diced
1 large carrot, peeled and grated
4 cloves garlic, peeled and chopped
1 (15-ounce) can crushed tomatoes
1 teaspoon dried rosemary
2 bay leaves
¼ cup extra-virgin olive oil

1　Add all ingredients to the Instant Pot® and stir well.

2　Close lid, set steam release to Sealing, press the Manual button, and set time to 20 minutes. When the timer beeps, quick-release the pressure until the float valve drops. Open lid and remove and discard bay leaves. Serve hot or cold.

Lentils with Artichoke, Tomato, and Feta

If you are not able to find any firm, ripe vine tomatoes, use halved cherry tomatoes. About 1 cup will work.

2 cups dried red lentils, rinsed and drained
½ teaspoon salt
4 cups water
1 (12-ounce) jar marinated artichokes, drained and chopped
2 medium vine-ripe tomatoes, chopped
½ medium red onion, peeled and diced

½ large English cucumber, diced
½ cup crumbled feta cheese
¼ cup chopped fresh flat-leaf parsley
3 tablespoons extra-virgin olive oil
2 tablespoons balsamic vinegar
½ teaspoon ground black pepper

SERVES 6	
Per Serving:	
Calories	332
Fat	13g
Protein	17g
Sodium	552mg
Fiber	6g
Carbohydrates	40g
Sugar	8g

1 Add lentils, salt, and water to the Instant Pot®. Close lid, set steam release to Sealing, press the Manual button, and set time to 12 minutes. When the timer beeps, quick-release the pressure until the float valve drops. Open lid and drain off any excess liquid. Let lentils cool to room temperature, about 30 minutes.

2 Add artichokes, tomatoes, onion, cucumber, feta, parsley, oil, vinegar, and pepper, and toss to mix. Transfer to a serving bowl. Serve at room temperature or refrigerate for at least 2 hours.

Lentil Pâté

Experiment with the cooking time for this dish; some cooks find the lentils take slightly less time to cook than the time provided.

2 tablespoons olive oil, divided
1 cup diced yellow onion
3 cloves garlic, peeled and minced
1 teaspoon red wine vinegar

2 cups dried green lentils, rinsed and drained
4 cups water
1 teaspoon salt
¼ teaspoon ground black pepper

SERVES 12	
Per Serving:	
Calories	138
Fat	3g
Protein	8g
Sodium	196mg
Fiber	10g
Carbohydrates	20g
Sugar	1g

1 Press the Sauté button on the Instant Pot® and heat 1 tablespoon oil. Add onion and cook until translucent, about 3 minutes. Add garlic and vinegar, and cook for 30 seconds. Add lentils, water, remaining 1 tablespoon oil, and salt to pot and stir to combine. Press the Cancel button.

2 Close lid, set steam release to Sealing, press the Bean button, and allow to cook for default time of 30 minutes. When the timer beeps, let pressure release naturally for 10 minutes. Quick-release any remaining pressure until the float valve drops, then open lid.

3 Transfer lentil mixture to a food processor or blender, and blend until smooth. Season with pepper and serve warm.

Lentil and Zucchini Boats

This dish is perfect for the Italian food lovers in your life. When hollowing out the zucchini, be sure to leave about ¼" of flesh inside so the zucchini will hold up during baking.

1 cup dried green lentils, rinsed and drained
¼ teaspoon salt
2 cups water
1 tablespoon olive oil
½ medium red onion, peeled and diced
1 clove garlic, peeled and minced
1 cup marinara sauce
¼ teaspoon crushed red pepper flakes
4 medium zucchini, trimmed and cut lengthwise
½ cup shredded part-skim mozzarella cheese
¼ cup chopped fresh flat-leaf parsley

1 Add lentils, salt, and water to the Instant Pot®. Close lid, set steam release to Sealing, press the Manual button, and set time to 12 minutes. When the timer beeps, quick-release the pressure until the float valve drops. Press the Cancel button. Open lid and drain off any excess liquid. Transfer lentils to a medium bowl. Set aside.

2 Press the Sauté button and heat oil. Add onion and cook until tender, about 3 minutes. Add garlic and cook until fragrant, about 30 seconds. Add marinara sauce and crushed red pepper flakes and stir to combine. Press the Cancel button. Stir in lentils.

3 Preheat oven to 350°F and spray a 9" × 13" baking dish with nonstick cooking spray.

4 Using a teaspoon, hollow out each zucchini half. Lay zucchini in prepared baking dish. Divide lentil mixture among prepared zucchini. Top with cheese. Bake for 30–35 minutes, or until zucchini are tender and cheese is melted and browned. Top with parsley and serve hot.

SERVES 4

Per Serving:

Calories	326
Fat	10g
Protein	22g
Sodium	568mg
Fiber	16g
Carbohydrates	39g
Sugar	6g

ALTERNATIVES TO ZUCCHINI

Not a fan of zucchini? No problem! You can use a variety of different vegetables instead. Yellow summer squash is a simple substitution. Or consider using large tomatoes. Slice off the top and scoop out the seeds and pulp with a spoon. If you have a little more time, use sweet potatoes. Roast them in the oven for 20–25 minutes at 400°F, or until they are tender throughout. Slice them in half, scoop out the flesh, and use the roasted skins as the boats. The roasted flesh can be reserved and later reheated and mashed with a little olive oil, orange juice, and cinnamon.

Lentil Soup with Quinoa

Lentils and quinoa are both considered superfoods (foods that are exceptionally dense with nutrients), and this soup may be the superhero of your weekly meal plan. Both lentils and quinoa are high in protein and fiber, and are good sources of vitamins and minerals.

HOW TO PEEL FRESH GINGER

With its uneven surface and knobby branches, fresh ginger can be difficult to peel. To keep your fingers safe, simply take the edge of a spoon and scrape the peel off of a fresh gingerroot before grating or mincing it.

2 tablespoons olive oil
1 medium yellow onion, peeled and chopped
1 medium carrot, peeled and chopped
1 stalk celery, chopped
1 large tomato, seeded and chopped
2 cups sliced button mushrooms
1 clove garlic, peeled and minced
1 teaspoon ground coriander
½ teaspoon ground turmeric
½ teaspoon grated fresh ginger
½ teaspoon ground black pepper
¼ teaspoon salt
2 cups dried brown lentils, rinsed and drained
1 cup quinoa, rinsed and drained
8 cups low-salt vegetable broth

1   Press the Sauté button on the Instant Pot® and heat oil. Add onion, carrot, and celery. Cook until just tender, about 5 minutes. Add tomato and mushrooms, and cook for 5 minutes, or until mushrooms soften and start to release their liquid. Add garlic, coriander, turmeric, ginger, pepper, and salt, and cook until fragrant, about 30 seconds. Press the Cancel button.

2   Add lentils, quinoa, and broth, then close lid, set steam release to Sealing, press the Manual button, and set time to 12 minutes. When the timer beeps, let pressure release naturally, about 15 minutes. Open lid and stir well. Serve warm.

CHAPTER 9

Vegetables

Dandelion Greens

SERVES 6

Per Serving:

Calories	39
Fat	12g
Protein	1g
Sodium	253mg
Fiber	3g
Carbohydrates	7g
Sugar	0g

Dandelion greens can be served warm or cold, as a side for grilled fish, or on their own with some crusty bread, Kalamata olives, and feta cheese. Garnish the greens with fresh minced garlic.

4 pounds dandelion greens, stalks cut and discarded, and greens washed
½ cup water
¼ cup extra-virgin olive oil
¼ cup lemon juice
½ teaspoon salt
½ teaspoon ground black pepper

1 Add dandelion greens and water to the Instant Pot®. Close lid, set steam release to Sealing, press the Manual button, and set time to 1 minute. When the timer beeps, quick-release the pressure until the float valve drops. Open lid and drain well.

2 Combine olive oil, lemon juice, salt, and pepper in a small bowl. Pour over greens and toss to coat.

Greek-Style Peas

SERVES 4

Per Serving:

Calories	377
Fat	15g
Protein	13g
Sodium	421mg
Fiber	11g
Carbohydrates	47g
Sugar	17g

We may think of peas as a side dish, but in Greece, peas with tomatoes and carrots is a popular plant-based main dish. Be sure to cut your potato into small, uniformly sized pieces so they cook evenly and are ready along with the peas.

3 tablespoons olive oil
1 large russet potato, peeled and cut into ½" pieces
1 medium white onion, peeled and diced
1 medium carrot, peeled and diced
3 medium tomatoes, seeded and diced
1 clove garlic, peeled and minced
1 pound fresh or frozen green peas
¼ cup chopped fresh dill
¼ teaspoon salt
¼ teaspoon ground black pepper
⅓ cup crumbled feta cheese

1 Press the Sauté button on the Instant Pot® and heat oil. Add potato, onion, and carrot, and cook until onion and carrot are tender, about 8 minutes. Add tomatoes and garlic, and cook until garlic is fragrant, about 1 minute. Press the Cancel button.

2 Add peas, close lid, set steam release to Sealing, press the Manual button, and set time to 1 minute. When the timer beeps, quick-release the pressure until the float valve drops. Press the Cancel button and open lid. Stir in dill, salt, and pepper. Top with feta and serve hot.

Melitzanes Yiahni (Braised Eggplant)

This eggplant dish is best served over a bed of rice and garnished with sesame seeds.

2 large eggplants, cut into 1" pieces
1¾ teaspoons salt, divided
3 tablespoons extra-virgin olive oil, divided
1 medium yellow onion, peeled and diced
3 cloves garlic, peeled and minced
2 cups diced fresh tomatoes
1 cup water
1 tablespoon dried oregano
½ teaspoon ground black pepper
2 tablespoons minced fresh basil

1. Place eggplant in a colander and sprinkle with 1½ teaspoons salt. Place colander over a plate. Let stand 30 minutes to drain.

2. Press the Sauté button on the Instant Pot® and heat 2 tablespoons oil. Add onion and cook until soft, about 5 minutes. Add garlic and cook until fragrant, about 30 seconds. Add tomatoes and water. Press the Cancel button.

3. Rinse eggplant well and drain. Add to pot. Close lid, set steam release to Sealing, press the Manual button, and set time to 8 minutes. Once timer beeps, quick-release the pressure until the float valve drops, press the Cancel button, and open lid. Add oregano, pepper, and remaining ¼ teaspoon salt.

4. Add remaining 1 tablespoon oil to pot and stir well. Press the Sauté button and simmer for 15 minutes to thicken. Add basil and serve hot.

SERVES 6	
Per Serving:	
Calories	121
Fat	7g
Protein	2g
Sodium	107mg
Fiber	7g
Carbohydrates	14g
Sugar	8g

AN EGGPLANT FOR YOUR THOUGHTS…

Though originally from India, the eggplant is likely the most widely used vegetable throughout the Mediterranean.

Roasted Garlic Spaghetti Squash

SERVES 4	
Per Serving:	
Calories	186
Fat	15g
Protein	6g
Sodium	531mg
Fiber	2g
Carbohydrates	8g
Sugar	3g

Roasting garlic mellows the flavor and adds a richness that is perfect as a dressing for pasta or, in this case, spaghetti squash. Be careful when you cut your spaghetti squash in half; the outer rind is quite tough. To soften the outer skin, you can place the squash in the microwave for 1 minute, then let stand for 5 minutes before cutting.

1 bulb garlic, top sliced off
3 tablespoons olive oil, divided
1 (3-pound) spaghetti squash
1 cup water
½ teaspoon salt
½ teaspoon ground black pepper
¼ cup chopped fresh flat-leaf parsley
¼ cup grated Parmesan cheese

1 Preheat oven to 400°F. Place garlic bulb on a sheet of aluminum foil. Drizzle with 1 tablespoon oil. Wrap bulb tightly and roast directly on the oven rack for 30–40 minutes, or until bulb is tender. Unwrap and let bulb rest while you prepare squash.

2 Slice spaghetti squash in half lengthwise. Scoop out seeds with a spoon and discard.

3 Place the rack in the Instant Pot®, add water, and place spaghetti squash on rack. Close lid, set steam release to Sealing, press the Manual button, and set time to 7 minutes.

4 When the timer beeps, quick-release the pressure until the float valve drops. Press the Cancel button and open lid. Carefully remove squash from pot and set aside to cool for 10 minutes, then take a fork and shred flesh into a large bowl.

5 Clean and dry pot. Press the Sauté button and heat remaining 2 tablespoons oil. Squeeze garlic into pot and cook for 30 seconds, then add squash, salt, and pepper and cook until squash is thoroughly coated in the garlic. Transfer to a serving bowl and top with parsley and cheese. Serve immediately.

Heirloom Tomato Basil Soup

If you love tomato soup, this dish is going to make your day. To make it even better, top the soup with grilled-cheese croutons. Make a grilled-cheese sandwich as you normally would and then cut the sandwich into little squares. Float these glorious croutons atop your soup and enjoy this new twist on an old classic.

1 tablespoon olive oil
1 small onion, peeled and diced
1 stalk celery, sliced
8 medium heirloom tomatoes, seeded and quartered
¼ cup julienned fresh basil
½ teaspoon salt
3 cups low-sodium chicken broth
1 cup heavy cream
1 teaspoon ground black pepper

SERVES 4	
Per Serving:	
Calories	282
Fat	24g
Protein	4g
Sodium	466mg
Fiber	1g
Carbohydrates	9g
Sugar	3g

1 Press the Sauté button on the Instant Pot® and heat oil. Add onion and celery and cook until translucent, about 5 minutes. Add tomatoes and cook for 3 minutes, or until tomatoes are tender and start to break down. Add basil, salt, and broth. Press the Cancel button.

2 Close lid, set steam release to Sealing, press the Manual button, and set time to 7 minutes. When the timer beeps, quick-release the pressure until the float valve drops and then open lid.

3 Add cream and pepper. Purée soup with an immersion blender, or purée in batches in a blender. Ladle into bowls and serve warm.

Artichokes Provençal

Cooking fresh artichokes may seem intimidating, but it is surprisingly easy to prepare them. These artichokes are cooked in a flavorful mixture of tomatoes, olives, garlic, and herbs for a burst of freshness.

SERVES 4

Per Serving:	
Calories	449
Fat	16g
Protein	20g
Sodium	762mg
Fiber	12g
Carbohydrates	40g
Sugar	4g

ARTICHOKES

Artichokes are enjoyed around the globe and come in a number of varieties, including green, purple, and white. When working with artichokes, it's a good idea to rub their cut surfaces with lemon to avoid browning. Artichokes should be firm, with closely fitted leaves and a plump stem.

4 large artichokes
1 medium lemon, cut in half
2 tablespoons olive oil
½ medium white onion, peeled and sliced
4 cloves garlic, peeled and chopped
2 tablespoons chopped fresh oregano
2 tablespoons chopped fresh basil
2 sprigs fresh thyme
2 medium tomatoes, seeded and chopped
¼ cup chopped Kalamata olives
¼ cup red wine
¼ cup water
¼ teaspoon salt
¼ teaspoon ground black pepper

1 Run artichokes under running water, making sure water runs between leaves to flush out any debris. Slice off top ⅓ of artichoke, trim stem, and pull away any tough outer leaves. Rub all cut surfaces with lemon.

2 Press the Sauté button on the Instant Pot® and heat oil. Add onion and cook until just tender, about 2 minutes. Add garlic, oregano, basil, and thyme, and cook until fragrant, about 30 seconds. Add tomatoes and olives and gently mix, then add wine and water and cook for 30 seconds. Press the Cancel button, then add artichokes cut side down to the Instant Pot®.

3 Close lid, set steam release to Sealing, press the Manual button, and set time to 5 minutes. When the timer beeps, quick-release the pressure until the float valve drops. Open lid and transfer artichokes to a serving platter. Pour sauce over top, then season with salt and pepper. Serve warm.

Hearty Minestrone Soup

SERVES 8

Per Serving:

Calories	207
Fat	1g
Protein	12g
Sodium	814mg
Fiber	10g
Carbohydrates	47g
Sugar	6g

This classic Italian soup is loaded with vegetables and robust Mediterranean flavors. Also included is orzo, a rice-shaped pasta, which adds to the heartiness of this scrumptious soup.

2 cups dried Great Northern beans, soaked overnight and drained
1 cup orzo
2 large carrots, peeled and diced
1 bunch Swiss chard, ribs removed and roughly chopped
1 medium zucchini, trimmed and diced
2 stalks celery, diced
1 medium onion, peeled and diced
1 teaspoon minced garlic
1 tablespoon Italian seasoning
1 teaspoon salt
½ teaspoon ground black pepper
2 bay leaves
1 (14.5-ounce) can diced tomatoes, including juice
4 cups vegetable broth
1 cup tomato juice

1 Place all ingredients in the Instant Pot® and stir to combine. Close lid, set steam release to Sealing, press the Soup button, and cook for the default time of 20 minutes.

2 When the timer beeps, let pressure release naturally for 10 minutes. Quick-release any remaining pressure until the float valve drops and open lid. Remove and discard bay leaves.

3 Ladle into bowls and serve warm.

Spaghetti Squash with Mushrooms

Mushrooms have a hearty flavor and a satisfying meaty texture. They are also a great source of plant-based protein and fiber, which makes you feel satisfied longer. Any mushrooms can work in this recipe, so use the ones you like best.

1 (3-pound) spaghetti squash
1 cup water
2 tablespoons olive oil
4 cups sliced button mushrooms
2 cloves garlic, peeled and minced
1 tablespoon chopped fresh oregano
1 tablespoon chopped fresh basil
¼ teaspoon crushed red pepper flakes
1 cup marinara sauce
½ cup shredded Parmesan cheese

SERVES 4	
Per Serving:	
Calories	289
Fat	13g
Protein	12g
Sodium	508mg
Fiber	8g
Carbohydrates	36g
Sugar	14g

1 Slice spaghetti squash in half lengthwise. Scoop out seeds with a spoon and discard.

2 Place the rack in the Instant Pot®, add water, and place spaghetti squash on rack. Close lid, set steam release to Sealing, press the Manual button, and set time to 7 minutes.

3 When the timer beeps, quick-release the pressure until the float valve drops. Press the Cancel button and open lid. Carefully remove squash from pot and set aside to cool for 10 minutes, then take a fork and shred flesh into a medium bowl.

4 Wash and dry pot. Press the Sauté button and heat oil. Add mushrooms and cook until tender and any juices have evaporated, about 8 minutes. Add garlic and cook until fragrant, about 30 seconds.

5 Add spaghetti squash to pot and toss to mix. Add oregano, basil, red pepper flakes, and marinara sauce and toss to coat. Press the Cancel button. Top with cheese and close the lid. Let stand 5 minutes until cheese melts. Serve hot.

Artichoke Soup

SERVES 8	
Per Serving:	
Calories	261
Fat	4g
Protein	9g
Sodium	1,099mg
Fiber	11g
Carbohydrates	51g
Sugar	8g

Artichokes are part of the thistle family and grow wild in the Mediterranean.

18 large fresh artichokes, trimmed, halved, and chokes removed
1 medium lemon, halved
6 tablespoons lemon juice, divided
2 tablespoons extra-virgin olive oil
6 medium leeks, trimmed, cut lengthwise, and sliced
¾ teaspoon salt, divided
½ teaspoon pepper, divided
3 large potatoes, peeled and quartered
10 cups vegetable stock
½ cup low-fat plain Greek yogurt
½ cup chopped fresh chives

1   Rinse artichokes under running water, making sure water runs between leaves to flush out any debris. Rub all cut surfaces with lemon. In a large bowl, combine artichokes, enough water to cover them, and 3 tablespoons lemon juice. Set aside.

2   Press the Sauté button on the Instant Pot® and heat oil. Add leeks, ½ teaspoon salt, and ¼ teaspoon pepper. Cook for 10 minutes or until leeks are softened.

3   Drain artichokes and add to leeks along with potatoes and stock. Add remaining ¼ teaspoon each salt and pepper.

4   Press the Cancel button, close lid, set steam release to Sealing, press the Soup button, and cook for default time of 20 minutes. When the timer beeps, let pressure release naturally, about 25 minutes. Press the Cancel button and open lid.

5   Using an immersion blender, or in batches in a regular blender, purée the soup until smooth. Stir in remaining 3 tablespoons lemon juice.

6   Serve soup with a dollop of yogurt and a sprinkle of chives.

Green Beans with Tomatoes and Potatoes

This dish is cooked in two stages, but don't let that worry you. All you are doing is adding ingredients to the pot so they are ready at the same time. Look for baby potatoes of roughly the same size, about 1" to 2" in diameter, to ensure even cooking.

1 pound small new potatoes

1 cup water

1 teaspoon salt

2 pounds fresh green beans, trimmed

2 medium tomatoes, seeded and diced

2 tablespoons olive oil

1 tablespoon red wine vinegar

1 clove garlic, peeled and minced

½ teaspoon dry mustard powder

¼ teaspoon smoked paprika

¼ teaspoon ground black pepper

1 Place potatoes in a steamer basket. Place the rack in the Instant Pot®, add water, and then top with the steamer basket. Close lid, set steam release to Sealing, press the Manual button, and set time to 4 minutes. When the timer beeps, quick-release the pressure until the float valve drops. Press the Cancel button and open lid.

2 Add salt, green beans, and tomatoes to the Instant Pot®. Close lid, set steam release to Sealing, press the Manual button, and set time to 1 minute. When the timer beeps, quick-release the pressure until the float valve drops, press the Cancel button, and open lid. Transfer mixture to a serving platter or large bowl.

3 In a small bowl, whisk oil, vinegar, garlic, mustard, paprika, and pepper. Pour dressing over vegetables and gently toss to coat. Serve hot.

SERVES 8	
Per Serving:	
Calories	112
Fat	4g
Protein	2g
Sodium	368mg
Fiber	5g
Carbohydrates	20g
Sugar	3g

EAT YOUR VEGGIES

In Mediterranean countries, vegetables are not only used as garnishes or sides to mains; they also comprise entire meals in themselves. Find ways to incorporate your favorite vegetables into salads, soups, and side dishes. Simply steamed vegetables make a great main meal with rice or pasta and a drizzle of olive oil.

Zesty Cabbage Soup

SERVES 8

Per Serving:

Calories	157
Fat	4g
Protein	7g
Sodium	360mg
Fiber	8g
Carbohydrates	25g
Sugar	9g

CABBAGE

Cabbage is an underrated vegetable that should be included in more meals. It's a good source of fiber and vitamin C. It's also a great colon cleanser and a detoxifier for the entire body.

Eliminate the chili pepper in this recipe if you don't like spicy food.

2 tablespoons extra-virgin olive oil
3 medium onions, peeled and chopped
1 large carrot, peeled, quartered, and sliced
1 stalk celery, chopped
3 bay leaves
1 teaspoon smoked paprika
3 cups sliced white cabbage
1 teaspoon fresh thyme leaves
3 cloves garlic, peeled and minced
½ cup chopped roasted red pepper
1 (15-ounce) can white navy beans, drained and rinsed
1½ cups low-sodium vegetable cocktail beverage
7 cups low-sodium vegetable stock
1 dried chili pepper
2 medium zucchini, trimmed, halved lengthwise, and thinly sliced
1 teaspoon salt
½ teaspoon ground black pepper

1 Press the Sauté button on the Instant Pot® and heat oil. Add onions, carrot, celery, and bay leaves. Cook for 7–10 minutes or until vegetables are soft.

2 Add paprika, cabbage, thyme, garlic, roasted red pepper, and beans. Stir to combine and cook for 2 minutes. Add vegetable cocktail beverage, stock, and chili pepper. Press the Cancel button.

3 Close lid, set steam release to Sealing, press the Soup button, and cook for default time of 20 minutes. When the timer beeps, quick-release the pressure until the float valve drops and open lid.

4 Remove and discard bay leaves. Add zucchini, close lid, and let stand on the Keep Warm setting for 15 minutes. Season with salt and pepper. Serve hot.

Eggplant Caponata

Caponata is similar to ratatouille except caponata includes a sweet element, such as the raisins used here.

1/4 cup extra-virgin olive oil
1/4 cup white wine
2 tablespoons red wine vinegar
1 teaspoon ground cinnamon
1 large eggplant, peeled and diced
1 medium onion, peeled and diced
1 medium green bell pepper, seeded and diced
1 medium red bell pepper, seeded and diced

2 cloves garlic, peeled and minced
1 (14.5-ounce) can diced tomatoes
3 stalks celery, diced
1/2 cup chopped oil-cured olives
1/2 cup golden raisins
2 tablespoons capers, rinsed and drained
1/2 teaspoon salt
1/2 teaspoon ground black pepper

SERVES 8	
Per Serving:	
Calories	90
Fat	1g
Protein	2g
Sodium	295mg
Fiber	4g
Carbohydrates	17g
Sugar	13g

1 Place all ingredients in the Instant Pot®. Stir well to mix. Close lid, set steam release to Sealing, press the Manual button, and set time to 5 minutes.

2 When the timer beeps, quick-release the pressure until the float valve drops. Open the lid and stir well. Serve warm or at room temperature.

Puréed Cauliflower Soup

This soup is easy to make but fancy enough to serve to guests, who will think you were in the kitchen all day. Serve the soup with additional Greek yogurt on the side for those who want a little extra tangy flavor.

2 tablespoons olive oil
1 medium onion, peeled and chopped
1 stalk celery, chopped
1 medium carrot, peeled and chopped
3 sprigs fresh thyme

4 cups cauliflower florets
2 cups vegetable stock
1/2 cup half-and-half
1/4 cup low-fat plain Greek yogurt
2 tablespoons chopped fresh chives

SERVES 6	
Per Serving:	
Calories	113
Fat	7g
Protein	3g
Sodium	236mg
Fiber	2g
Carbohydrates	9g
Sugar	5g

1 Press the Sauté button on the Instant Pot® and heat oil. Add onion, celery, and carrot. Cook until just tender, about 6 minutes. Add thyme, cauliflower, and stock. Stir well, then press the Cancel button.

2 Close lid, set steam release to Sealing, press the Manual button, and set time to 5 minutes. When the timer beeps, let pressure release naturally, about 15 minutes.

3 Open lid, remove and discard thyme stems, and with an immersion blender, purée soup until smooth. Stir in half-and-half and yogurt. Garnish with chives and serve immediately.

Spicy Corn on the Cob

SERVES 4	
Per Serving:	
Calories	180
Fat	9g
Protein	5g
Sodium	300mg
Fiber	4g
Carbohydrates	27g
Sugar	8g

If you are serving these along with other grilled foods, toss the ears of corn on a very hot grill after they come out of the Instant Pot®. Just grill them long enough to get a slight char, then brush with the olive oil mixture.

2 tablespoons olive oil
¼ teaspoon smoked paprika
¼ teaspoon ground cumin
¼ teaspoon ground black pepper
⅛ teaspoon cayenne pepper
1 cup water
4 large ears corn, husk and silks removed
½ teaspoon flaky sea salt

1   In a small bowl, whisk together olive oil, paprika, cumin, black pepper, and cayenne pepper. Set aside.

2   Place the rack in the Instant Pot®, pour in water, and place corn on the rack. Close lid, set steam release to Sealing, press the Manual button, and set time to 2 minutes.

3   When the timer beeps, quick-release the pressure until the float valve drops. Press the Cancel button and open lid. Carefully transfer corn to a platter and brush with spiced olive oil. Serve immediately with sea salt.

Gingered Sweet Potatoes

SERVES 6	
Per Serving:	
Calories	219
Fat	6g
Protein	3g
Sodium	304mg
Fiber	9g
Carbohydrates	39g
Sugar	6g

This comforting side dish is begging to be put on your holiday table. Depending on the dairy limitations of you or your guests, feel free to use your milk of choice—regular, soy, or almond. Or get creative—try using canned coconut milk for a fun twist on the taste of these sweet potatoes.

2½ pounds sweet potatoes, peeled and chopped (about 3 large sweet potatoes)
2 cups water
1 tablespoon minced fresh ginger
½ teaspoon salt
1 tablespoon maple syrup
1 tablespoon unsalted butter
¼ cup whole milk

1   Place sweet potatoes and water in the Instant Pot®. Close lid, set steam release to Sealing, press the Manual button, and set time to 10 minutes. When the timer beeps, let the pressure release naturally, about 20 minutes, and open lid.

2   Drain water from the Instant Pot®. Add ginger, salt, maple syrup, butter, and milk to sweet potatoes. Using an immersion blender, cream the potatoes until desired consistency is reached. Serve warm.

Zucchini Pomodoro

This recipe calls for spiralized zucchini, but if you don't have a vegetable spiralizer, you can manually cut the zucchini into long strips. However, the spiralizer is a great, inexpensive kitchen gadget that gives you a lot of bang for the buck. It can spiral apples, jicama, and carrots for summer salads as well as any root vegetable you'd like to substitute for pasta.

1 tablespoon vegetable oil
1 large onion, peeled and diced
3 cloves garlic, peeled and minced
1 (28-ounce) can diced tomatoes, including juice
½ cup water
1 tablespoon Italian seasoning
½ teaspoon salt
½ teaspoon ground black pepper
2 medium zucchini, trimmed and spiralized

SERVES 4	
Per Serving:	
Calories	72
Fat	4g
Protein	2g
Sodium	476mg
Fiber	2g
Carbohydrates	9g
Sugar	5g

1   Press the Sauté button on the Instant Pot® and heat oil. Add onion and cook until translucent, about 5 minutes. Add garlic and cook for an additional 30 seconds. Add tomatoes, water, Italian seasoning, salt, and pepper. Add zucchini and toss to combine. Press the Cancel button.

2   Close lid, set steam release to Sealing, press the Manual button, and set time to 1 minute. When the timer beeps, let pressure release naturally for 5 minutes. Quick-release any remaining pressure until the float valve drops and open lid. Press the Cancel button.

3   Transfer zucchini to four bowls. Press the Sauté button, then press the Adjust button to change the temperature to Less, and simmer sauce in the Instant Pot® uncovered for 5 minutes. Ladle over zucchini and serve immediately.

Burgundy Mushrooms

These mushrooms are a side dish you'll make again and again. Don't skip the bacon in this recipe—its meatiness and saltiness adds depth to this richly flavored, earthy side dish. Serve alongside a grilled steak with some garlicky mashed potatoes and you'll have a meal to be proud of.

SERVES 8	
Per Serving:	
Calories	110
Fat	8g
Protein	5g
Sodium	410mg
Fiber	1g
Carbohydrates	5g
Sugar	1g

¼ cup olive oil

3 cloves garlic, peeled and halved

16 ounces whole white mushrooms

16 ounces whole baby bella mushrooms

1½ cups dry red wine

1 teaspoon Worcestershire sauce

1 teaspoon dried thyme

1 tablespoon Dijon mustard

1 teaspoon ground celery seed

½ teaspoon ground black pepper

3 cups beef broth

2 slices bacon

1　Press the Sauté button on the Instant Pot® and heat oil. Add garlic and mushrooms, and cook until mushrooms start to get tender, about 3 minutes. Add wine and simmer for 3 minutes.

2　Add Worcestershire sauce, thyme, mustard, celery seed, pepper, broth, and bacon to pot. Press the Cancel button.

3　Close lid, set steam release to Sealing, press the Manual button, and set time to 20 minutes. When the timer beeps, let pressure release naturally, about 20 minutes, and open lid. Remove and discard bacon and garlic halves.

4　Transfer mushrooms to a serving bowl. Serve warm.

Wild Mushroom Soup

This broth-based mushroom soup makes a light but flavorful first course or a comforting side dish for when you are feeling under the weather. If you are unable to find fresh wild mushrooms, use whatever fresh mushrooms are available at your market.

3 tablespoons olive oil

1 stalk celery, diced

1 medium carrot, peeled and diced

½ medium yellow onion, peeled and diced

1 clove garlic, peeled and minced

1 (8-ounce) container hen of the woods mushrooms, sliced

1 (8-ounce) container porcini or chanterelle mushrooms, sliced

2 cups sliced shiitake mushrooms

2 tablespoons dry sherry

4 cups vegetable broth

2 cups water

1 tablespoon chopped fresh tarragon

½ teaspoon salt

½ teaspoon ground black pepper

1   Press the Sauté button on the Instant Pot® and heat oil. Add celery, carrot, and onion. Cook, stirring often, until softened, about 5 minutes. Add garlic and cook 30 seconds until fragrant, then add mushrooms and cook until beginning to soften, about 5 minutes.

2   Add sherry, broth, water, tarragon, salt, and pepper to pot, and stir well. Press the Cancel button. Close lid, set steam release to Sealing, press the Manual button, and set time to 5 minutes.

3   When the timer beeps, let pressure release naturally, about 15 minutes. Press the Cancel button, open lid, and stir well. Serve hot.

SERVES 8

Per Serving:

Calories	98
Fat	6g
Protein	1g
Sodium	759mg
Fiber	2g
Carbohydrates	11g
Sugar	5g

WILD MUSHROOMS

Wild mushrooms have flavors that range from mildly floral to meaty and earthy. If fresh varieties are unavailable, you can often find small bags of dried wild mushrooms that just need a quick soak in hot water to be ready. It is unadvisable to forage or pick mushrooms in the wild unless you are well trained or are with a mushroom expert, as some can be deadly when eaten.

Stuffed Acorn Squash

SERVES 2

Per Serving:	
Calories	558
Fat	27g
Protein	9g
Sodium	594mg
Fiber	9g
Carbohydrates	78g
Sugar	39g

If you're looking to include more plant-based main dishes to your diet, this fall dish is a great addition to a Thanksgiving or other holiday table. Top the squash with feta or Parmesan cheese if you prefer them instead of goat cheese.

1 cup water
1 (1-pound) acorn squash, halved and seeded
2 tablespoons olive oil
½ medium white onion, peeled and sliced
1 stalk celery, sliced
2 cloves garlic, peeled and chopped
1 tablespoon chopped fresh sage
1 tablespoon chopped fresh flat-leaf parsley

1 teaspoon chopped fresh rosemary
1 teaspoon fresh thyme leaves
¼ teaspoon salt
¼ teaspoon ground black pepper
½ cup wild rice
¾ cup vegetable stock
¼ cup chopped toasted walnuts
¼ cup golden raisins
¼ cup dried cranberries
¼ cup crumbled goat cheese

1 Place the rack in the Instant Pot® and add water. Place squash halves on the rack, close lid, set steam release to Sealing, press the Manual button, and set time to 10 minutes. When the timer beeps, let pressure release naturally for 10 minutes, then quick-release any reserved pressure until the float valve drops and open lid. Check squash for doneness by inserting a paring knife into the skin. When it pierces easily, it's done. Transfer squash to a platter and cover with foil to keep warm.

2 Wash and dry pot. Press the Sauté button and heat oil. Add onion and celery. Cook until just tender, about 3 minutes. Add garlic, sage, parsley, rosemary, and thyme. Cook until fragrant, about 30 seconds. Add salt and pepper, and stir well, then add wild rice and stock. Press the Cancel button.

3 Close lid, set steam release to Sealing, press the Manual button, and set time to 25 minutes. When the timer beeps, quick-release the pressure until the float valve drops. Open lid, add walnuts, raisins, and cranberries, and stir well. Close lid and let stand on the Keep Warm setting for 10 minutes. Spoon mixture into acorn squash halves and top with goat cheese. Serve warm.

Herb Vinaigrette Potato Salad

This zesty potato salad is a nice change of pace from the typically heavier potato salad.

1/4 cup olive oil

3 tablespoons red wine vinegar

1/4 cup chopped fresh flat-leaf parsley

2 tablespoons chopped fresh dill

2 tablespoons chopped fresh chives

1 clove garlic, peeled and minced

1/2 teaspoon dry mustard powder

1/4 teaspoon ground black pepper

2 pounds baby Yukon Gold potatoes

1 cup water

1 teaspoon salt

SERVES 10	
Per Serving:	
Calories	116
Fat	6g
Protein	2g
Sodium	239mg
Fiber	1g
Carbohydrates	16g
Sugar	1g

1 Whisk together oil, vinegar, parsley, dill, chives, garlic, mustard, and pepper in a small bowl. Set aside.

2 Place potatoes in a steamer basket. Place the rack in the Instant Pot®, add water and salt, then top with the steamer basket. Close lid, set steam release to Sealing, press the Manual button, and set time to 4 minutes. When the timer beeps, quick-release the pressure until the float valve drops. Press the Cancel button and open lid.

3 Transfer hot potatoes to a serving bowl. Pour dressing over potatoes and gently toss to coat. Serve warm or at room temperature.

Steamed Cauliflower with Olive Oil and Herbs

Cauliflower is gaining in popularity because of its versatility, flavor, and nutrition. In this recipe, steamed cauliflower is reverse-marinated, meaning the cauliflower is soaked in a flavorful herb and olive oil marinade after cooking.

1 head cauliflower, cut into florets (about 6 cups)

1 cup water

4 tablespoons olive oil

1 clove garlic, peeled and minced

2 tablespoons chopped fresh oregano

1 teaspoon chopped fresh thyme leaves

1 teaspoon chopped fresh sage

1/4 teaspoon salt

1/4 teaspoon ground black pepper

SERVES 6	
Per Serving:	
Calories	105
Fat	9g
Protein	0g
Sodium	128mg
Fiber	2g
Carbohydrates	0g
Sugar	0g

1 Place cauliflower florets in a steamer basket. Place the rack in the Instant Pot®, add water, then top with the steamer basket. Close lid, set steam release to Sealing, press the Manual button, and set time to 0 minutes.

2 While cauliflower cooks, prepare the dressing. Whisk together olive oil, garlic, oregano, thyme, sage, salt, and pepper.

3 When the timer beeps, quick-release the pressure until the float valve drops. Press the Cancel button and open lid. Carefully transfer cauliflower to a serving bowl and immediately pour dressing over cauliflower. Carefully toss to coat. Let stand for 5 minutes. Serve hot.

Maple Dill Carrots

A little sweet and a little savory, these carrots are a delight. If you have some leftover turkey or chicken in your refrigerator and need a quick and healthy side dish, this recipe has you covered. It is also worthy to accompany those other glorious side dishes at your holiday feast—especially if you garnish it with a bit of extra dill.

1 pound carrots, peeled and cut into quarters, or whole baby carrots
1 tablespoon minced fresh dill
1 tablespoon maple syrup
1 tablespoon ghee
½ teaspoon salt
½ cup water

1 Place all ingredients in the Instant Pot®.

2 Close lid, set steam release to Sealing, press the Manual button, and set time to 5 minutes. When the timer beeps, let the pressure release naturally for 5 minutes, then quick-release remaining pressure until the float valve drops, and open lid.

3 Transfer to a serving dish and serve warm.

SERVES 6	
Per Serving:	
Calories	54
Fat	3g
Protein	1g
Sodium	249mg
Fiber	2g
Carbohydrates	7g
Sugar	4g

MAPLE SYRUP

Maple syrup is made by boiling sap from maple trees until the water evaporates and a thick syrup remains. Maple sap is harvested at the end of winter when the ground begins to thaw. Maple syrup is graded by color from Vermont Fancy, which is the lightest, to Grade B, the darkest. Each grade has the same sugar content, but different flavor profiles. The higher the grade, the more subtle and delicate the flavor. Grade B maple syrup adds the most flavor, which means you can use less. Be sure to check that your maple syrup is pure, and the only ingredient listed is "maple syrup." If you see corn syrup or any other sweeteners or colors, you should pass.

Ratatouille

Originating from Nice, France, ratatouille is a vegetable stew whose name is derived from the French word touiller, *meaning "to toss" or "to stir up." If you want to make this stew more authentic to its French roots, substitute the Italian seasoning with herbes de Provence.*

SALTING EGGPLANT

You can reduce or even eliminate the bitter flavor sometimes found in eggplant by salting it prior to cooking. Salting draws out the bitter liquid in eggplant, making it easy to rinse away. Younger, firm eggplants are less likely to be bitter, but if you want to be sure to get rid of any bitterness, it is best to use salt.

1 medium eggplant, cut into 1" pieces
2 teaspoons salt
4 tablespoons olive oil, divided
1 medium white onion, peeled and chopped
1 medium green bell pepper, seeded and chopped
1 medium red bell pepper, seeded and chopped
1 medium zucchini, trimmed and chopped
1 medium yellow squash, chopped
4 cloves garlic, peeled and minced
4 large tomatoes, cut into 1" pieces
2 teaspoons Italian seasoning
¼ teaspoon crushed red pepper flakes
6 fresh basil leaves, thinly sliced

1 Place eggplant in a colander and sprinkle evenly with salt. Let stand 30 minutes, then rinse and dry eggplant. Set aside.

2 Press the Sauté button on the Instant Pot® and heat 1 tablespoon oil. Add onion and bell peppers. Cook, stirring often, until vegetables are just tender, about 5 minutes. Transfer to a large bowl and set aside.

3 Add 1 tablespoon oil to pot and heat for 30 seconds, then add zucchini and squash. Cook, stirring constantly, until vegetables are tender, about 5 minutes. Add garlic and cook until fragrant, about 30 seconds. Transfer to bowl with onion and peppers.

4 Add 1 tablespoon oil to pot and heat for 30 seconds. Add eggplant and cook, stirring constantly, until eggplant is golden brown, about 8 minutes. Add tomatoes and cook until they are tender and releasing juice, about 4 minutes.

5 Return reserved vegetables to pot and stir in Italian seasoning and red pepper flakes. Press the Cancel button. Close lid, set steam release to Sealing, press the Manual button, and set time to 5 minutes.

6 When the timer beeps, quick-release the pressure until the float valve drops. Press the Cancel button, open lid, and stir well. Serve topped with basil and remaining 1 tablespoon oil.

CHAPTER 10

Seafood

Linguine with Clams and White Wine

This elegant pasta dish is perfect for a stay-at-home date night, a dinner party with friends, or anytime you want a meal that feels special. Serve torn hunks of crusty bread as the perfect accompaniment to soak up the sauce.

HOW DO YOU PURGE CLAMS?

To get rid of, or purge, the sand and grit in fresh clams, soak them in water with 1–2 tablespoons of cornmeal for 20 minutes. Rinse and drain until there is no more sand in the water.

2 tablespoons olive oil
4 cups sliced mushrooms
1 medium yellow onion, peeled and diced
2 tablespoons chopped fresh oregano
3 cloves garlic, peeled and minced
¼ teaspoon salt
¼ teaspoon ground black pepper
½ cup white wine
1½ cups water
8 ounces linguine, broken in half
1 pound fresh clams, rinsed and purged
3 tablespoons lemon juice
¼ cup grated Parmesan cheese
2 tablespoons chopped fresh parsley

1 Press the Sauté button on the Instant Pot® and heat oil. Add mushrooms and onion. Cook until tender, about 5 minutes. Add oregano, garlic, salt, and pepper, and cook until very fragrant, about 30 seconds. Add wine, water, and pasta, pushing pasta down until submerged in liquid. Press the Cancel button.

2 Top pasta with clams and sprinkle lemon juice on top. Close lid, set steam release to Sealing, press the Manual button, and set time to 5 minutes. When the timer beeps, quick-release the pressure until the float valve drops and open lid. Transfer to a serving bowl and top with cheese and parsley. Serve immediately.

Mussels with Potatoes

If you choose fresh mussels for this dish, make sure that all your mussels close when gently tapped, and that you scrub them well and pull out the attached beard before cooking.

2 pounds baby Yukon Gold potatoes, cut in half
½ cup water
2 tablespoons olive oil, divided
1 medium yellow onion, peeled and diced
1 tablespoon chopped fresh oregano
½ teaspoon paprika
4 cloves garlic, peeled and minced
¼ teaspoon salt
¼ teaspoon ground black pepper
1 (15-ounce) can diced tomatoes
1½ cups water
2 pounds mussels, scrubbed and beards removed
½ cup sliced green olives
2 tablespoons chopped fresh parsley

SERVES 6	
Per Serving:	
Calories	272
Fat	8g
Protein	15g
Sodium	560mg
Fiber	4g
Carbohydrates	35g
Sugar	4g

1 Place potatoes, water, and 1 tablespoon oil in the Instant Pot®. Close lid, set steam release to Sealing, press the Manual button, and set time to 2 minutes. When the timer beeps, quick-release the pressure until the float valve drops. Press the Cancel button. Open lid and drain potatoes. Set aside. Wash and dry pot.

2 Press the Sauté button and heat remaining 1 tablespoon oil. Add onion and cook until tender, about 4 minutes. Add oregano, paprika, garlic, salt, and pepper, and cook until very fragrant, about 30 seconds. Add tomatoes and water, and stir well. Press the Cancel button.

3 Stir in mussels, olives, and potatoes. Close lid, set steam release to Sealing, press the Manual button, and set time to 5 minutes. When the timer beeps, quick-release the pressure until the float valve drops and open lid. Discard any mussels that haven't opened. Garnish with parsley and serve immediately.

Steamed Shrimp and Asparagus

SERVES 4	
Per Serving:	
Calories	145
Fat	8g
Protein	19g
Sodium	295mg
Fiber	0g
Carbohydrates	1g
Sugar	1g

In a busy world and a busy kitchen, this dish of shrimp and asparagus is simplicity itself.

1 cup water
1 bunch asparagus, trimmed
½ teaspoon salt, divided
1 pound shrimp (21/25 count), peeled
   and deveined

1½ tablespoons lemon juice
2 tablespoons olive oil

1 Pour water into the Instant Pot®. Insert rack and place steamer basket onto rack.

2 Spread asparagus on the bottom of the steamer basket. Sprinkle with ¼ teaspoon salt. Add shrimp. Drizzle with lemon juice and sprinkle with remaining ¼ teaspoon salt. Drizzle olive oil over shrimp.

3 Close lid, set steam release to Sealing, press the Manual button, and set time to 1 minute. When the timer beeps, quick-release the pressure until the float valve drops and open lid.

4 Transfer shrimp and asparagus to a platter and serve.

Tomato-Stewed Calamari

SERVES 6	
Per Serving:	
Calories	394
Fat	7g
Protein	62g
Sodium	505mg
Fiber	3g
Carbohydrates	12g
Sugar	4g

If you have fresh parsley and basil on hand, omit the dried herbs and stir 1 tablespoon of each into the calamari after you quick-release the pressure.

2 tablespoons olive oil
1 small carrot, peeled and grated
1 stalk celery, finely diced
1 small white onion, peeled and diced
3 cloves garlic, peeled and minced
2½ pounds calamari
1 (28-ounce) can diced tomatoes

½ cup white wine
⅓ cup water
1 teaspoon dried parsley
1 teaspoon dried basil
½ teaspoon salt
½ teaspoon ground black pepper

1 Press the Sauté button on the Instant Pot® and heat oil. Add carrot and celery, and cook until just tender, about 2 minutes.

2 Add onion and cook until tender, about 3 minutes. Stir in garlic and cook until fragrant, about 30 seconds. Press the Cancel button.

3 Add calamari, tomatoes, wine, water, parsley, basil, salt, and pepper to the Instant Pot®. Close lid, set steam release to Sealing, press the Manual button, and set time to 10 minutes. When the timer beeps, quick-release the pressure until the float valve drops and open lid. Serve immediately.

Mediterranean Seafood Chowder

If you have scallops, clams, or other firm white fish on hand, you can use them instead of the shrimp and cod called for in this chowder. Similarly, use water or vegetable stock if you don't have seafood stock.

2 tablespoons olive oil

1 medium yellow onion, peeled and chopped

1 stalk celery, chopped

1 medium carrot, peeled and chopped

3 cloves garlic, peeled and minced

1 tablespoon tomato paste

1 teaspoon fresh thyme leaves

1 teaspoon chopped fresh oregano

¼ teaspoon crushed red pepper flakes

¼ teaspoon salt

¼ teaspoon ground black pepper

1 (28-ounce) can diced tomatoes

½ cup seafood stock

1 pound medium shrimp, peeled and deveined

8 ounces cod fillets, cut into 1" pieces

2 cups cooked white rice

2 tablespoons chopped fresh parsley

SERVES 6	
Per Serving:	
Calories	239
Fat	7g
Protein	21g
Sodium	701mg
Fiber	3g
Carbohydrates	25g
Sugar	5g

1 Press the Sauté button on the Instant Pot® and heat oil. Add onion, celery, and carrot, and cook until tender, about 5 minutes. Add garlic, tomato paste, thyme, oregano, red pepper flakes, salt, and pepper, and cook until fragrant, about 30 seconds. Add tomatoes and stock, and stir well. Press the Cancel button.

2 Close lid, set steam release to Sealing, press the Manual button, and set time to 5 minutes. When the timer beeps, quick-release the pressure until the float valve drops and open lid. Add shrimp and fish. Close lid, set steam release to Sealing, press the Manual button, and set time to 0 minutes.

3 When the timer beeps, quick-release the pressure until the float valve drops. Open lid and stir gently to combine. Serve over rice and garnish with parsley.

Shrimp Pasta with Basil and Feta

This easy and elegant pasta dish is perfect for summer; the bright flavors are particularly enjoyable when the weather is warm. You can use Parmesan cheese instead, but tangy feta cheese pairs well with the basil.

SHRIMP SIZES

Shrimp are sold by their quantity per pound. That means that when buying shrimp, you will see a range of numbers that indicate the approximate number of shrimp per pound. Very small shrimp are labeled as 61/70, while the largest shrimp are listed as U-10, meaning under 10 per pound. Some packages will also list names, such as Extra Jumbo, Colossal, and Super Colossal. These names are not regulated, so use the numbers as a guide. Most recipes will call for large shrimp, which are 31/35 count.

3 tablespoons olive oil, divided
4 cloves garlic, peeled and minced
¼ teaspoon salt
¼ teaspoon ground black pepper
2 cups water
8 ounces whole-wheat penne pasta
2 pounds tail-on shrimp (31/35 count)
1 tablespoon lemon juice
1 teaspoon grated lemon zest
2 tablespoons chopped fresh basil
¼ cup crumbled feta cheese

1 Press the Sauté button on the Instant Pot® and heat 1 tablespoon oil. Add garlic, salt, and pepper. Cook until garlic is very fragrant, about 30 seconds. Add water and pasta and stir well. Press the Cancel button.

2 Close lid, set steam release to Sealing, press the Manual button, and set time to 4 minutes. When the timer beeps, quick-release the pressure until the float valve drops and open lid. Drain off any excess water, then transfer pasta to a serving bowl and cover with foil. Press the Cancel button.

3 Clean and dry pot. Press the Sauté button and heat remaining 2 tablespoons oil. Add shrimp and cook, stirring often, until shrimp are just cooked through, about 2 minutes. Add lemon juice, lemon zest, and basil, and cook for 30 seconds more. Pour shrimp over pasta and top with feta. Serve immediately.

Steamed Clams

Serve these clams atop a pile of linguine with a piece of crusty bread on the side. Or substitute a can of diced tomatoes, including juice, for the water to create a warm, hearty pasta sauce.

SERVES 4	
Per Serving:	
Calories	205
Fat	6g
Protein	30g
Sodium	135mg
Fiber	0g
Carbohydrates	7g
Sugar	1g

2 pounds fresh clams, rinsed
1 tablespoon olive oil
1 small white onion, peeled and diced
1 clove garlic, peeled and quartered
½ cup Chardonnay
½ cup water

1. Place clams in the Instant Pot® steamer basket. Set aside.
2. Press the Sauté button and heat oil. Add onion and cook until tender, about 3 minutes. Add garlic and cook about 30 seconds. Pour in Chardonnay and water. Insert steamer basket with clams. Press the Cancel button.
3. Close lid, set steam release to Sealing, press the Manual button, and set time to 4 minutes. When the timer beeps, quick-release the pressure until the float valve drops. Open lid.
4. Transfer clams to four bowls and top with a generous scoop of cooking liquid.

Shrimp Scampi

This super-quick Shrimp Scampi is rich and buttery. Pressure cooking infuses the buttery sauce into the shrimp, so they are extra decadent.

SERVES 6	
Per Serving:	
Calories	326
Fat	25g
Protein	22g
Sodium	1,062mg
Fiber	0g
Carbohydrates	0g
Sugar	0g

3 tablespoons unsalted butter
3 tablespoons olive oil
3 cloves garlic, peeled and minced
½ teaspoon salt
½ teaspoon ground black pepper
½ cup white wine
½ cup low-sodium chicken broth
2 pounds tail-on shrimp (21/25 count)
1 tablespoon lemon juice
2 tablespoons chopped fresh flat-leaf parsley

1. Press the Sauté button on the Instant Pot® and heat butter and olive oil. Add garlic, salt, and pepper. Cook 30 seconds until garlic is very fragrant. Add white wine and broth, and stir quickly to combine. Press the Cancel button.
2. Add shrimp to pot and toss to coat in garlic mixture. Close lid, set steam release to Sealing, press the Manual button, and set time to 1 minute.
3. When the timer beeps, quick-release the pressure until the float valve drops. Press the Cancel button and open lid. Add lemon juice and parsley. Serve immediately.

Shrimp Risotto

Risotto is a magical dish that is made with Arborio rice, a short-grain rice that, when cooked properly, releases starch to make a creamy sauce. Cooking risotto on the stove can take almost an hour from start to finish. In this recipe, you work for a few minutes and the Instant Pot® does the rest.

4 tablespoons olive oil, divided
1 medium yellow onion, peeled and chopped
1 clove garlic, peeled and minced
1 teaspoon fresh thyme leaves
1½ cups Arborio rice
½ cup white wine
4 cups low-sodium chicken broth
1 pound medium shrimp, peeled and deveined
½ teaspoon ground black pepper
½ cup grated Parmesan cheese

SERVES 6	
Per Serving:	
Calories	412
Fat	16g
Protein	27g
Sodium	670mg
Fiber	4g
Carbohydrates	37g
Sugar	2g

1 Press the Sauté button on the Instant Pot® and heat 2 tablespoons oil. Add onion and cook until tender, about 3 minutes. Add garlic and thyme, and cook 30 seconds. Add rice and cook, stirring so each grain is coated in fat, for 3 minutes.

2 Add wine to the Instant Pot® and cook, stirring constantly, until it is almost completely evaporated, about 2 minutes. Add broth and bring to a simmer, stirring constantly, about 3 minutes.

3 Press the Cancel button. Close lid, set steam release to Sealing, press the Manual button, and set time to 6 minutes. When the timer beeps, let pressure release naturally for 15 minutes, then quick-release remaining pressure until the float valve drops and open lid. Press the Cancel button.

4 Stir in shrimp and pepper. Press the Sauté button and cook until shrimp are pink, opaque, and curled into a C shape, about 4 minutes. Divide risotto among six bowls and top with cheese and remaining 2 tablespoons oil. Serve immediately.

Mixed Seafood Soup

SERVES 8	
Per Serving:	
Calories	172
Fat	7g
Protein	15g
Sodium	481mg
Fiber	1g
Carbohydrates	9g
Sugar	2g

The seafood departments in many grocery stores sell frozen mixed seafood that can be used in place of the seafood listed here. The mixture usually includes shrimp, scallops, calamari rings, and mussels. If you use frozen seafood, add one minute to the cook time.

2 tablespoons light olive oil
1 medium yellow onion, peeled and diced
1 medium red bell pepper, seeded and diced
3 cloves garlic, peeled and minced
1 tablespoon chopped fresh oregano
½ teaspoon Italian seasoning
½ teaspoon ground black pepper
2 tablespoons tomato paste
½ cup white wine
2 cups seafood stock
1 bay leaf
½ pound medium shrimp, peeled and deveined
½ pound fresh scallops
½ pound fresh calamari rings
1 tablespoon lemon juice

1 Press the Sauté button on the Instant Pot® and heat oil. Add onion and bell pepper and cook until just tender, about 5 minutes. Add garlic, oregano, Italian seasoning, and pepper. Cook until fragrant, about 30 seconds. Add tomato paste and cook for 1 minute, then slowly pour in wine and scrape bottom of pot well. Press the Cancel button.

2 Add stock and bay leaf. Stir well. Close lid and set steam release to Sealing, then press the Manual button and set time to 5 minutes.

3 When the timer beeps, quick-release the pressure until the float valve drops. Open lid and stir in shrimp, scallops, calamari rings, and lemon juice. Press the Cancel button, then press the Sauté button and allow soup to simmer until seafood is cooked through, about 10 minutes. Remove and discard bay leaf. Serve hot.

Seafood Paella

Saffron is the most expensive spice in the world. If it is a little over your budget, swap it for ½ teaspoon of ground turmeric. It will provide the same vibrant color without breaking the bank.

½ teaspoon saffron threads
2 cups vegetable broth
2 tablespoons olive oil
1 medium yellow onion, peeled and diced
1 cup diced carrot
1 medium green bell pepper, seeded and diced
1 cup fresh or frozen green peas
2 cloves garlic, peeled and minced
1 cup basmati rice
¼ cup chopped fresh flat-leaf parsley
½ pound medium shrimp, peeled and deveined
½ pound mussels, scrubbed and beards removed
½ pound clams, rinsed
¼ teaspoon ground black pepper

SERVES 4	
Per Serving:	
Calories	555
Fat	12g
Protein	58g
Sodium	1,266mg
Fiber	3g
Carbohydrates	49g
Sugar	6g

1 Add saffron and broth to a medium microwave-safe bowl and stir well. Microwave for 30 seconds on High to just warm broth. Set aside.

2 Press the Sauté button on the Instant Pot® and heat oil. Add onion, carrot, bell pepper, and peas, and cook until they begin to soften, about 5 minutes. Add garlic and rice. Stir until well coated. Add saffron broth and parsley. Press the Cancel button.

3 Close lid, set steam release to Sealing, press the Manual button, and set time to 7 minutes. When the timer beeps, quick-release the pressure until the float valve drops and open lid. Press the Cancel button.

4 Stir rice mixture, then top with shrimp, mussels, and clams. Close lid, set steam release to Sealing, press the Manual button, and set time to 1 minute. When the timer beeps, let pressure release naturally for 10 minutes. Quick-release the remaining pressure until the float valve drops and open lid. Discard any mussels that haven't opened. Season with black pepper before serving.

Garlic Shrimp

SERVES 6

Per Serving:

Calories	151
Fat	5g
Protein	25g
Sodium	691mg
Fiber	0g
Carbohydrates	0g
Sugar	0g

Serve these shrimp on skewers for a party or over a slice of toasted crusty bread, accompanied by a crisp green salad and lemony dressing.

2 tablespoons light olive oil
1 small shallot, peeled and minced
6 cloves garlic, peeled and thinly sliced
1 tablespoon chopped fresh dill
1 tablespoon chopped fresh chives
½ teaspoon ground black pepper
¼ teaspoon salt
¼ cup white wine
¼ cup low-sodium chicken broth
2 pounds large tail-on shrimp
2 tablespoons lemon juice
2 tablespoons chopped fresh parsley

1 Press the Sauté button on the Instant Pot® and heat oil. Add shallot and garlic. Sauté 1 minute. Add dill, chives, pepper, and salt, and cook 30 seconds. Stir in wine and broth. Press the Cancel button.

2 Add shrimp and toss to coat in sauce. Close lid, set steam release to Sealing, press the Manual button, and set time to 1 minute.

3 When the timer beeps, quick-release the pressure until the float valve drops. Press the Cancel button and open lid. Add lemon juice and parsley. Serve immediately.

Mussels Saganaki

SERVES 2

Per Serving:

Calories	250
Fat	21g
Protein	18g
Sodium	1,140mg
Fiber	1g
Carbohydrates	7g
Sugar	2g

This mussel dish is a specialty of Thessaloniki, Greece, where much of the local cuisine is spicy. Use sweet peppers if you wish to tone down the heat.

2 tablespoons extra-virgin olive oil
1 medium banana pepper, stemmed, seeded, and thinly sliced
2 medium tomatoes, chopped
½ teaspoon salt
1 pound mussels, scrubbed and beards removed
⅓ cup white wine
⅓ cup crumbled feta cheese
2 teaspoons dried oregano

1 Press the Sauté button on the Instant Pot® and heat oil. Add pepper, tomatoes, and salt, and cook until tender, about 3 minutes. Press the Cancel button.

2 Add mussels and wine. Close lid, set steam release to Sealing, press the Manual button, and set time to 3 minutes. When the timer beeps, quick-release the pressure until the float valve drops. Open lid and discard any mussels that haven't opened.

3 Add feta and oregano and shake the pot to combine them with the sauce. Serve hot.

Mussels with White Wine Garlic Sauce

One of the best parts of cooking mussels in the shell is the delicious broth they leave behind. Serve this with soup spoons and plenty of toasted crusty bread for enjoying the broth after the mussels have been devoured.

2 tablespoons light olive oil

2 shallots, peeled and minced

4 cloves garlic, peeled and minced

½ teaspoon ground black pepper

3 pounds mussels, scrubbed and beards removed

2 cups white wine

¼ cup chopped fresh chives

¼ cup chopped fresh tarragon

2 tablespoons chopped fresh dill

SERVES 6	
Per Serving:	
Calories	146
Fat	7g
Protein	14g
Sodium	321mg
Fiber	0g
Carbohydrates	6g
Sugar	0g

1 Press the Sauté button on the Instant Pot® and heat oil. Add shallots and cook until tender, about 1 minute. Add garlic and pepper and cook until the garlic is fragrant, about 30 seconds. Press the Cancel button.

2 Add mussels and wine. Stir to combine. Close lid, set steam release to Sealing, press the Manual button, and set time to 3 minutes. When the timer beeps, quick-release the pressure until the float valve drops and open lid. Discard any mussels that haven't opened, then transfer mussels to a serving bowl, leaving broth behind.

3 Press the Cancel button, then press the Sauté button. Bring cooking liquid to a simmer and whisk in chives, tarragon, and dill. Cook for 3 minutes, or until broth has reduced slightly. Pour the liquid over the mussels and serve immediately.

Mussels with Tomatoes and Herbs

Not only are mussels an excellent source of protein, but they are also low in fat and packed with iron. It is believed that mussels can improve brain function because of their vitamin A and vitamin B_{12} content.

2 tablespoons light olive oil

1 medium white onion, peeled and chopped

2 cloves garlic, peeled and minced

2 tablespoons chopped fresh dill

2 tablespoons chopped fresh tarragon

½ teaspoon ground fennel

½ teaspoon ground black pepper

3 pounds mussels, scrubbed and beards removed

½ cup vegetable broth

1 (14.5-ounce) can diced tomatoes, drained

1 Press the Sauté button on the Instant Pot® and heat oil. Add onion and cook until tender, about 3 minutes. Add garlic, dill, tarragon, fennel, and pepper, and cook until garlic is fragrant, about 30 seconds. Press the Cancel button.

2 Add mussels, broth, and tomatoes. Stir to combine. Close lid, set steam release to Sealing, press the Manual button, and set time to 3 minutes. When the timer beeps, quick-release the pressure until the float valve drops and open lid. Discard any mussels that haven't opened. Serve immediately.

SERVES 6	
Per Serving:	
Calories	162
Fat	7g
Protein	14g
Sodium	435mg
Fiber	2g
Carbohydrates	10g
Sugar	3g

MUSSELS

Mussels are found in both fresh and salt water. About seventeen species of mussels are edible, and for thousands of years humans have been enjoying them. Mussels can be prepared a variety of ways, including smoked, steamed, boiled, and roasted. Discard any mussels with unopened or broken shells before cooking, and be sure the shells have fully opened before eating. Besides having a mild flavor and tender chewiness, mussels are a good source of vitamin B_{12}, zinc, and folate.

Cioppino

SERVES 6	
Per Serving:	
Calories	384
Fat	11g
Protein	47g
Sodium	671mg
Fiber	3g
Carbohydrates	14g
Sugar	6g

This version of cioppino (an Italian fish stew) uses only shellfish, but you can also add cubed white fish if you have some on hand. Just add it with the shellfish and simmer until it is opaque and flakes when gently pressed with a fork.

3 tablespoons light olive oil
1 medium yellow onion, peeled and chopped
1 medium red bell pepper, seeded and chopped
2 cloves garlic, peeled and minced
1 (28-ounce) can crushed tomatoes
1 cup red wine
1 cup seafood stock
1 tablespoon lemon juice
1 bay leaf
¼ cup chopped fresh basil
½ teaspoon ground black pepper
1 pound fresh mussels, scrubbed and beards removed
1 pound large shrimp, peeled and deveined
1 pound clams, scrubbed

1 Press the Sauté button on the Instant Pot® and heat oil. Add onion and bell pepper. Cook until just tender, about 3 minutes. Add garlic and cook until fragrant, about 30 seconds. Add tomatoes, wine, stock, lemon juice, bay leaf, basil, and black pepper. Stir well. Press the Cancel button.

2 Close lid, set steam release to Sealing, press the Manual button, and set time to 5 minutes. When the timer beeps, quick-release the pressure until the float valve drops. Press the Cancel button and open lid. Remove bay leaf and add mussels, shrimp, and clams. Press the Sauté button and cook until shrimp are pink and shellfish have opened, about 3 minutes. Discard any mussels that haven't opened. Serve hot.

Seasoned Steamed Crab

Crab is a great source of omega-3 fatty acids, calcium, and phosphorus, so it's also a food that is good for boosting immunity, reducing inflammation, and lowering your cholesterol.

1 tablespoon extra-virgin olive oil
½ teaspoon Old Bay seafood seasoning
½ teaspoon smoked paprika
¼ teaspoon cayenne pepper

2 cloves garlic, peeled and minced
2 (2-pound) Dungeness crabs
1 cup water

SERVES 2	
Per Serving:	
Calories	185
Fat	8g
Protein	25g
Sodium	434mg
Fiber	0g
Carbohydrates	1g
Sugar	0g

1 In a medium bowl, combine oil, seafood seasoning, smoked paprika, cayenne pepper, and garlic. Mix well. Coat crabs in seasoning mixture and place in the steamer basket.

2 Add water to the Instant Pot® and place steamer basket inside. Close lid, set steam release to Sealing, press the Manual button, and set time to 3 minutes.

3 When the timer beeps, quick-release the pressure until the float valve drops. Press the Cancel button and open lid. Transfer crabs to a serving platter. Serve hot.

Spicy Steamed Chili Crab

Part of the fun of eating whole crabs is the process of cracking, hammering, and pulling to get all of the tasty meat out. Serve a little melted butter for dipping.

2 tablespoons garlic chili sauce
1 tablespoon hoisin sauce
1 tablespoon minced fresh ginger
1 teaspoon fish sauce

2 cloves garlic, peeled and minced
2 small bird's eye chilies, minced
2 (2-pound) Dungeness crabs
1 cup water

SERVES 2	
Per Serving:	
Calories	128
Fat	1g
Protein	25g
Sodium	619mg
Fiber	0g
Carbohydrates	1g
Sugar	1g

1 In a medium bowl, combine garlic chili sauce, hoisin sauce, ginger, fish sauce, garlic, and chilies. Mix well. Coat crabs in chili mixture.

2 Add water to the Instant Pot® and insert steamer basket. Add crabs to basket. Close lid, set steam release to Sealing, press the Manual button, and set time to 3 minutes.

3 When the timer beeps, quick-release the pressure until the float valve drops. Press the Cancel button and open lid. Transfer crabs to a serving platter. Serve hot.

Poached Octopus

Let the octopus defrost for a day in the refrigerator before using it for this recipe.

SERVES 8	
Per Serving:	
Calories	301
Fat	15g
Protein	15g
Sodium	883mg
Fiber	2g
Carbohydrates	30g
Sugar	1g

TENDERIZE IT!

When you buy fresh octopus, you need to either freeze and thaw it or beat it vigorously to tenderize it before cooking. If your fishmonger has fresh octopus, ask him if he will tenderize the octopus for you. Otherwise, spend about half an hour banging on it with a meat tenderizer or just put it in the freezer overnight.

2 pounds potatoes (about 6 medium)
3 teaspoons salt, divided
1 (2-pound) frozen octopus, thawed, cleaned, and rinsed
3 cloves garlic, peeled, divided
1 bay leaf
2 teaspoons whole peppercorns
½ cup olive oil
¼ cup white wine vinegar
½ teaspoon ground black pepper
½ cup chopped fresh parsley

1 Place potatoes in the Instant Pot® with 2 teaspoons salt and enough water to just cover the potatoes halfway. Close lid, set steam release to Sealing, press the Manual button, and set time to 6 minutes. When the timer beeps, quick-release the pressure until the float valve drops and open lid. Press the Cancel button.

2 Remove potatoes with tongs (reserve the cooking water), and peel them as soon as you can handle them. Dice potatoes into bite-sized pieces. Set aside.

3 Add octopus to potato cooking water in the pot and add more water to cover if needed. Add 1 garlic clove, bay leaf, and peppercorns. Close lid, set steam release to Sealing, press the Manual button, and set time to 10 minutes. When the timer beeps, quick-release the pressure until the float valve drops and open lid. Remove and discard bay leaf.

4 Check octopus for tenderness by seeing if a fork will sink easily into the thickest part of the flesh. If not, close the top and bring it to pressure for another minute or two and check again.

5 Remove octopus and drain. Chop head and tentacles into small, bite-sized chunks.

6 Crush remaining 2 garlic cloves and place in a small jar or plastic container. Add olive oil, vinegar, remaining 1 teaspoon salt, and pepper. Close the lid and shake well.

7 In a large serving bowl, mix potatoes with octopus, cover with vinaigrette, and sprinkle with parsley.

Lobster Tails with Herbs

Lobster is a special occasion food that is delicious and impressive. This version is simply steamed and served with an herbed olive oil dressing.

¼ cup extra-virgin olive oil
¼ teaspoon salt
¼ teaspoon ground black pepper
1 clove garlic, peeled and minced
1 tablespoon grated lemon zest
1 teaspoon chopped fresh tarragon
1 teaspoon chopped fresh dill
1 cup low-sodium chicken broth
2 tablespoons Old Bay seafood seasoning
2 pounds fresh cold-water lobster tails

SERVES 4	
Per Serving:	
Calories	230
Fat	15g
Protein	22g
Sodium	534mg
Fiber	0g
Carbohydrates	0g
Sugar	0g

1 In a small saucepan, heat oil, salt, pepper, garlic, and lemon zest over low heat until oil is warm. Stir in tarragon and dill, and immediately turn off heat. Cover, set aside, and keep warm.

2 Add broth and seafood seasoning to the Instant Pot® and stir well. Place rack inside pot. Place lobster tails shell side down on rack. Close lid, set steam release to Sealing, press the Manual button, and set time to 3 minutes.

3 When the timer beeps, quick-release the pressure until the float valve drops. Press the Cancel button and open lid. Transfer lobster tails to a platter. Carefully cut bottom of each shell with kitchen shears and pull tail meat out in one piece. Slice into ½"-thick pieces. Serve immediately with herbed olive oil.

Lemon Orzo with Crab and Herbs

SERVES 4

Per Serving:	
Calories	367
Fat	12g
Protein	24g
Sodium	531mg
Fiber	3g
Carbohydrates	43g
Sugar	1g

PASTEURIZED CRABMEAT

Most grocery stores sell fresh crabmeat packed in containers and kept in the seafood department. In areas that are landlocked, pasteurized crabmeat is a better option than fresh crabs, which can quickly go from fresh to funky. Pasteurized crab is fully cooked and ready to eat. It has a fairly long shelf life when sealed, but once opened, the clock starts ticking and you have 2–3 days to enjoy it.

Crabmeat can be purchased in your grocery store's seafood department in vacuum-sealed containers. Although it is checked for bits of shell when processed, it is always wise to check it again before using in recipes.

2 tablespoons light olive oil
1 medium shallot, peeled and minced
1 clove garlic, peeled and minced
¼ cup chopped fresh flat-leaf parsley
2 tablespoons chopped fresh basil
¼ teaspoon salt
¼ teaspoon ground black pepper
2 cups water
8 ounces orzo
8 ounces jumbo lump crabmeat
1 tablespoon lemon juice
¼ cup grated Parmesan cheese

1 Press the Sauté button on the Instant Pot® and heat oil. Add shallot and garlic. Cook until garlic is very fragrant, about 1 minute. Add parsley, basil, salt, and pepper. Stir well. Add water and pasta. Press the Cancel button.

2 Close lid, set steam release to Sealing, press the Manual button, and set time to 4 minutes. When the timer beeps, quick-release the pressure until the float valve drops and open lid.

3 Add crab and lemon juice. Stir gently to combine, then let stand, uncovered, on the Keep Warm setting for 10 minutes to heat crab. Top with cheese and serve immediately.

Kakavia (Fish Soup)

Feel free to add some shrimp, scallops, or any other favorite seafood to this recipe for variation.

SERVES 12

Per Serving:

Calories	163
Fat	6g
Protein	18g
Sodium	171mg
Fiber	2g
Carbohydrates	10g
Sugar	3g

8 cups water
2 medium onions, peeled and diced
2 medium potatoes, cubed
2 stalks celery, diced
2 medium carrots, peeled and chopped
1 tablespoon dried marjoram
½ teaspoon salt
½ teaspoon ground black pepper
2 pounds fresh cod, cut into pieces
2 pounds fresh grey mullet, deboned and cut into pieces
1 pound mussels, scrubbed and beards removed
¼ cup chopped fresh parsley
¼ cup extra-virgin olive oil
2 tablespoons lemon juice

1 Add water, onions, potatoes, celery, carrots, marjoram, salt, and pepper to the Instant Pot®. Close lid, set steam release to Sealing, press the Manual button, and set time to 10 minutes. When the timer beeps, quick-release the pressure until the float valve drops and open lid. Press the Cancel button.

2 Add cod, mullet, mussels, and parsley to pot. Close lid, set steam release to Sealing, press the Manual button, and set time to 4 minutes. When the timer beeps, quick-release the pressure until the float valve drops and open lid. Discard any mussels that haven't opened.

3 Using a slotted spoon, remove fish and mussels from pot. Set aside on a plate.

4 Strain stock through a sieve. Push softened vegetables through sieve using a wooden spoon. Return strained stock to pot. Press the Sauté button, add olive oil and lemon juice, and bring to boil. Add fish and mussels to pot and simmer 3–5 minutes. Serve hot.

CHAPTER 11

Fish

Pistachio-Crusted Halibut

The pistachios that encrust this dish give it a unique flavor. Pistachios have a rich and nutty quality, and add a distinct texture that complements the sweetness of the halibut.

1 tablespoon Dijon mustard
1 teaspoon lemon juice
2 tablespoons panko bread crumbs
¼ cup chopped unsalted pistachios
¼ teaspoon salt
2 (5-ounce) halibut fillets
1 cup water

1 Preheat broiler. Line a baking sheet with parchment paper.

2 In a small bowl, combine mustard, lemon juice, bread crumbs, pistachios, and salt to form a thick paste.

3 Pat fillets dry with a paper towel. Rub paste on the top of each fillet and place in the steamer basket.

4 Pour water in the Instant Pot® and insert rack. Place steamer basket on rack. Close lid, set steam release to Sealing, press the Manual button, and set time to 5 minutes. When the timer beeps, quick-release the pressure until the float valve drops and then open lid. Transfer fillets to prepared baking sheet.

5 Broil for approximately 1–2 minutes until tops are browned. Remove from oven and serve hot.

Basil Cod Kebabs

Check that your wooden skewers fit into your Instant Pot® before you start threading your fish and vegetables on them. If they are too long, you can easily trim them to fit.

1 cup water

4 (4-ounce) cod or other white fish fillets, cut into 1" pieces

½ medium onion, peeled and cut into 1" pieces

½ medium red bell pepper, seeded and cut into 1" pieces

2 tablespoons extra-virgin olive oil

2 tablespoons chopped fresh basil

½ teaspoon salt

½ teaspoon ground black pepper

1 small lemon, cut into wedges

SERVES 4	
Per Serving:	
Calories	93
Fat	7g
Protein	5g
Sodium	312mg
Fiber	1g
Carbohydrates	2g
Sugar	1g

1 Place rack inside the Instant Pot® and add water.

2 Thread fish, onion, and bell pepper alternately onto four wooden skewers. Brush skewers with olive oil, then top with basil, salt, and black pepper. Place skewers on rack. Close lid, set steam release to Sealing, press Steam, and set time to 2 minutes.

3 When the timer beeps, quick-release the pressure until the float valve drops. Press the Cancel button and open lid. Serve with lemon.

Lemon Salmon with Dill

If you are looking to add more omega-3 fatty acids to your diet, then you will want to check out this recipe. Salmon is an excellent source of omega-3 fatty acids, as well as vitamin B and protein.

1 cup water

4 (4-ounce) skin-on salmon fillets

½ teaspoon salt

½ teaspoon ground black pepper

¼ cup chopped fresh dill

1 small lemon, thinly sliced

2 tablespoons extra-virgin olive oil

1 tablespoon chopped fresh parsley

SERVES 4	
Per Serving:	
Calories	160
Fat	9g
Protein	19g
Sodium	545mg
Fiber	0g
Carbohydrates	0g
Sugar	0g

1 Add water to the Instant Pot® and place rack inside.

2 Season fish fillets with salt and pepper. Place fillets on rack. Top each fillet with dill and two or three lemon slices. Close lid, set steam release to Sealing, press the Steam button, and set time to 3 minutes.

3 When the timer beeps, quick-release the pressure until the float valve drops. Press the Cancel button and open lid. Place fillets on a serving platter, drizzle with olive oil, and garnish with parsley. Serve immediately.

Cod Stew with Olives

Delicate fish does not take long to cook, but the Instant Pot® helps you save time by simmering the vegetable and herb broth in less time than it would take on the stove. You can make the broth base a day or two ahead of time—just return it to the pot, heat it using the Sauté setting, and add the fish.

3 tablespoons olive oil
1 medium onion, peeled and diced
1 stalk celery, diced
1 medium carrot, peeled and chopped
2 cloves garlic, peeled and minced
1 tablespoon chopped fresh oregano
½ teaspoon ground fennel
1 sprig fresh thyme
1 (14.5-ounce) can diced tomatoes
1½ cups vegetable broth
1 pound cod fillets, cut into 1" pieces
⅓ cup sliced green olives
¼ teaspoon ground black pepper
2 tablespoons chopped fresh dill

1 Press the Sauté button on the Instant Pot® and heat oil. Add onion, celery, and carrot. Cook until vegetables are soft, about 6 minutes. Add garlic, oregano, fennel, and thyme. Cook for 30 seconds, then add tomatoes and vegetable broth. Stir well. Press the Cancel button.

2 Close lid, set steam release to Sealing, press the Manual button, and set time to 3 minutes.

3 When the timer beeps, quick-release the pressure until the float valve drops and open lid. Press the Cancel button, then press the Sauté button and add fish, olives, and pepper. Cook until fish is opaque, 3–5 minutes. Sprinkle with dill and serve hot.

Italian Fish

Pressure cooking rehydrates the dried seasonings and keeps the fish moist. This dish is delicious served over couscous, orzo, pasta, rice, or steamed cabbage, or alongside polenta.

1 (14.5-ounce) can diced tomatoes
¼ teaspoon dried minced onion
¼ teaspoon onion powder
¼ teaspoon dried minced garlic
¼ teaspoon garlic powder
¼ teaspoon dried basil
¼ teaspoon dried parsley
⅛ teaspoon dried oregano
¼ teaspoon sugar
⅛ teaspoon dried lemon granules, crushed
⅛ teaspoon chili powder
⅛ teaspoon dried red pepper flakes
1 tablespoon grated Parmesan cheese
4 (4-ounce) cod fillets, rinsed and patted dry

1   Add tomatoes, minced onion, onion powder, minced garlic, garlic powder, basil, parsley, oregano, sugar, lemon granules, chili powder, red pepper flakes, and cheese to the Instant Pot® and stir to mix. Arrange the fillets over the tomato mixture, folding thin tail ends under to give the fillets even thickness. Spoon some of the tomato mixture over the fillets.

2   Close lid, set steam release to Sealing, press the Manual button, and set time to 3 minutes. When the timer beeps, quick-release the pressure until the float valve drops and open lid. Serve immediately.

SERVES 4	
Per Serving:	
Calories	116
Fat	3g
Protein	20g
Sodium	400mg
Fiber	2g
Carbohydrates	5g
Sugar	3g

SEASONING SENSE

You can enhance flavors without salt by using a variety of complementary seasonings like the combination of dried ingredients and powders used in the Italian Fish recipe. Mix things up by substituting 1 teaspoon grated lemon zest for the dried lemon granules and garnish the sauce with minced fresh parsley or basil.

Mustard and Herb Fish Fillets

White fish is a broad term that includes fish like cod, sole, halibut, and sea bass. The flesh is firm, white, and rather lean. The mild flavor is a great canvas for flavorful additions like, in this recipe, mustard and fresh herbs.

1 cup water
4 (4-ounce) cod or other white fish fillets
2 tablespoons Dijon mustard
2 tablespoons chopped fresh dill
2 tablespoons chopped fresh chives
½ teaspoon salt
½ teaspoon ground black pepper
1 small lemon, cut into wedges

1   Add water to the Instant Pot® and place rack inside.

2   Brush fish fillets with mustard. Sprinkle each with dill and chives, then season with salt and pepper. Place fillets on rack. Close lid, set steam release to Sealing, press the Steam button, and set time to 2 minutes.

3   When the timer beeps, quick-release the pressure until the float valve drops. Press the Cancel button and open lid. Place fillets on a serving platter with lemon wedges. Serve immediately.

SERVES 4	
Per Serving:	
Calories	80
Fat	3g
Protein	14g
Sodium	765mg
Fiber	0g
Carbohydrates	0g
Sugar	0g

DIJON MUSTARD

Arguably the most famous French condiment, Dijon mustard is popular for its sharp, tangy taste. Unlike champagne, Dijon mustard is not required to be grown or produced in a specific domain in France, and 80 percent of the mustard seeds used in its production are grown in Canada.

Trout in Parsley Sauce

This recipe is a good way to use up lettuce that's no longer crisp enough for a salad but isn't totally past its prime. In addition, using the lettuce to steam the fish keeps the fish firm and adds a bit of extra taste to the poaching liquid.

PARSLEY SAUCE ALTERNATIVES

For a reduced-calorie parsley sauce, replace the mayonnaise with water or Greek yogurt. For a richer sauce, substitute extra-virgin olive oil for the mayonnaise.

4 (½-pound) river trout, rinsed and patted dry
¾ teaspoon salt, divided
4 cups torn lettuce leaves, divided
1 teaspoon white wine vinegar
½ cup water
½ cup minced fresh flat-leaf parsley
1 small shallot, peeled and minced
2 tablespoons olive oil mayonnaise
½ teaspoon lemon juice
¼ teaspoon sugar
2 tablespoons toasted sliced almonds

1 Season trout with ½ teaspoon salt inside and out. Put 3 cups lettuce leaves in the bottom of the Instant Pot®. Arrange trout over lettuce and top trout with remaining 1 cup lettuce. Stir vinegar into water and pour into pot.

2 Close lid, set steam release to Sealing, press the Manual button, and set time to 3 minutes. When the timer beeps, quick-release the pressure until the float valve drops and open lid.

3 Use a spatula to move fish to a serving plate. Peel and discard skin from fish. Remove and discard fish heads if desired.

4 In a small bowl, mix together parsley, shallot, mayonnaise, lemon juice, sugar, and remaining ¼ teaspoon salt. Evenly divide among the fish, spreading it over them. Sprinkle toasted almonds over the sauce. Serve immediately.

Steamed Cod with Capers and Lemon

Capers, the pickled flower buds of the Flinders Rose, have a tangy, salty flavor that pairs well with seafood. In this recipe, the capers (used in place of salt), olive oil, lemon, and herbs make an elegant fish dish.

1 cup water
4 (4-ounce) cod fillets, rinsed and patted dry
½ teaspoon ground black pepper
1 small lemon, thinly sliced
2 tablespoons extra-virgin olive oil
¼ cup chopped fresh parsley
2 tablespoons capers
1 tablespoon chopped fresh chives

SERVES 4	
Per Serving:	
Calories	140
Fat	10g
Protein	14g
Sodium	370mg
Fiber	0g
Carbohydrates	0g
Sugar	0g

1 Add water to the Instant Pot® and place the rack inside.

2 Season fish fillets with pepper. Top each fillet with three slices of lemon. Place fillets on rack. Close lid, set steam release to Sealing, press the Steam button, and set time to 3 minutes.

3 While fish cooks, combine olive oil, parsley, capers, and chives in a small bowl and mix well. Set aside.

4 When the timer beeps, quick-release the pressure until the float valve drops. Press the Cancel button and open lid. Place cod fillets on a serving platter. Remove and discard lemon slices and drizzle fish with olive oil mixture, making sure each fillet has herbs and capers on top. Serve immediately.

Fish and Potato Stew

SERVES 4

Per Serving:

Calories	363
Fat	11g
Protein	24g
Sodium	295mg
Fiber	6g
Carbohydrates	38g
Sugar	11g

This rustic stew is sure to fill you up since it is packed with vegetables and tender chunks of fish. If you prefer, you can omit the fresh fennel bulb and substitute ½ teaspoon ground fennel seeds instead.

3 tablespoons olive oil

2 stalks celery, sliced

2 medium carrots, peeled and sliced

1 medium onion, peeled and chopped

½ fennel bulb, trimmed and chopped

2 cloves garlic, peeled and minced

1 tablespoon chopped fresh oregano

3 sprigs fresh thyme

1 (14.5-ounce) can diced tomatoes

1½ cups vegetable broth

2 medium russet potatoes, peeled and diced

1 pound cod or other white fish fillets, cut into 1" pieces

¼ teaspoon ground black pepper

2 tablespoons chopped fresh parsley

1 Press the Sauté button on the Instant Pot® and heat oil. Add celery, carrots, onion, and fennel. Cook until vegetables are soft, about 8 minutes. Add garlic, oregano, and thyme. Cook for 30 seconds, then add tomatoes, vegetable broth, and potatoes. Stir well. Press the Cancel button.

2 Close lid, set steam release to Sealing, press the Manual button, and set time to 4 minutes.

3 When the timer beeps, quick-release the pressure until the float valve drops and open lid. Press the Cancel button, then press the Sauté button and add fish and pepper. Cook until fish is opaque, 3–5 minutes. Sprinkle with parsley and serve hot.

Salmon Poached in Red Wine

You can prepare this dish without alcohol by substituting raspberry apple juice for the red wine.

1 medium onion, peeled and quartered
2 cloves garlic, peeled and smashed
1 stalk celery, diced
1 bay leaf
½ teaspoon dried thyme
3½ cups water
2 cups dry red wine
2 tablespoons red wine vinegar
½ teaspoon salt
½ teaspoon black peppercorns
1 (2½-pound) center-cut salmon roast
1 medium lemon, cut into wedges

SERVES 6	
Per Serving:	
Calories	435
Fat	24g
Protein	43g
Sodium	213mg
Fiber	0g
Carbohydrates	4g
Sugar	3g

1. Add all ingredients except salmon and lemon to the Instant Pot®. Close lid, set steam release to Sealing, press the Manual button, and set time to 10 minutes. When the timer beeps, quick-release the pressure until the float valve drops and open lid. Press the Cancel button.

2. Set the rack in the pot and put steamer basket on rack. Wrap salmon in cheesecloth, leaving ends long enough to extend about 3". Use two sets of tongs to hold on to the 3" cheesecloth extensions and place the salmon on the rack. Close lid, set steam release to Sealing, press the Manual button, and set time to 6 minutes. When the timer beeps, let pressure release naturally for 20 minutes.

3. Quick-release any remaining pressure until the float valve drops and open lid. Use tongs to hold on to the 3" cheesecloth extensions to lift salmon out of the Instant Pot®. Set in a metal colander to allow extra moisture to drain away. When salmon is cool enough to handle, unwrap the cheesecloth. Peel away and discard any skin.

4. Transfer salmon to a serving platter. Garnish with lemon wedges.

Tomato-Poached Fish

Poaching fish leaves it soft, tender, and very juicy. This fish is poached in an herb-infused tomato sauce that can then be spooned over the fish. Serve with crusty bread for soaking up the sauce.

WHAT IS POACHING?

Poaching is a method of cooking that uses boiling or simmering liquid to cook food. Liquids can vary from water and broth to juices and even milk. As the food cooks, the simmering liquid helps the meat, seafood, eggs, or vegetables retain moisture, promoting a soft texture. Poached foods retain a great deal of flavor while using a minimum of fat.

2 tablespoons olive oil
1 medium onion, peeled and chopped
2 cloves garlic, peeled and minced
1 tablespoon chopped fresh oregano
1 teaspoon fresh thyme leaves
½ teaspoon ground fennel
¼ teaspoon ground black pepper
¼ teaspoon crushed red pepper flakes
1 (14.5-ounce) can diced tomatoes
1 cup vegetable broth
1 pound halibut fillets
2 tablespoons chopped fresh parsley

1　Press the Sauté button on the Instant Pot® and heat oil. Add onion and cook until soft, about 4 minutes. Add garlic, oregano, thyme, and fennel. Cook until fragrant, about 30 seconds, then add black pepper, red pepper flakes, tomatoes, and vegetable broth. Press the Cancel button.

2　Top vegetables with fish, close lid, set steam release to Sealing, press the Manual button, and set time to 3 minutes.

3　When the timer beeps, quick-release the pressure until the float valve drops and open lid. Carefully transfer fillets to a serving platter and spoon sauce over fillets. Sprinkle with parsley and serve hot.

Catfish in Creole Sauce

SERVES 4

Per Serving:

Calories	284
Fat	9g
Protein	31g
Sodium	696mg
Fiber	3g
Carbohydrates	7g
Sugar	4g

Serve this over cooked rice and be sure to have hot sauce available at the table for those who want it.

1 (1½-pound) catfish fillet, rinsed in cold water, patted dry, cut into bite-sized pieces

1 (14.5-ounce) can diced tomatoes

2 teaspoons dried minced onion

¼ teaspoon onion powder

1 teaspoon dried minced garlic

¼ teaspoon garlic powder

1 teaspoon hot paprika

¼ teaspoon dried tarragon

1 medium green bell pepper, seeded and diced

1 stalk celery, finely diced

¼ teaspoon sugar

½ cup chili sauce

½ teaspoon salt

½ teaspoon ground black pepper

1 Add all ingredients to the Instant Pot® and stir to mix.

2 Close lid, set steam release to Sealing, press the Manual button, and set time to 5 minutes. When the timer beeps, quick-release the pressure until the float valve drops and open lid. Gently stir and serve.

Salmon with Cilantro and Lime

SERVES 4

Per Serving:

Calories	100
Fat	3g
Protein	19g
Sodium	398mg
Fiber	0g
Carbohydrates	0g
Sugar	0g

If you enjoy the flavors of cilantro and cumin, you will love this salmon. Pair it with black beans, rice, and a scattering of freshly chopped fresh cilantro leaves.

1 cup water

4 (4-ounce) skin-on salmon fillets, about 1 pound

¼ teaspoon ground cumin

¼ teaspoon smoked paprika

¼ teaspoon salt

¼ teaspoon ground black pepper

¼ cup chopped fresh cilantro

1 small lime, thinly sliced

2 tablespoons extra-virgin olive oil

1 Add water to the Instant Pot® and place rack inside.

2 Season fish fillets with cumin, paprika, salt, and pepper. Top each fillet with cilantro and two to three slices of lime. Place fillets on rack. Close lid, set steam release to Sealing, press the Steam button, and set time to 3 minutes.

3 When the timer beeps, quick-release the pressure until the float valve drops. Press the Cancel button and open lid. Place salmon fillets on a serving platter and drizzle with olive oil. Serve immediately.

Provençal Fish Soup

This refreshing fish soup is perfect anytime, but is particularly great in the fall when there is a crisp bite to the air—which also happens to be the start of fennel season, so you should be able to find fresh fennel in your produce department.

3 tablespoons olive oil

1 fennel bulb, white part only, chopped

1 medium onion, peeled and chopped

1 medium zucchini, trimmed and chopped

4 cloves garlic, peeled and minced

1 tablespoon tomato paste

1 (14.5-ounce) can diced tomatoes

3 sprigs fresh thyme

1 tablespoon chopped fresh oregano

2 teaspoons grated orange zest

½ cup white wine

3 cups low-sodium chicken broth

1 pound russet potatoes, peeled and chopped

1 pound cod fillets, cut into 1" pieces

¼ cup chopped Kalamata olives

3 basil leaves, roughly torn

SERVES 6	
Per Serving:	
Calories	198
Fat	10g
Protein	9g
Sodium	279mg
Fiber	2g
Carbohydrates	17g
Sugar	6g

1 Press the Sauté button on the Instant Pot® and heat oil. Add fennel and onion. Cook until soft, about 8 minutes. Add zucchini, garlic, and tomato paste and cook until garlic is fragrant, about 1 minute. Add tomatoes, thyme, oregano, and orange zest and stir well. Press the Cancel button.

2 Add wine, broth, and potatoes. Close lid, set steam release to Sealing, press the Manual button, and set time to 5 minutes.

3 When the timer beeps, quick-release the pressure until the float valve drops and open lid. Press the Cancel button and remove and discard thyme. Press the Sauté button and add fish and olives. Cook until fish is opaque, 3–5 minutes. Top with basil and serve hot.

Mediterranean Cod

The flavors of the Mediterranean are spotlighted in this simple yet elegant dish. The richness of the olive oil, the freshness of the basil and tomatoes, and the brininess of the Kalamata olives all come together to dress up this understated, flaky piece of cod.

SERVES 2	
Per Serving:	
Calories	148
Fat	9g
Protein	18g
Sodium	1,202mg
Fiber	0g
Carbohydrates	1g
Sugar	1g

1 cup water
2 (5-ounce) cod fillets
2 teaspoons olive oil
½ teaspoon salt
10 Kalamata olives, pitted and halved
1 small Roma tomato, diced
3 tablespoons chopped fresh basil leaves, divided

1   Add water to the Instant Pot® and place the rack inside.

2   Place each piece of cod on a 10" × 10" square of aluminum foil. Drizzle each fillet with 1 teaspoon oil and sprinkle with ¼ teaspoon salt. Add 5 olives, half of the tomatoes, and 1 tablespoon basil on top of each fillet. Bring up the sides of the foil and crimp at the top to create a foil pocket.

3   Place both fish packets on rack. Close lid, set steam release to Sealing, press the Manual button, and set time to 6 minutes. When the timer beeps, quick-release the pressure until the float valve drops and open lid.

4   Remove foil packets and transfer fish and toppings to two plates. Garnish each serving with half of the remaining 1 tablespoon basil.

Halibut Fillets with Vegetables

Omit the nutmeg and turn this steamed meal into a hot fish and vegetable salad by serving it over salad greens.

1 cup chopped broccoli
1 large potato, peeled and diced
1 large carrot, peeled and grated
1 small zucchini, trimmed and grated
4 ounces mushrooms, sliced
¼ teaspoon dried thyme
¼ teaspoon grated lemon zest
1 (½-pound) halibut fillet
½ cup white wine
½ cup lemon juice
1 teaspoon dried parsley
¼ teaspoon salt
¼ teaspoon ground black pepper
⅛ teaspoon ground nutmeg

1 Place the rack and steamer basket in the Instant Pot®. Place broccoli, potato, carrot, zucchini, and mushrooms in layers in the basket. Sprinkle thyme and lemon zest over vegetables.

2 Place fish over vegetables. Pour wine and lemon juice over fish. Sprinkle parsley, salt, and pepper over the fish and vegetables.

3 Close lid, set steam release to Sealing, press the Manual button, and set time to 5 minutes. When the timer beeps, quick-release the pressure until the float valve drops and open lid. Divide fish and vegetables between two plates. Sprinkle nutmeg over each serving.

SERVES 2

Per Serving:

Calories	278
Fat	3g
Protein	31g
Sodium	409mg
Fiber	5g
Carbohydrates	23g
Sugar	4g

SAVE THE STEAMING LIQUID

The liquid used to steam the fish and vegetables can form the base of a light salad dressing. Whisk 1 teaspoon Dijon mustard into ¼ cup strained pan juices and 1 tablespoon lemon juice. Slowly whisk in 1–2 tablespoons extra-virgin olive oil. Add salt and ground black pepper to taste.

Lemon and Herb Fish Packets

SERVES 4

Per Serving:

Calories	185
Fat	9g
Protein	23g
Sodium	355mg
Fiber	0g
Carbohydrates	0g
Sugar	0g

Cooking fish in a foil packet will infuse it with the flavors of the herbs and lemon and will also leave the fish tender and moist.

1 cup water
4 (4-ounce) halibut or other white fish fillets
½ teaspoon salt
½ teaspoon ground black pepper

1 small lemon, thinly sliced
¼ cup chopped fresh dill
¼ cup chopped fresh chives
2 tablespoons chopped fresh tarragon
2 tablespoons extra-virgin olive oil

1 Add water to the Instant Pot® and place the rack inside.

2 Season fish fillets with salt and pepper. Measure out four pieces of foil large enough to wrap around fish fillets. Lay fish fillets on foil. Top with lemon, dill, chives, and tarragon, and drizzle each with olive oil. Carefully wrap fish loosely in foil.

3 Place packets on rack. Close lid, set steam release to Sealing, press the Steam button, and set time to 5 minutes.

4 When the timer beeps, quick-release the pressure until the float valve drops. Press the Cancel button and open lid. Serve immediately.

Orange Roughy in Black Olive Sauce

SERVES 2

Per Serving:

Calories	337
Fat	21g
Protein	37g
Sodium	650mg
Fiber	0g
Carbohydrates	1g
Sugar	0g

If fresh dill isn't available, sprinkle ¼ teaspoon dried dill over each fillet when you salt it. Add more dried dill to the sauce, if desired.

⅜ cup dry white wine
⅜ cup water
2 (8-ounce) orange roughy fillets, rinsed and patted dry
¼ teaspoon salt

4 thin slices white onion, divided
6 sprigs fresh dill, divided
3 tablespoons unsalted butter, melted
4 teaspoons lime juice
6 Kalamata olives, pitted and chopped

1 Pour wine and water into the Instant Pot® and add rack. Sprinkle fish with salt. Place 2 onion slices on rack and top each slice with a sprig of dill.

2 Place fish over the onion and dill, put a sprig of dill on top of each fillet, and top with remaining 2 onion slices. Close lid, set steam release to Sealing, press the Manual button, and set time to 5 minutes. When the timer beeps, let pressure release naturally for 5 minutes. Quick-release any remaining pressure until the float valve drops. Open lid.

3 In a small bowl, whisk butter, lime juice, and ½ tablespoon cooking liquid from the fish; stir in the olives. Pour sauce over fish and garnish with remaining 2 dill sprigs.

Fish with Spinach and Rice

This is a super-easy weeknight dish, with everything cooked in one pot at once. If you prefer, you can replace the white fish with salmon.

1 cup water
1 cup white rice
1 tablespoon light olive oil
4 (4-ounce) cod or other white fish fillets
½ teaspoon salt
½ teaspoon ground black pepper
2 cups baby spinach
2 tablespoons extra-virgin olive oil
4 lemon wedges

SERVES 4	
Per Serving:	
Calories	266
Fat	18g
Protein	16g
Sodium	799mg
Fiber	1g
Carbohydrates	12g
Sugar	0g

1 Add water, rice, and light olive oil to the Instant Pot® and stir well. Place rack and steamer basket inside the pot.

2 Season fish fillets with salt and pepper. Measure out four pieces of foil large enough to wrap around fish fillets. Lay spinach on foil, top with fish fillets, drizzle with extra-virgin olive oil, and squeeze juice from lemon wedges. Carefully wrap loosely in foil, making sure to seal seams well.

3 Place packets in steamer basket. Close lid, set steam release to Sealing, press the Steam button, and set time to 5 minutes.

4 When the timer beeps, quick-release the pressure until the float valve drops. Press the Cancel button and open lid. Carefully remove packets and set aside. Divide rice between four bowls. Open packets and place fish with spinach on rice. Serve hot.

Rosemary Salmon

The aromatic and slightly bitter flavor of rosemary pairs well with the rich flavor of salmon in this dish. Rosemary is a powerful herb, so don't be tempted to add too much or it will overpower the fish.

1 cup water
4 (4-ounce) salmon fillets
½ teaspoon salt
½ teaspoon ground black pepper
1 sprig rosemary, leaves stripped off and minced
2 tablespoons chopped fresh thyme
2 tablespoons extra-virgin olive oil
4 lemon wedges

1 Add water to the Instant Pot® and place rack inside.

2 Season fish fillets with salt and pepper. Measure out four pieces of foil large enough to wrap around fish fillets. Lay fish fillets on foil. Top with rosemary and thyme, then drizzle each with olive oil. Carefully wrap loosely in foil.

3 Place foil packets on rack. Close lid, set steam release to Sealing, press the Steam button, and set time to 5 minutes.

4 When the timer beeps, quick-release the pressure until the float valve drops. Press the Cancel button and open lid. Carefully remove packets to plates. Serve immediately with lemon wedges.

SERVES 4	
Per Serving:	
Calories	160
Fat	8g
Protein	24g
Sodium	445mg
Fiber	0g
Carbohydrates	0g
Sugar	0g

BENEFITS OF ROSEMARY

Native to the Mediterranean, rosemary packs a surprising number of health benefits. Rosemary is an excellent source of calcium, vitamin B_6, and iron. In ancient times, rosemary was considered a medicinal herb and was used to help with circulatory problems, to boost the immune system, and to ease muscle pain. Rosemary may also aid in memory and concentration, so if you are looking for ways to help your brain health, you may want to consider adding more rosemary to your diet.

River Trout with Herb Sauce

SERVES 4

Per Serving:

Calories	344
Fat	18g
Protein	45g
Sodium	581mg
Fiber	0g
Carbohydrates	1g
Sugar	0g

If the trout haven't already been gutted, your fishmonger will be happy to do this for you. All you have to do is ask. Once home, cook the fish within 1–2 days with this incredibly fresh and creamy traditional herb sauce.

4 (½-pound) fresh river trout, rinsed and patted dry
1 teaspoon salt, divided
1 teaspoon white wine vinegar
½ cup water
½ cup minced fresh flat-leaf parsley
2 tablespoons chopped fresh oregano
1 teaspoon fresh thyme leaves
1 small shallot, peeled and minced
2 tablespoons olive oil
½ teaspoon lemon juice

1 Sprinkle trout with ¾ teaspoon salt inside and out. Combine vinegar and water, pour into the Instant Pot®, and place rack inside. Place trout on rack.

2 Close lid, set steam release to Sealing, press the Manual button, and set time to 3 minutes. When the timer beeps, let pressure release naturally for 3 minutes. Quick-release any remaining pressure until the float valve drops and then open lid.

3 Transfer fish to a serving plate. Peel and discard skin from fish. Remove and discard the heads if desired.

4 In a small bowl, mix together parsley, oregano, thyme, shallot, olive oil, lemon juice, and remaining ¼ teaspoon salt. Pour evenly over fish. Serve immediately.

Citrus Fish Tacos

There's no need for cooking deep-fried fish when you can easily make these fresh fish tacos. You can even change up the flavors to go with your current mood. Add a mango salsa for your staycation or a grilled pineapple salsa when dining alfresco. Switch up the guacamole and tomatoes for fresh avocado slices and a pico de gallo.

½ cup grated cabbage
1 large carrot, peeled and grated
1 small jicama, peeled and julienned
2 tablespoons lime juice, divided
2 tablespoons olive oil, divided
⅛ teaspoon hot sauce
¼ cup chopped fresh cilantro
½ teaspoon salt
1 pound cod, cut into 2" pieces
2 tablespoons orange juice
1 teaspoon garlic salt
1 teaspoon ground cumin
1 cup water
½ cup guacamole
½ cup diced tomatoes
8 (6") soft corn tortillas

1 Combine cabbage, carrot, jicama, 1 tablespoon lime juice, 1 tablespoon oil, hot sauce, cilantro, and salt in a medium bowl. Cover and refrigerate for 30 minutes or overnight.

2 In a large bowl, combine fish, remaining 1 tablespoon lime juice, orange juice, garlic salt, cumin, and remaining 1 tablespoon oil, and refrigerate for 15 minutes.

3 Add 1 cup water to the Instant Pot® and insert rack. Place steamer basket on top of rack. Add cod in an even row in steamer basket. Pour in remaining marinade.

4 Close lid, set steam release to Sealing, press the Manual button, and set time to 3 minutes. When the timer beeps, quick-release the pressure until the float valve drops and then open lid. Transfer fish to a serving bowl.

5 Assemble fish tacos by adding equal amounts of fish, slaw, guacamole, and tomatoes to each corn tortilla.

SERVES 8	
Per Serving:	
Calories	240
Fat	8g
Protein	14g
Sodium	564mg
Fiber	5g
Carbohydrates	25g
Sugar	3g

HOMEMADE GUACAMOLE

Combine the following ingredients in a medium bowl for a quick and easy guacamole: 2 diced avocados, 2 tablespoons lime juice, 3 minced garlic cloves, 1 teaspoon hot sauce, 1 diced Roma tomato, 1 teaspoon salt, and 3 tablespoons chopped cilantro. Refrigerate, covered, until ready to serve. Use within 1–2 days.

Mediterranean Fish Stew

Fish stew can be made with just about any bits of white fish you have available; add shrimp, mussels, or clams, if you like. Serve this with thick slices of crusty bread for soaking up all the delicious broth.

4 tablespoons olive oil
1 medium yellow onion, peeled and diced
2 cloves garlic, peeled and minced
½ teaspoon dried oregano leaves
½ teaspoon ground fennel
¼ teaspoon dried thyme leaves
1 (14.5-ounce) can diced tomatoes
1 cup seafood stock
½ cup white wine
1 pound white fish fillets, such as halibut or sea bass, cut into 2" pieces
¼ teaspoon salt
¼ teaspoon ground black pepper
½ teaspoon hot sauce

1 Press the Sauté button on the Instant Pot® and heat oil. Add onion and cook until soft, about 4 minutes. Add garlic, oregano, fennel, and thyme. Cook 30 seconds, then add tomatoes, seafood stock, and wine. Stir well and press the Cancel button.

2 Close lid, set steam release to Sealing, press the Manual button, and set time to 3 minutes.

3 When the timer beeps, quick-release the pressure until the float valve drops and open lid. Press the Cancel button, then press the Sauté button and add fish. Cook until fish is opaque, about 5 minutes. Season with salt and pepper. Add hot sauce just before serving.

CHAPTER 12

Poultry

Chicken with Lemon Asparagus

Browning chicken, or any meat cooked in the Instant Pot®, will add a lot of extra flavor, giving you more bang for your buck. So, don't skimp on the browning time, even if you're in a hurry.

2 tablespoons olive oil
4 (6-ounce) boneless, skinless chicken breasts
½ teaspoon ground black pepper
¼ teaspoon salt
¼ teaspoon smoked paprika
2 cloves garlic, peeled and minced
2 sprigs thyme
2 sprigs oregano
1 tablespoon grated lemon zest
¼ cup lemon juice
¼ cup low-sodium chicken broth
1 bunch asparagus, trimmed
¼ cup chopped fresh parsley
4 lemon wedges

1 Press Sauté on the Instant Pot® and heat oil. Season chicken with pepper, salt, and smoked paprika. Brown chicken on both sides, about 4 minutes per side. Add garlic, thyme, oregano, lemon zest, lemon juice, and chicken broth. Press the Cancel button.

2 Close lid, set steam release to Sealing, press the Manual button, and set time to 5 minutes.

3 When the timer beeps, quick-release the pressure until the float valve drops. Press the Cancel button and open lid. Transfer chicken breasts to a serving platter. Tent with foil to keep warm.

4 Add asparagus to the Instant Pot®. Close lid, set steam release to Sealing, press the Manual button, and set time to 0. When the timer beeps, quick-release the pressure until the float valve drops. Open lid and remove asparagus. Arrange asparagus around chicken and garnish with parsley and lemon wedges. Serve immediately.

Chicken and Mushroom Marsala

Marsala, a fortified wine that originates in Sicily, is commonly used for deglazing pans and making sauces. While you can find wine labeled as "marsala" grouped with the cooking wines at the grocery store, the best quality marsala is usually found in the wine aisle.

3 tablespoons all-purpose flour
½ teaspoon ground black pepper
¼ teaspoon salt
2 (6-ounce) boneless, skinless chicken breasts
2 tablespoons olive oil
1 medium white onion, peeled and diced
1 pound sliced button mushrooms
2 cloves garlic, peeled and minced
2 sprigs thyme
2 sprigs oregano
¼ cup marsala wine
¼ cup low-sodium chicken broth
¼ cup chopped fresh parsley

SERVES 4	
Per Serving:	
Calories	525
Fat	14g
Protein	37g
Sodium	218mg
Fiber	8g
Carbohydrates	9g
Sugar	2g

1 Combine flour, pepper, and salt in a shallow dish. Dredge chicken breasts in flour, shaking to remove excess. Press the Sauté button on the Instant Pot® and heat oil. Brown chicken on both sides, about 4 minutes per side. Transfer chicken to a plate and set aside.

2 Add onion to the pot and cook until just tender, about 3 minutes. Add mushrooms and cook, stirring often, until mushrooms are tender, about 8 minutes. Add garlic, thyme, and oregano, and cook until fragrant, about 30 seconds.

3 Stir in wine and chicken broth, and scrape bottom of pot to release any browned bits. Top with chicken. Press the Cancel button, close lid, set steam release to Sealing, press the Manual button, and set time to 5 minutes.

4 When the timer beeps, let pressure release naturally, about 20 minutes. Press the Cancel button and open lid. Transfer chicken breasts to a cutting board and slice into ½" pieces. Arrange on serving platter. Pour mushrooms and cooking liquid over chicken. Sprinkle with parsley and serve hot.

Chicken Cacciatore

Chicken Cacciatore is an Italian stew flavored with fresh herbs, onion, and wine. Serve this dish with hot cooked pasta or rice, garlic bread, and a tossed green salad.

ITALIAN MEDLEY SEASONING BLEND

Mrs. Dash Italian Medley Seasoning Blend is a mixture of garlic, basil, oregano, rosemary, parsley, marjoram, white pepper, sage, savory, cayenne pepper, thyme, bay leaf, cumin, mustard powder, coriander, onion, and red bell pepper. All of the Mrs. Dash blends are salt-free, which makes them a healthy addition to any dish.

1 (3-pound) chicken, cut up

3 tablespoons all-purpose flour

½ teaspoon salt

⅛ teaspoon ground black pepper

2 tablespoons olive oil

2 ounces diced salt pork

1 large onion, peeled and sliced

2 cloves garlic, peeled and minced

1 tablespoon dried parsley

2 teaspoons Mrs. Dash Italian Medley Seasoning Blend

2 large carrots, peeled and diced

1 stalk celery, diced

1 (14.5-ounce) can diced tomatoes

½ teaspoon salt

½ teaspoon ground black pepper

½ cup white wine

1 (6-ounce) can tomato paste

1 Trim and discard any extra fat from chicken. Add flour, salt, and pepper to a large zip-top plastic bag. Add chicken, seal the bag, and shake to coat chicken.

2 Press the Sauté button on the Instant Pot® and heat oil. Add pork and cook until it begins to render its fat, about 3 minutes.

3 Add chicken, skin side down, and brown until crisp, about 3 minutes. Add onion, garlic, parsley, seasoning blend, carrots, celery, tomatoes, salt, pepper, and wine. Press the Cancel button.

4 Close lid, set steam release to Sealing, press the Manual button, and set time to 20 minutes.

5 When the timer beeps, quick-release the pressure until the float valve drops. Open lid. Place chicken on a serving platter and keep warm. Press the Cancel button.

6 Press the Sauté button, stir in tomato paste, and simmer for 5 minutes or until thickened. Pour sauce over chicken and serve.

Chicken and Orzo Soup

This soup is simple to make, super comforting, and extra-super filling.

1 pound boneless, skinless chicken breast
3 stalks celery, sliced
2 medium carrots, peeled and chopped
1 medium onion, peeled and chopped
2 cups baby spinach
1 clove garlic, peeled and minced

1 bay leaf
2 sprigs sage
2 sprigs thyme
¼ teaspoon ground black pepper
4 cups low-sodium chicken broth
1 cup orzo

SERVES 8	
Per Serving:	
Calories	176
Fat	1g
Protein	11g
Sodium	176mg
Fiber	3g
Carbohydrates	27g
Sugar	5g

1 Place all ingredients except orzo in the Instant Pot®. Close lid, set steam release to Sealing, and press the Soup button and cook for default time of 20 minutes. When the timer beeps, quick-release the pressure until the float valve drops. Press the Cancel button and open lid.

2 With tongs or a slotted spoon transfer chicken to a cutting board. Carefully shred meat, then return to pot. Remove and discard thyme and bay leaf.

3 Add orzo, close lid, set steam release to Sealing, press the Manual button, and set time to 4 minutes. When the timer beeps, quick-release the pressure until the float valve drops. Press the Cancel button and open lid. Serve hot.

Turkey Thighs in Fig Sauce

Balsamic vinegar brings out the flavor of the figs in the sauce, imparting a tart, wine-like flavor. If you have room in the Instant Pot®, add four halved Yukon Gold potatoes and cook them along with the thighs.

4 (¾-pound) bone-in turkey thighs, skin removed
1 large onion, peeled and quartered
2 large carrots, peeled and sliced
½ stalk celery, finely diced
½ cup balsamic vinegar

2 tablespoons tomato paste
1 cup low-sodium chicken broth
½ teaspoon salt
¾ teaspoon ground black pepper
12 dried figs, cut in half

SERVES 4	
Per Serving:	
Calories	565
Fat	17g
Protein	68g
Sodium	685mg
Fiber	5g
Carbohydrates	26g
Sugar	18g

1 Add the turkey, onion, carrots, and celery to the Instant Pot®. Whisk vinegar, tomato paste, broth, salt, and pepper in a small bowl. Pour into pot. Add figs. Close lid, set steam release to Sealing, press the Manual button, and set time to 14 minutes. When the timer beeps, let pressure release naturally, about 25 minutes.

2 Open the lid. Transfer thighs, carrots, and figs to a serving platter. Tent loosely with aluminum foil and keep warm while you finish the sauce.

3 Strain pan juices. Discard onion and celery. Skim and discard fat. Pour strained sauce over the thighs. Serve immediately.

Vegetable Bowls with Turkey and Hummus

SERVES 4	
Per Serving:	
Calories	563
Fat	23g
Protein	37g
Sodium	1,304mg
Fiber	6g
Carbohydrates	37g
Sugar	18g

WHAT IS A VEGETABLE BOWL?

If you think a vegetable bowl is just a salad, you are only half right. While it is true that a vegetable bowl and a salad have a lot in common, there are a few distinct differences that make a vegetable bowl unique. First is presentation. A salad is typically mixed before serving, while a vegetable bowl is artfully arranged to be pleasing to the eyes. Next, vegetable bowls are usually lightly dressed with simple vinaigrettes or topped with purées like hummus in place of creamy dressings. Finally, vegetable bowls are more fun! Sure, a salad is great, but a vegetable bowl looks and feels special. Treat yourself to a good-for-you vegetable bowl today!

Reserve the turkey cooking liquid—it's packed with flavor. Strain the broth in a fine-mesh strainer, chill, and use it for making soup within three days; or freeze it and keep for up to three months for longer storage.

1 pound boneless, skinless turkey breast cutlets
1 stalk celery, cut into 1" pieces
1 medium carrot, peeled and cut into 1" pieces
1 medium white onion, peeled and quartered
1 teaspoon poultry seasoning
1 clove garlic, peeled and crushed
1 bay leaf
¼ teaspoon ground black pepper
4 cups low-sodium chicken broth
8 cups mixed salad greens
1 large English cucumber, chopped
1 medium yellow bell pepper, seeded and chopped
½ medium red onion, peeled and chopped
16 cherry tomatoes, quartered
1 cup pitted Kalamata olives
1 cup Red Pepper Hummus (see recipe in Chapter 3)

1   Place turkey, celery, carrot, white onion, poultry seasoning, garlic, bay leaf, black pepper, and broth in the Instant Pot®. Close lid, set steam release to Sealing, press the Manual button, and set time to 6 minutes. When the timer beeps, quick-release the pressure until the float valve drops. Press the Cancel button and open lid. Remove and discard bay leaf.

2   With tongs or a slotted spoon, transfer turkey to a cutting board. Carefully shred meat.

3   Divide salad greens among four bowls. Top with cucumber, bell pepper, red onion, tomatoes, olives, hummus, and shredded turkey. Serve immediately.

Citrus and Spice Chicken

This ridiculously delicious and juicy chicken is spiced just right with a balanced combination of paprika, cinnamon, ginger, nutmeg, and citrus. Serve with a plate of steamed vegetables or add a scoop of rice to make it a full meal.

2 tablespoons olive oil
3 pounds boneless, skinless chicken thighs
1 teaspoon smoked paprika
½ teaspoon salt
⅛ teaspoon ground cinnamon
⅛ teaspoon ground ginger
⅛ teaspoon ground nutmeg
½ cup golden raisins
½ cup slivered almonds
1 cup orange juice
⅛ cup lemon juice
⅛ cup lime juice
1 pound carrots, peeled and chopped
2 tablespoons water
1 tablespoon arrowroot powder

1 Press the Sauté button on the Instant Pot® and heat oil. Fry chicken thighs for 2 minutes on each side until browned.

2 Add paprika, salt, cinnamon, ginger, nutmeg, raisins, almonds, orange juice, lemon juice, lime juice, and carrots. Press the Cancel button.

3 Close lid, set steam release to Sealing, press the Manual button, and set time to 10 minutes. When the timer beeps, let pressure release naturally for 5 minutes. Quick-release any remaining pressure until the float valve drops and then open lid. Check chicken using a meat thermometer to make sure the internal temperature is at least 165°F.

4 Use a slotted spoon to remove chicken, carrots, and raisins, and transfer to a serving platter. Press the Cancel button.

5 In a small bowl, whisk together water and arrowroot to create a slurry. Add to liquid in the Instant Pot® and stir to combine. Press the Sauté button, press the Adjust button to change the temperature to Less, and simmer uncovered for 3 minutes until sauce is thickened. Pour sauce over chicken and serve.

Kale and Orzo Chicken

Light olive oil does not refer to the amount of fat or calories in the oil, but its lighter flavor. It also has a higher smoke point or burning point than regular olive oil, so it is more suitable for sautéing or frying.

3 tablespoons light olive oil
1 pound boneless, skinless chicken breasts
½ teaspoon salt
½ teaspoon ground black pepper
½ medium yellow onion, peeled and chopped
4 cups chopped kale
¼ teaspoon crushed red pepper flakes
2 cups low-sodium chicken broth
1½ cups orzo
½ cup crumbled feta cheese

SERVES 4	
Per Serving:	
Calories	690
Fat	19g
Protein	56g
Sodium	835mg
Fiber	7g
Carbohydrates	72g
Sugar	4g

1 Press the Sauté button on the Instant Pot® and heat oil. Season chicken with salt and pepper and add to the pot. Brown well on both sides, about 4 minutes per side. Transfer chicken to a plate and set aside.

2 Add onion and cook until just tender, about 2 minutes. Add kale and crushed red pepper flakes, and cook until kale is just wilted, about 2 minutes. Press the Cancel button.

3 Add broth and orzo to the Instant Pot® and stir well. Top with chicken breasts. Close lid, set steam release to Sealing, press the Manual button, and set time to 4 minutes. When the timer beeps, quick-release the pressure until the float valve drops. Press the Cancel button and open lid. Transfer chicken to a cutting board and cut into ½" slices. Arrange slices on a platter along with orzo and kale. Top with feta and serve hot.

Chicken Breasts Stuffed with Feta and Spinach

SERVES 4

Per Serving:

Calories	304
Fat	17g
Protein	40g
Sodium	772mg
Fiber	1g
Carbohydrates	2g
Sugar	0g

This dish looks like a million bucks and could not be easier to make. If you prefer, you can replace the feta with shredded mozzarella or goat cheese. Make sure to wring as much water from the spinach as you can to keep the filling firm.

1 cup chopped frozen spinach, thawed and drained well
½ cup crumbled feta cheese
4 (6-ounce) boneless, skinless chicken breasts
¼ teaspoon salt
¼ teaspoon ground black pepper
2 tablespoons light olive oil, divided
1 cup water

1 In a small bowl, combine spinach and feta. Slice a pocket into each chicken breast along one side. Stuff one-quarter of the spinach and feta mixture into the pocket of each breast. Season chicken on all sides with salt and pepper. Set aside.

2 Press the Sauté button on the Instant Pot® and add 1 tablespoon oil. Add two chicken breasts and brown on both sides, about 3 minutes per side. Transfer to a plate and repeat with remaining 1 tablespoon oil and chicken.

3 Add water to pot and place rack inside. Place chicken breasts on rack. Close lid, set steam release to Sealing, press the Manual button, and set time to 8 minutes.

4 When the timer beeps, quick-release the pressure until the float valve drops. Press the Cancel button and open lid. Transfer chicken to a serving platter. Serve hot.

Lemony Chicken Soup

This bright and refreshing soup is a wonderful meal when you want something warm and comforting, or if you need a pick-me-up when you're feeling under the weather.

2 tablespoons light olive oil

2 stalks celery, sliced

1 medium carrot, peeled and chopped

1 medium yellow onion, peeled and chopped

2 cloves garlic, peeled and minced

2 sprigs thyme

1 sprig sage

1 bay leaf

1 tablespoon grated lemon zest

8 cups low-sodium chicken broth

12 ounces cooked chicken breast, shredded

½ cup white rice

¼ cup lemon juice

2 tablespoons chopped fresh flat-leaf parsley

1 teaspoon ground black pepper

SERVES 8	
Per Serving:	
Calories	231
Fat	5g
Protein	17g
Sodium	248mg
Fiber	1g
Carbohydrates	23g
Sugar	3g

1. Press the Sauté button on the Instant Pot® and heat oil. Add celery, carrot, and onion, and cook until tender, about 5 minutes. Add garlic and cook until fragrant, about 30 seconds. Add thyme, sage, bay leaf, and lemon zest, and stir well. Press the Cancel button.

2. Add broth, chicken, and rice. Stir well, then close lid, set steam release to Sealing, press the Manual button, and set time to 5 minutes.

3. When the timer beeps, let pressure release naturally for 15 minutes, then quick-release any remaining pressure until the float valve drops. Open lid and remove and discard thyme, sage, and bay leaf. Stir in lemon juice, parsley, and pepper. Serve hot.

Turkey Breast in Yogurt Sauce

SERVES 6	
Per Serving:	
Calories	146
Fat	6g
Protein	17g
Sodium	554mg
Fiber	1g
Carbohydrates	7g
Sugar	4g

Serve over cooked rice or couscous with a cucumber and yogurt salad on the side. To make the salad, combine plain yogurt, garlic, mint, salt, and ginger. Spritz with lemon juice and add thinly sliced cucumbers.

1 cup plain low-fat yogurt
1 teaspoon ground turmeric
1 teaspoon ground cumin
1 teaspoon yellow mustard seeds
¼ teaspoon salt

½ teaspoon ground black pepper
1 pound boneless turkey breast, cut into bite-sized pieces
1 tablespoon olive oil
1 (1-pound) bag frozen baby peas and pearl onions, thawed

1 In a large bowl, mix together yogurt, turmeric, cumin, mustard seeds, salt, and pepper. Stir in in turkey. Cover and refrigerate for 4 hours.

2 Press the Sauté button on the Instant Pot® and heat oil. Add turkey and yogurt mixture. Press the Cancel button, close lid, set steam release to Sealing, press the Manual button, and set time to 8 minutes. When the timer beeps, quick-release the pressure and open lid.

3 Stir in peas and onions. Press the Cancel button, then press the Sauté button and simmer until sauce is thickened, about 8 minutes. Serve hot.

Roasted Red Pepper Chicken

SERVES 6	
Per Serving:	
Calories	357
Fat	21g
Protein	32g
Sodium	516mg
Fiber	1g
Carbohydrates	9g
Sugar	3g

A touch of heavy cream adds a little luxury to this chicken dish.

1 cup chopped roasted red peppers
½ teaspoon Italian seasoning
3 tablespoons olive oil
1 medium white onion, peeled and chopped
2 cloves garlic, peeled and minced
½ teaspoon ground black pepper

1 pound boneless, skinless chicken breast, cut into 1" pieces
½ cup low-sodium chicken broth
¼ cup heavy cream
½ cup grated Parmesan cheese
¼ cup chopped fresh basil

1 In a blender or food processor, purée roasted red peppers and Italian seasoning until smooth, about 1 minute. Set aside.

2 Press the Sauté button on the Instant Pot® and heat oil. Add onion and sauté 2 minutes. Add garlic and black pepper, and cook 30 seconds. Stir in red pepper purée. Press the Cancel button.

3 Add chicken and broth. Close lid, set steam release to Sealing, press the Manual button, and set time to 6 minutes. When the timer beeps, let pressure release naturally, about 15 minutes, then press the Cancel button. Open lid, stir in cream, and top with cheese and basil.

Balsamic Chicken Thighs with Tomato and Basil

Balsamic vinegar has a rich, sweet, complex flavor, and cooking with it only enhances its deep caramel notes. Serve this dish with extra balsamic vinegar on the table so your guests can drizzle a little on their plates.

1 pound boneless, skinless chicken thighs
¼ teaspoon salt
¼ teaspoon ground black pepper
¼ teaspoon Italian seasoning
3 tablespoons olive oil
1 medium white onion, peeled and chopped
1 medium red bell pepper, seeded and chopped
2 cloves garlic, peeled and minced
4 medium tomatoes, seeded and diced
½ cup red wine
¼ cup balsamic vinegar
½ cup grated Parmesan cheese
¼ cup chopped fresh basil

SERVES 6	
Per Serving:	
Calories	239
Fat	13g
Protein	20g
Sodium	447mg
Fiber	1g
Carbohydrates	8g
Sugar	7g

1   Season chicken on both sides with salt, black pepper, and Italian seasoning. Press the Sauté button on the Instant Pot® and heat oil. Add chicken and brown well on both sides, about 4 minutes per side. Transfer chicken to a plate and set aside.

2   Add onion and bell pepper to the Instant Pot®. Cook until just tender, about 2 minutes. Add garlic and cook until fragrant, about 30 seconds. Stir in tomatoes and wine, and scrape any brown bits from the bottom of the pot. Press the Cancel button.

3   Stir in chicken and balsamic vinegar. Close lid, set steam release to Sealing, press the Manual button, and set time to 6 minutes. When the timer beeps, let pressure release naturally, about 15 minutes. Press the Cancel button and open lid. Top with cheese and basil, and serve hot.

Mediterranean Chicken Lettuce Wraps

Nothing beats a crisp, cool piece of lettuce surrounding a hot, savory filling. This is a Mediterranean take on lettuce wraps that includes a tangy yogurt dipping sauce and plenty of fresh toppings.

1 cup low-fat plain Greek yogurt
¼ cup chopped fresh parsley
2 teaspoons lemon juice
¼ teaspoon sea salt
¼ teaspoon ground black pepper
1 pound boneless, skinless chicken breasts, cut into 1" pieces
1 teaspoon chopped fresh rosemary
1 teaspoon fresh thyme leaves
1 cup water
8 butter lettuce leaves
½ large English cucumber, chopped
½ medium red onion, peeled and chopped
1 large tomato, seeded and chopped
½ cup sliced black olives

1 Place yogurt, parsley, lemon juice, salt, and pepper in a small bowl. Mix well, then cover and refrigerate until ready to serve.

2 In a medium bowl, toss chicken with rosemary and thyme. Add water to the Instant Pot® and insert steamer basket. Transfer chicken to steamer basket. Close lid, set steam release to Sealing, press the Poultry button, and cook for the default time of 15 minutes. When the timer beeps, quick-release the pressure until the float valve drops and open lid.

3 Place chicken on a platter with lettuce leaves. Serve cucumber, onion, tomato, olives, and yogurt sauce in small bowls so that guests can make their own wraps.

SERVES 6	
Per Serving:	
Calories	150
Fat	3g
Protein	27g
Sodium	148mg
Fiber	0g
Carbohydrates	2g
Sugar	2g

LETTUCE WRAPS

Lettuce wraps turn dinner into a fun party activity, allowing guests to build their own delicious, crunchy creations. Use your favorite green or try a new one. If you like an extra-crisp lettuce wrap, go for iceberg lettuce. Looking for something crisp yet tender? Butter lettuce is for you. Want a hearty lettuce with a bit of green flavor? Use romaine. No matter how you build it, a lettuce wrap is sure to please you and your friends and family.

Mini Turkey Loaves

SERVES 6	
Per Serving:	
Calories	110
Fat	4g
Protein	8g
Sodium	190mg
Fiber	2g
Carbohydrates	11g
Sugar	4g

Serve these little loaves with mashed potatoes and a steamed vegetable. You can also serve slices hot or cold in sandwiches.

1½ pounds lean ground turkey	1 tablespoon mayonnaise
1 small onion, peeled and diced	¼ teaspoon salt
1 stalk celery, minced	¼ teaspoon ground black pepper
1 medium carrot, peeled and grated	1 large egg
½ cup butter cracker crumbs	3 tablespoons ketchup
1 clove garlic, peeled and minced	1 tablespoon light brown sugar
½ teaspoon dried basil	1 cup water

1 Combine all ingredients except water in a large bowl. Divide the mixture between two mini loaf pans. Pack the mixture down into the pans. Add 1 cup water to Instant Pot® and insert rack. Place pans on the rack.

2 Close lid, set steam release to Sealing, press the Manual button, and set time to 20 minutes. When the timer beeps, let pressure release naturally, about 25 minutes.

3 Open lid. Use oven mitts to lift the pans from the pot. Serve directly hot.

Chicken Marinara and Zucchini

SERVES 4	
Per Serving:	
Calories	407
Fat	13g
Protein	42g
Sodium	1,293mg
Fiber	5g
Carbohydrates	27g
Sugar	16g

Whether you use homemade or jarred marinara sauce, this quick recipe uses what you already have on hand, turning basic ingredients into an Italian dream meal in minutes.

2 large zucchini, trimmed and chopped	1 tablespoon Italian seasoning
4 (6-ounce) chicken breast halves	½ teaspoon salt
3 cups marinara sauce	1 cup shredded mozzarella cheese

1 Place zucchini on the bottom of the Instant Pot®. Place chicken on zucchini. Pour marinara sauce over chicken. Sprinkle with Italian seasoning and salt.

2 Close lid, set steam release to Sealing, press the Poultry button, and cook for the default time of 15 minutes. When the timer beeps, let pressure release naturally for 10 minutes. Quick-release any remaining pressure until the float valve drops and then open lid. Check chicken using a meat thermometer to ensure the internal temperature is at least 165°F.

3 Sprinkle chicken with cheese. Close lid and let stand on the Keep Warm setting for 5 minutes to allow the cheese to melt.

4 Transfer chicken and zucchini to a serving platter. Serve hot.

Easy Pesto Chicken and Potatoes

This dish not only tastes and smells delicious, but it's incredibly quick and easy to make.

3 pounds boneless, skinless chicken thighs
¾ cup pesto

2 pounds red potatoes, quartered
1 large sweet onion, peeled and chopped
1 cup low-sodium chicken broth

SERVES 8	
Per Serving:	
Calories	372
Fat	16g
Protein	38g
Sodium	396mg
Fiber	4g
Carbohydrates	18g
Sugar	2g

1 Place chicken in a large bowl or zip-top plastic bag. Add pesto. Toss or shake chicken to distribute the pesto evenly over the thighs. Set aside.

2 Layer potatoes and onion in the Instant Pot®. Pour in chicken broth. Place chicken on top.

3 Close lid, set steam release to Sealing, press the Manual button, and set time to 10 minutes. When the timer beeps, let pressure release naturally for 10 minutes. Quick-release any remaining pressure until the float valve drops and then open lid. Check the chicken using a meat thermometer to ensure the internal temperature is at least 165°F.

4 Transfer chicken and potatoes to a platter. Serve warm.

Kale, Chickpea, and Chicken Stew

Stirring in a little tahini at the end of cooking adds a subtle richness.

2 tablespoons light olive oil
2 large red bell peppers, seeded and chopped
1 medium yellow onion, peeled and chopped
4 cups chopped kale
2 cloves garlic, peeled and minced
3 medium tomatoes, seeded and chopped

2 sprigs thyme
1 pound boneless, skinless chicken breast, cut into 1" pieces
2 (15-ounce) cans chickpeas, drained and rinsed
2 cups low-sodium chicken broth
½ cup tahini
¼ cup chopped fresh parsley

SERVES 8	
Per Serving:	
Calories	310
Fat	14g
Protein	25g
Sodium	359mg
Fiber	9g
Carbohydrates	30g
Sugar	6g

1 Press the Sauté button on the Instant Pot® and heat oil. Add bell peppers and onion and sauté 5 minutes. Add kale and cook until just wilted, about 2 minutes. Add garlic and cook until fragrant, about 30 seconds. Add tomatoes and thyme. Press the Cancel button.

2 Add chicken, chickpeas, and broth. Stir well, then close lid, set steam release to Sealing, press the Manual button, and set time to 5 minutes.

3 When the timer beeps, let pressure release naturally for 15 minutes, then quick-release any remaining pressure until the float valve drops. Open lid and stir in tahini. Sprinkle with parsley and serve hot.

Chicken in Lemon and Herb Sauce

SERVES 4

Per Serving:

Calories	235
Fat	11g
Protein	35g
Sodium	371mg
Fiber	0g
Carbohydrates	0g
Sugar	0g

There is a reason that herbs, lemon, and chicken have been a trinity for so long—they just taste so good together. Add the Instant Pot® to this threesome, and you'll get bright, fresh flavors and tender, moist chicken in minutes.

2 tablespoons olive oil
1 pound boneless, skinless chicken breast, cut in 1" pieces
½ cup low-sodium chicken broth
2 tablespoons lemon juice
2 cloves garlic, peeled and minced
2 teaspoons Dijon mustard
1 tablespoon Italian seasoning
½ teaspoon salt
1 tablespoon grated lemon zest
¼ cup chopped fresh parsley

1 Press the Sauté button on the Instant Pot® and heat oil. Add chicken and cook for about 4 minutes or until lightly browned on all sides. Stir in broth, lemon juice, garlic, mustard, Italian seasoning, and salt. Press the Cancel button.

2 Close lid, set steam release to Sealing, press the Poultry button, and cook for the default time of 15 minutes. When the timer beeps, let pressure release naturally for 10 minutes. Quick-release any remaining pressure until the float valve drops and then open lid. Check chicken using a meat thermometer to ensure the internal temperature is at least 165°F. Transfer chicken to a serving platter. Press the Cancel button.

3 Press the Sauté button, press the Adjust button to change the temperature to Less, and simmer uncovered for 5 minutes to thicken sauce, then pour sauce over chicken.

4 Garnish with lemon zest and chopped parsley. Serve warm.

Herbed Turkey Breast with Mushroom Gravy

If you don't have time to prepare an entire Thanksgiving feast, make this recipe, which provides the holiday flavors in about an hour.

SERVES 8	
Per Serving:	
Calories	222
Fat	15g
Protein	7g
Sodium	682mg
Fiber	1g
Carbohydrates	22g
Sugar	7g

1 tablespoon olive oil

3 tablespoons unsalted room temperature butter, divided

1 large sweet onion, peeled and diced

1 pound button mushrooms, sliced

4 cloves garlic, peeled and minced

2 teaspoons Mrs. Dash Garlic & Herb Seasoning Blend

1 (2-pound) boneless rolled turkey breast

1¾ cups low-sodium chicken broth

½ cup sweet Madeira or port wine

1 bay leaf

¼ cup all-purpose flour

½ teaspoon salt

½ teaspoon ground black pepper

1 Press the Sauté button on the Instant Pot® and heat oil and 1 tablespoon butter. Add onion and cook until tender, about 3 minutes.

2 Add mushrooms and cook for 3 minutes. Stir in garlic and seasoning blend. Push sautéed vegetables to the sides of the pot and add turkey breast.

3 Brown turkey for 3 minutes per side. Use tongs to lift turkey out of pot. Spread sautéed mixture over the bottom of the pot and then insert rack.

4 Nestle turkey on the rack. Add broth, Madeira, and bay leaf. Press the Cancel button.

5 Close lid, set steam release to Sealing, press the Manual button, and set time to 25 minutes. When the timer beeps, let pressure release naturally, about 20 minutes. Press the Cancel button.

6 Open the lid and transfer turkey to a serving platter. Tent turkey in aluminum foil and let it rest for at least 10 minutes before you carve it.

7 While the turkey rests, remove the rack from pot. Remove and discard bay leaf. Skim off any excess fat from the top of broth.

8 In a small bowl or measuring cup, mix remaining 2 tablespoons butter with flour. Stir in some of the broth to form a paste free of any lumps.

9 Press the Sauté button. Bring pan juices in the Instant Pot® to a boil. Stir in flour mixture, and stir and cook for 3 minutes or until gravy is thickened. Season with salt and pepper, and pour into a gravy boat. Serve turkey and gravy hot.

Curried Chicken and Lentil Salad

This main dish salad gets its salt from the roasted cashews. If you're using unsalted cashews, you may need to add some salt or have it available at the table.

SERVES 8

Per Serving:	
Calories	404
Fat	18g
Protein	41g
Sodium	177mg
Fiber	3g
Carbohydrates	21g
Sugar	10g

SWEETEN THE DRESSING

Cooking the apples with the lentils cuts some of the heat of the curry powder. The raw apple and grapes in the salad will also sweeten the curry powder taste. But if you still find the taste of the curry powder in the dressing too strong, stir a little sugar, honey, or applesauce into the dressing to soften the taste.

1 teaspoon olive oil
2 pounds boneless, skinless chicken breasts, cut into ½" pieces
1 cup dried lentils, rinsed and drained
2 cups water
2½ teaspoons curry powder, divided
2 small Golden Delicious apples, divided
1 teaspoon lemon juice
2 cups halved seedless grapes
1 cup roasted salted cashews
2 stalks celery, diced
½ small red onion, peeled and diced
¾ cup plain low-fat yogurt
¼ cup mayonnaise
11 ounces baby salad greens

1   Press the Sauté button on the Instant Pot® and heat oil. Add chicken and cook for 5 minutes or until browned. Stir in lentils, water, and 1 teaspoon curry powder. Halve one of the apples; core and dice 1 half and add it to the pot. Coat the cut side of the other half of the apple with lemon juice to prevent it from turning brown and set aside. Press the Cancel button.

2   Close lid, set steam release to Sealing, press the Manual button, and set time to 8 minutes. When the timer beeps, let pressure release naturally, about 20 minutes. Open lid.

3   Transfer the contents of the Instant Pot® to a large bowl and set aside to cool.

4   Dice reserved apple half, and core and dice remaining apple. Add to chicken and lentil mixture along with grapes, cashews, celery, and red onion.

5   In a small bowl, mix together yogurt, mayonnaise, and remaining 1½ teaspoons curry powder. Drizzle over chicken and lentil mixture, and stir to combine. Serve over salad greens.

Turkey Breast Romano

You can substitute chicken breast tenders in this recipe if you are not able to find boneless turkey breast. Serve with a crisp green salad and toasted crusty bread.

½ cup all-purpose flour
½ teaspoon salt
½ teaspoon ground black pepper
2 pounds boneless, skinless turkey breast, cut into bite-sized pieces
2 tablespoons olive oil
1 large sweet onion, peeled and diced
4 cloves garlic, peeled and minced
1 tablespoon dried oregano
1 teaspoon dried basil
2 tablespoons tomato paste
½ cup low-sodium chicken broth
1 (8-ounce) can tomato sauce
1 teaspoon balsamic vinegar
2 (4-ounce) cans sliced mushrooms, drained
1 tablespoon sugar
1 pound spaghetti, cooked
8 ounces Romano cheese, grated

SERVES 8	
Per Serving:	
Calories	498
Fat	11g
Protein	47g
Sodium	734mg
Fiber	4g
Carbohydrates	53g
Sugar	6g

1 Place flour, salt, and pepper in a large zip-top plastic bag. Seal and shake to mix. Add turkey to the bag, seal, and shake to coat turkey in flour mixture.

2 Press the Sauté button on the Instant Pot® and heat oil. Add turkey and onion, and cook until turkey begins to brown and onion is translucent, about 5 minutes.

3 Stir in garlic, oregano, basil, and tomato paste, and cook for 2 minutes. Stir in broth, tomato sauce, vinegar, mushrooms, and sugar. Press the Cancel button.

4 Close lid, set steam release to Sealing, press the Manual button, and set time to 12 minutes. When the timer beeps, let pressure release naturally for 10 minutes.

5 Quick-release any remaining pressure until the float valve drops. Open lid and stir turkey and sauce, pour over pasta, and top with grated Romano cheese.

Whole Roasted Chicken with Herbs

SERVES 6

Per Serving:	
Calories	498
Fat	11g
Protein	47g
Sodium	768mg
Fiber	4g
Carbohydrates	53g
Sugar	6g

You might not think that an Instant Pot® would be an effective roaster, but it is! Make sure you brown the bird well on all sides before cooking so there is some color to the skin.

1 tablespoon unsalted butter, softened
1 teaspoon poultry seasoning
1 teaspoon salt, divided
½ teaspoon ground black pepper
1 (4-pound) whole chicken
2 tablespoons olive oil
1 medium lemon, halved
5 sprigs fresh thyme
4 sprigs fresh sage
1 branch fresh rosemary, broken in half
1 medium yellow onion, peeled and quartered
1 cup low-sodium chicken broth

1 In a small bowl, combine butter, poultry seasoning, ½ teaspoon salt, and pepper. Separate skin from chicken breast by hand and spread seasoned butter under skin. Season outside of the bird with remaining ½ teaspoon salt.

2 Press the Sauté button on the Instant Pot® and heat oil. Add chicken breast side down and brown 6 minutes. Flip and brown back of bird 4 minutes. Remove from pot. Press the Cancel button.

3 Add juice from half of lemon to pot, then place rack in pot. Add thyme, sage, rosemary, 1 juiced lemon half, and two pieces onion to cavity of chicken. Add remaining lemon half and onion to pot and pour in broth.

4 Place chicken breast side up on rack. Close lid, set steam release to Sealing, press the Manual button, and set time to 25 minutes.

5 When the timer beeps, let the pressure release naturally, about 20 minutes. Press the Cancel button and open lid. Carefully transfer bird to a serving platter. Serve hot.

CHAPTER 13

Pork, Lamb, and Beef

Mediterranean Braised Lamb Shanks

SERVES 4	
Per Serving:	
Calories	636
Fat	27g
Protein	72g
Sodium	1,186mg
Fiber	9g
Carbohydrates	20g
Sugar	5g

This is a meal to be savored, so take your time and enjoy it. Serve with a tossed salad, baked potatoes, whole-wheat dinner rolls, and of course, a glass of red wine.

¼ cup all-purpose flour
¼ teaspoon salt
¼ teaspoon ground black pepper
4 (12-ounce) lamb shanks
1 tablespoon olive oil
1 large carrot, peeled and diced
1 medium onion, peeled and diced
2 cloves garlic, peeled and minced
1 tablespoon herbes de Provence

1 (14.5-ounce) can diced tomatoes
½ cup dry white wine
½ cup chicken or beef broth
1 bay leaf
1 (12-ounce) jar pimiento-stuffed olives, drained
1 (8-ounce) package frozen artichokes, thawed

1 Add flour, salt, and pepper to a large zip-top plastic bag. Shake to mix. Add lamb shanks to the bag, seal, and shake to coat them in flour mixture.

2 Press the Sauté button on the Instant Pot® and heat oil. Remove 2 lamb shanks from the bag, shaking off any excess flour, and add to the pot. Brown on all sides, about 3 minutes per side. Transfer to a platter and keep warm. Repeat with remaining 2 lamb shanks.

3 Add carrot to pot and cook until just tender, about 1 minute. Add onion and cook for 3 minutes, or until onion begins to soften. Stir in garlic and cook until fragrant, about 30 seconds. Stir in herbes de Provence, undrained tomatoes, wine, broth, and bay leaf. Press the Cancel button.

4 Return lamb and juices to the Instant Pot®. Close lid, set steam release to Sealing, press the Manual button, and set time to 25 minutes. When the timer beeps, let pressure release naturally for 10 minutes. Quick-release any remaining pressure until the float valve drops. Press the Cancel button and open lid.

5 Transfer lamb shanks to a large ovenproof platter and tent loosely with aluminum foil. Place in a warm (200°F) oven.

6 Press the Sauté button and bring the pan juices to a simmer. Stir in olives and artichokes. Simmer, stirring occasionally, for 15 minutes. Remove and discard bay leaf.

7 Remove lamb shanks from the oven, uncover, and pour sauce over lamb shanks. Serve.

Herbs and Lamb Stew

Cooking with fresh herbs gives this dish a bright flavor. If you can't find fresh herbs, you can swap them for ½ teaspoon of dried herbs. Remember, dried herbs are always more concentrated and more potent than fresh ones.

1 pound boneless lamb shoulder, trimmed and cut into 1" pieces
2 tablespoons all-purpose flour
¼ teaspoon salt
¼ teaspoon ground black pepper
2 tablespoons olive oil, divided
2 medium carrots, peeled and sliced
2 stalks celery, sliced
1 medium onion, peeled and chopped
3 cloves garlic, peeled and minced
4 thyme sprigs
1 sprig rosemary
2 tablespoons chopped fresh oregano
1 bay leaf
2 cups low-sodium chicken broth
1 cup tomato sauce
1 medium russet potato, cut into 1" pieces
¼ cup chopped fresh parsley

SERVES 8	
Per Serving:	
Calories	222
Fat	11g
Protein	18g
Sodium	285mg
Fiber	2g
Carbohydrates	11g
Sugar	6g

1 In a medium bowl, add lamb, flour, salt, and pepper. Toss until lamb is thoroughly coated. Set aside.

2 Press the Sauté button on the Instant Pot® and heat 1 tablespoon oil. Add half of the lamb pieces in a single layer, leaving space between each piece to prevent steaming, and brown well on all sides, about 3 minutes per side. Transfer lamb to a large bowl and repeat with remaining 1 tablespoon oil and lamb.

3 Add carrots, celery, and onion to the pot. Cook until tender, about 8 minutes. Add garlic and cook until fragrant, about 30 seconds. Add thyme, rosemary, oregano, and bay leaf. Stir well.

4 Slowly add chicken broth, scraping the bottom of the pot well to release any brown bits. Add tomato sauce, potato, and browned lamb along with any juices. Press the Cancel button.

5 Close lid, set steam release to Sealing, press the Stew button, and set time to 40 minutes. When the timer beeps, quick-release the pressure until the float valve drops, open lid, and stir well. Remove and discard thyme, rosemary, and bay leaf. Sprinkle with parsley and serve hot.

Minty Lamb Meatballs in Spicy Red Pepper Ragu

These meatballs make a fantastic appetizer or party snack. You can also slice them and use them as a topping for flatbread topped with some crumbled feta cheese.

1 pound ground lamb
1 large egg
½ cup plus 1 tablespoon chopped fresh mint, divided
¼ cup bread crumbs
2 tablespoons minced white onion
¼ teaspoon salt
¼ teaspoon ground black pepper
2 tablespoons light olive oil, divided
2 medium red bell peppers, seeded and chopped
2 cloves garlic, peeled and minced
¼ teaspoon crushed red pepper flakes
1 tablespoon chopped fresh oregano
1 (14.5-ounce) can diced tomatoes, drained
¼ cup water

1 In a medium bowl, combine lamb, egg, ½ cup mint, bread crumbs, onion, salt, and black pepper. Form into 16 golf ball–sized meatballs. Set aside.

2 Press the Sauté button on the Instant Pot® and heat 1 tablespoon oil. Place half of the meatballs around the edges of the Instant Pot®. Sear all sides of meatballs for a total of 4 minutes. Remove first batch and set aside. Add remaining 1 tablespoon oil and meatballs, and sear 4 minutes. Remove meatballs.

3 Add bell peppers to the Instant Pot® and cook until tender, about 5 minutes. Add garlic and red pepper flakes and cook until garlic is fragrant, about 30 seconds. Add oregano, tomatoes, water, and remaining 1 tablespoon mint to the Instant Pot®, and stir well. Press the Cancel button.

4 Top red pepper mixture with browned meatballs. Close lid, set steam release to Sealing, press the Manual button, and set time to 3 minutes. When the timer beeps, quick-release the pressure until the float valve drops and open lid. Transfer meatballs and sauce to bowls and serve warm.

Quinoa Pilaf–Stuffed Pork

Served with plenty of fresh vegetables, this pork dish would make a welcome addition to a holiday table or special occasion.

1 (1½-pound) pork tenderloin
2 tablespoons olive oil, divided
1 clove garlic, peeled and minced
½ medium tomato, diced
¼ cup chopped fresh flat-leaf parsley
1 tablespoon lemon juice
½ cup quinoa, rinsed and drained
2 cups water, divided
¼ cup crumbled goat cheese
¼ teaspoon salt

SERVES 6	
Per Serving:	
Calories	207
Fat	9g
Protein	25g
Sodium	525mg
Fiber	1g
Carbohydrates	11g
Sugar	0g

1 Butterfly pork tenderloin. Open tenderloin and top with a sheet of plastic wrap. Pound pork out to ½" thick. Wrap and refrigerate until ready to use.

2 Press the Sauté button on the Instant Pot® and heat 1 tablespoon oil. Add garlic and cook 30 seconds, then add tomato, parsley, and lemon juice. Cook an additional minute. Transfer mixture to a small bowl. Press the Cancel button.

3 Add quinoa and 1 cup water to the pot. Close lid, set steam release to Sealing, press the Multigrain button, and set time to 20 minutes. When the timer beeps, let pressure release naturally, about 20 minutes, then open lid. Press the Cancel button. Fluff quinoa with a fork. Transfer quinoa to bowl with tomato mixture and mix well.

4 Spread quinoa mixture over pork. Top with goat cheese. Season with salt. Roll pork over filling. Tie pork every 2" with butcher's twine to secure.

5 Press Sauté on the Instant Pot® and heat remaining 1 tablespoon oil. Brown pork on all sides, about 2 minutes per side. Press the Cancel button. Remove pork and clean out pot. Return to machine, add remaining 1 cup water, place rack in pot, and place pork on rack.

6 Close lid, set steam release to Sealing, Press the Manual button, and set time to 20 minutes. When the timer beeps, quick-release the pressure until the float valve drops. Open lid and transfer pork to cutting board. Let rest for 10 minutes, then remove twine and cut into 1" slices. Serve hot.

Balsamic Beef and Vegetable Stew

This rich stew is perfect for cold days when you need something comforting to warm you from the inside out. Use the leftover stew to make a delicious lunch the next day as well.

SERVES 8

Per Serving:

Calories	332
Fat	17g
Protein	16g
Sodium	404mg
Fiber	5g
Carbohydrates	15g
Sugar	6g

TAKE A WALK

Taking a 30-minute walk every day, an exercise that almost anyone can do, offers major improvements to your health. Walking is also an excellent opportunity for social activity, so round up your friends and family and, while your stew is cooking, take a turn around the neighborhood. It will help the time pass while you wait for dinner, allow you to connect with your friends and family, and improve your cardiovascular health.

1 pound beef stew meat, cut into 1" pieces
2 tablespoons all-purpose flour
¼ teaspoon salt
¼ teaspoon ground black pepper
2 tablespoons olive oil, divided
2 medium carrots, peeled and sliced
2 stalks celery, sliced
1 medium onion, peeled and chopped
8 ounces whole crimini mushrooms, quartered
3 cloves garlic, peeled and minced
4 sprigs thyme
2 tablespoons chopped fresh oregano
2 bay leaves
¼ cup balsamic vinegar
1½ cups beef broth
1 (14.5-ounce) can diced tomatoes, drained
1 medium russet potato, cut into 1" pieces
1 (6-ounce) can large black olives, drained and quartered
¼ cup chopped fresh parsley

1 In a medium bowl, add beef, flour, salt, and pepper. Toss meat with seasoned flour until thoroughly coated. Set aside.

2 Press the Sauté button on the Instant Pot® and heat 1 tablespoon oil. Place half of the beef pieces in a single layer, leaving space between each piece to prevent steaming, and brown well on all sides, about 3 minutes per side. Transfer beef to a medium bowl and repeat with remaining 1 tablespoon oil and beef.

3 Add carrots, celery, and onion to the pot. Cook until tender, about 8 minutes. Add mushrooms, garlic, thyme, oregano, and bay leaves. Stir well.

4 Slowly add balsamic vinegar and beef broth, scraping bottom of pot well to release any brown bits. Add tomatoes, potato, and browned beef along with any juices. Press the Cancel button.

5 Close lid, set steam release to Sealing, press the Stew button, and set time to 40 minutes. When the timer beeps, quick-release the pressure until the float valve drops, open lid, and stir well. Remove and discard thyme and bay leaves. Stir in olives and parsley. Serve immediately.

Balsamic Pork Tenderloin

Cipollini onions are small and mild sweet onions that were at one time found only in fancy restaurants. Today, they are available in most produce departments. If you can't find them, swap them for sweet onions cut into 1" pieces.

2 pounds pork tenderloin, cut into 1" pieces
¼ teaspoon salt
¼ teaspoon ground black pepper
2 tablespoons olive oil
1 medium carrot, peeled and sliced
2 cloves garlic, peeled and minced
2 sprigs thyme
1 sprig rosemary
½ cup balsamic vinegar
¼ cup water
1 pound cipollini onions, peeled
2 tablespoons cornstarch
¼ cup chopped fresh parsley

SERVES 6	
Per Serving:	
Calories	331
Fat	10g
Protein	29g
Sodium	840mg
Fiber	1g
Carbohydrates	18g
Sugar	5g

1 In a medium bowl, toss pork with salt and pepper until thoroughly coated. Set aside.

2 Press the Sauté button on the Instant Pot® and heat oil. Add carrot and cook until tender, about 5 minutes. Add garlic, thyme, and rosemary, and stir well.

3 Slowly add balsamic vinegar and water, scraping bottom of pot well to release any brown bits. Add cipollini and pork, and stir to combine. Press the Cancel button.

4 Close lid, set steam release to Sealing, press the Stew button, and set time to 30 minutes. When the timer beeps, quick-release the pressure until the float valve drops, open lid, and stir well. Remove and discard thyme and rosemary. Press the Cancel button.

5 Remove ¼ cup liquid from pot and whisk in cornstarch. Stir mixture back into pot. Press the Sauté button and bring sauce to a boil to thicken, about 4 minutes. Press the Cancel button. Remove pork and sauce. Sprinkle with parsley and serve hot.

One-Pot Pork Loin Dinner

SERVES 6

Per Serving:

Calories	271
Fat	4g
Protein	14g
Sodium	316mg
Fiber	5g
Carbohydrates	30g
Sugar	7g

One of the joys of cooking in the Instant Pot® is that you can do all the cooking in one pot. Serve this dinner with warm bread and a tossed green salad.

1 tablespoon olive oil
1 small onion, peeled and diced
1 pound boneless pork loin, cut into 1" pieces
½ teaspoon salt
¼ teaspoon ground black pepper
½ cup white wine
1 cup low-sodium chicken broth
1 large rutabaga, peeled and diced
1 large turnip, peeled and diced
4 small Yukon Gold or red potatoes, quartered
4 medium carrots, peeled and diced
1 stalk celery, finely diced
½ cup sliced leeks, white part only
½ teaspoon mild curry powder
¼ teaspoon dried thyme
2 teaspoons dried parsley
3 tablespoons lemon juice
2 large Granny Smith apples, peeled, cored, and diced

1 Press the Sauté button on the Instant Pot® and heat oil. Add onion and cook until tender, about 3 minutes. Add pork and season with salt and pepper. Cook until pork begins to brown, about 5 minutes. Add wine, broth, rutabaga, and turnip and stir well. Add potatoes, carrots, celery, leeks, curry powder, thyme, parsley, and lemon juice to the pot. Stir to combine. Press the Cancel button.

2 Close lid, set steam release to Sealing, press the Manual button, and set time to 15 minutes. When the timer beeps, let pressure release naturally, about 25 minutes. Press the Cancel button.

3 Open lid and add diced apples. Press the Sauté button and simmer for 5 minutes or until apples are tender. Serve immediately in large bowls.

Ground Pork and Eggplant Casserole

Ground black pepper contains anticaking agents, additives that can cause stomach upset for some people and can also change the flavor of the dish. That's why food always tastes better when you grind the pepper yourself. Serve with a tossed salad and toasted garlic bread.

2 pounds lean ground pork
1 large yellow onion, peeled and diced
1 stalk celery, diced
1 medium green bell pepper, seeded and diced
2 medium eggplants, cut into ½" pieces
4 cloves garlic, peeled and minced
⅛ teaspoon dried thyme
1 tablespoon freeze-dried parsley
3 tablespoons tomato paste
½ teaspoon hot sauce
2 teaspoons Worcestershire sauce
1 teaspoon salt
½ teaspoon ground black pepper
1 large egg, beaten
½ cup low-sodium chicken broth

SERVES 8	
Per Serving:	
Calories	292
Fat	18g
Protein	22g
Sodium	392mg
Fiber	4g
Carbohydrates	10g
Sugar	5g

1 Press the Sauté button on the Instant Pot® and add pork, onion, celery, and bell pepper to the pot. Cook until pork is no longer pink, breaking it apart as it cooks, about 8 minutes.

2 Drain and discard any fat rendered from pork. Add eggplant, garlic, thyme, parsley, tomato paste, hot sauce, Worcestershire sauce, salt, pepper, and egg. Stir well, then press the Cancel button.

3 Pour in chicken broth. Close lid, set steam release to Sealing, press the Manual button, and set time to 10 minutes. When the timer beeps, let pressure release naturally, about 25 minutes. Open lid and serve hot.

Pork Tenderloin with Vegetable Ragu

If you like, serve this hearty dish with balsamic vinegar and grated Parmesan cheese so your guests can add more flavor to their own plates. A loaf of crusty bread would also be a nice addition to the meal.

2 tablespoons light olive oil, divided
1 (1½-pound) pork tenderloin
¼ teaspoon salt
¼ teaspoon ground black pepper
1 medium zucchini, trimmed and sliced
1 medium yellow squash, sliced
1 medium onion, peeled and chopped
1 medium carrot, peeled and grated
1 (14.5-ounce) can diced tomatoes, drained
2 cloves garlic, peeled and minced
¼ teaspoon crushed red pepper flakes
1 tablespoon chopped fresh basil
1 tablespoon chopped fresh oregano
1 sprig fresh thyme
½ cup red wine

1   Press the Sauté button on the Instant Pot® and heat 1 tablespoon oil. Season pork with salt and black pepper. Brown pork lightly on all sides, about 2 minutes per side. Transfer pork to a plate and set aside.

2   Add remaining 1 tablespoon oil to the pot. Add zucchini and squash, and cook until tender, about 5 minutes. Add onion and carrot, and cook until just softened, about 5 minutes. Add tomatoes, garlic, crushed red pepper flakes, basil, oregano, thyme, and red wine to pot, and stir well. Press the Cancel button.

3   Top vegetable mixture with browned pork. Close lid, set steam release to Sealing, press the Manual button, and set time to 3 minutes. When the timer beeps, quick-release the pressure until the float valve drops and open lid. Transfer pork to a cutting board and cut into 1" slices. Pour sauce on a serving platter and arrange pork slices on top. Serve immediately.

Caldo Verde

This version of the Portuguese classic green soup has less sausage and more kale, so you can feel good about enjoying as much of this soup as you like.

3 tablespoons olive oil

6 ounces Spanish chorizo or Portuguese chouriço, sliced

6 cups chopped kale

6 medium Yukon Gold potatoes, cut into 1" pieces

1 medium white onion, peeled and chopped

1 clove garlic, peeled and minced

½ teaspoon salt

½ teaspoon ground black pepper

1 bay leaf

4 cups water

SERVES 6	
Per Serving:	
Calories	381
Fat	17g
Protein	16g
Sodium	475mg
Fiber	3g
Carbohydrates	45g
Sugar	2g

1 Press the Sauté button on the Instant Pot® and heat oil. Add chorizo and cook until edges of sausage start to brown, about 5 minutes. Drain off excess fat and return pot to machine. Add kale and stir to mix with chorizo. Add potatoes, onion, garlic, salt, pepper, bay leaf, and water, and stir well. Press the Cancel button.

2 Close lid, set steam release to Sealing, press the Manual button, and set time to 6 minutes. When the timer beeps, let pressure release naturally, about 15 minutes, then press the Cancel button. Open lid and remove and discard bay leaf. Serve hot.

Spaghetti with Meaty Mushroom Sauce

This spaghetti dish has a bold, meaty flavor but uses half the beef of most traditional recipes. Mushrooms add extra flavor, richness, and a hearty texture to the sauce.

SERVES 6

Per Serving:

Calories	188
Fat	7g
Protein	23g
Sodium	595mg
Fiber	2g
Carbohydrates	8g
Sugar	3g

BUYING MARINARA SAUCE

Using jarred marinara and pasta sauce is quick and easy, but be sure to check that label! Look for an ingredient list that is short and easy to read. It should not include sugar, corn syrup, high-fructose corn syrup, or other forms of added sweeteners. Also avoid jarred sauces that do not use olive oil. Some companies will use cheaper oils instead of heart-healthy olive oil. Spending a little time in the pasta sauce section checking labels will lead to a higher-quality sauce for you and your family.

1 tablespoon olive oil
1 medium onion, peeled and diced
1 pound sliced crimini mushrooms
½ pound 90% lean ground beef
1 (14.5-ounce) can fire-roasted tomatoes, drained
1 clove garlic, peeled and minced
½ teaspoon ground fennel
2 sprigs thyme
2 sprigs oregano
1 pound spaghetti, broken in half
1 (25-ounce) jar marinara sauce
2 cups low-sodium chicken broth
1 cup grated Parmesan cheese

1 Press the Sauté button on the Instant Pot® and heat oil. Add onion and mushrooms, and cook until vegetables are tender, about 10 minutes. Add beef and cook, crumbling well, until no longer pink, about 5 minutes. Add tomatoes, garlic, fennel, thyme, and oregano. Stir well, then press the Cancel button.

2 Add spaghetti, sauce, and broth, and stir well. Close lid, set steam release to Sealing, press the Manual button, and set time to 8 minutes.

3 When the timer beeps, quick-release the pressure until the float valve drops, open lid, and stir well. Top with cheese and serve hot.

Greek Meatballs in Tomato Sauce

SERVES 8

Per Serving:	
Calories	334
Fat	13g
Protein	21g
Sodium	299mg
Fiber	1g
Carbohydrates	31g
Sugar	3g

You can serve the meatballs and sauce over pasta, beans, or a combination of both. Serve with pita bread and with a salad tossed in a lemon and olive oil vinaigrette, sprinkled with some feta cheese.

½ cup all-purpose flour
1½ pounds lean ground beef or lamb
1 cup rice
1 small yellow onion, peeled and diced
3 cloves garlic, peeled and minced
2 teaspoons dried parsley
½ tablespoon dried oregano
1 large egg
2 cups tomato juice
1 (14.5-ounce) can diced tomatoes
2 tablespoons extra-virgin olive oil
½ teaspoon salt
½ teaspoon ground black pepper

1 Place flour in a shallow dish and set aside.

2 In a large bowl, mix ground beef or lamb together with rice, onion, garlic, parsley, oregano, and egg. Shape into small meatballs and roll each one in flour.

3 Add tomato juice and diced tomatoes to the Instant Pot®. Carefully add meatballs. If necessary, pour in enough water to completely cover the meatballs, making sure not to take the liquid above the fill line. Add oil.

4 Close lid, set steam release to Sealing, press the Manual button, and set time to 10 minutes. When the timer beeps, let pressure release naturally for 10 minutes. Quick-release any remaining pressure until the float valve drops and open lid. Season with salt and pepper, and serve immediately.

Pork and White Bean Chili

Tender chunks of pork and creamy beans make this chili deeply satisfying. If you do not like pork, replace it with beef stew meat or boneless, skinless chicken thighs.

1 cup dried cannellini beans, soaked overnight and drained
1 (1-pound) pork loin roast, cut into 1" pieces
4 cups vegetable broth
½ cup chopped fresh cilantro
2 cloves garlic, peeled and minced
1 tablespoon olive oil
1 tablespoon chili powder
1 teaspoon ground cumin
1 teaspoon ground coriander
½ teaspoon salt
½ teaspoon ground black pepper
1 (10-ounce) can tomatoes with green chilies, drained

1 Add beans, pork, broth, cilantro, garlic, oil, chili powder, cumin, coriander, salt, and pepper to the Instant Pot®, and stir well. Close lid, set steam release to Sealing, press the Manual button, and set time to 30 minutes. When the timer beeps, quick-release the pressure until the float valve drops, open lid, and stir. Press the Cancel button.

2 Press the Sauté button, then press the Adjust button to change the temperature to Less. Add tomatoes and simmer uncovered for 10 minutes. Serve hot.

SERVES 6	
Per Serving:	
Calories	250
Fat	9g
Protein	27g
Sodium	859mg
Fiber	3g
Carbohydrates	15g
Sugar	3g

Balsamic Pork Chops with Figs and Pears

SERVES 2	
Per Serving:	
Calories	672
Fat	32g
Protein	27g
Sodium	773mg
Fiber	13g
Carbohydrates	68g
Sugar	36g

The flavors in this recipe are so sophisticated that your guests will never know you took less than 30 minutes to whip up this juicy master-piece. Figs—a superfood high in potassium and fiber—are one of those underused fruits that pair so nicely with pork chops and a good wine. You may never pay for fine dining again!

2 (8-ounce) bone-in pork chops
½ teaspoon salt
1 teaspoon ground black pepper
¼ cup balsamic vinegar
¼ cup low-sodium chicken broth
1 tablespoon dried mint
2 tablespoons olive oil
1 medium sweet onion, peeled and sliced
3 medium pears, peeled, cored, and chopped
5 dried figs, stems removed and halved

1 Pat pork chops dry with a paper towel and season both sides with salt and pepper. Set aside.

2 In a small bowl, whisk together vinegar, broth, and mint. Set aside.

3 Press the Sauté button on the Instant Pot® and heat oil. Brown pork chops for 5 minutes per side. Remove chops and set aside.

4 Add vinegar mixture and scrape any brown bits from sides and bottom of pot. Layer onion slices in the pot, then scatter pears and figs over slices. Place pork chops on top. Press the Cancel button.

5 Close lid, set steam release to Sealing, press the Steam button, and set time to 3 minutes. When the timer beeps, let pressure release naturally for 10 minutes. Quick-release any remaining pressure until the float valve drops and then open lid.

6 Using a slotted spoon, transfer pork, onion, figs, and pears to a serving platter. Serve warm.

Beef Stew with Red Wine

If you find the stew thinner than you like, press the Sauté button and let the stew simmer until it reaches your preferred thickness. Usually, simmering for 10 minutes will thicken most soups and stews sufficiently.

1 pound beef stew meat, cut into 1" pieces
2 tablespoons all-purpose flour
¼ teaspoon salt
¼ teaspoon ground black pepper
2 tablespoons olive oil, divided
1 pound whole crimini mushrooms
2 cloves garlic, peeled and minced
4 sprigs thyme
2 bay leaves
8 ounces baby carrots
8 ounces frozen pearl onions, thawed
1 cup red wine
½ cup beef broth
¼ cup chopped fresh parsley

SERVES 8	
Per Serving:	
Calories	206
Fat	13g
Protein	12g
Sodium	186mg
Fiber	1g
Carbohydrates	6g
Sugar	3g

1 In a medium bowl, toss beef with flour, salt, and pepper until thoroughly coated. Set aside.

2 Press the Sauté button on the Instant Pot® and heat 1 tablespoon oil. Add half of the beef pieces in a single layer, leaving space between each piece to prevent steaming, and brown well on all sides, about 3 minutes per side. Transfer beef to a medium bowl and repeat with remaining 1 tablespoon oil and beef. Press the Cancel button.

3 Add mushrooms, garlic, thyme, bay leaves, carrots, onions, wine, and broth to the Instant Pot®. Stir well. Close lid, set steam release to Sealing, press the Stew button, and set time to 40 minutes. When the timer beeps, quick-release the pressure until the float valve drops, open lid, and stir well. Remove and discard thyme and bay leaves. Sprinkle with parsley and serve hot.

Green Beans with Pork and Tomatoes

SERVES 8	
Per Serving:	
Calories	165
Fat	11g
Protein	7g
Sodium	483mg
Fiber	5g
Carbohydrates	11g
Sugar	4g

This lighter take on Southern-style green beans swaps out fatty bacon for leaner ground pork.

1 cup water
1 teaspoon salt
2 pounds fresh green beans, trimmed
2 tablespoons olive oil
½ pound ground pork
1 medium onion, peeled and chopped

2 cups halved cherry tomatoes
1 clove garlic, peeled and minced
1 teaspoon packed light brown sugar
½ teaspoon dry mustard powder
¼ teaspoon smoked paprika
¼ teaspoon ground black pepper

1 Add water and salt to the Instant Pot®, and insert steamer basket. Add green beans to basket. Close lid, set steam release to Sealing, press the Manual button, and set time to 1 minute. When the timer beeps, quick-release the pressure until the float valve drops. Press the Cancel button and open lid. Transfer to a medium bowl, remove basket, and clean out pot.

2 Press the Sauté button and heat oil in the Instant Pot®. Add pork and sauté 5 minutes. Add onion and sauté 3 minutes. Add tomatoes, garlic, brown sugar, dry mustard, paprika, and pepper. Cook 30 seconds. Add green beans to pot and toss to coat. Serve hot.

Pork and Cabbage Egg Roll in a Bowl

SERVES 6	
Per Serving:	
Calories	283
Fat	24g
Protein	12g
Sodium	507mg
Fiber	2g
Carbohydrates	5g
Sugar	3g

This recipe is made with the same ingredients that would be used to fill egg rolls. This version uses ground pork, but you can substitute ground beef or ground chicken, or use meat-free soy crumbles.

1 tablespoon light olive oil
1 pound ground pork
1 medium yellow onion, peeled and chopped
1 clove garlic, peeled and minced
2 teaspoons minced fresh ginger

¼ cup low-sodium chicken broth
2 tablespoons soy sauce
2 (10-ounce) bags shredded coleslaw mix
1 teaspoon sesame oil
1 teaspoon garlic chili sauce

1 Press the Sauté button on the Instant Pot® and heat olive oil. Add pork and sauté until cooked through, about 8 minutes. Add onion, garlic, and ginger, and cook until fragrant, about 2 minutes. Stir in chicken broth and soy sauce. Press the Cancel button.

2 Spread coleslaw mix over pork, but do not mix. Close lid, set steam release to Sealing, press the Manual button, and set time to 0 minutes.

3 When the timer beeps, quick-release the pressure until the float valve drops and open lid. Stir in sesame oil and garlic chili sauce. Serve hot.

Beef and Mushroom Stroganoff

The classic stroganoff has a sour cream sauce, but this version uses Greek yogurt instead. The result has the same tang and creaminess as sour cream, but with fewer calories and more protein.

2 tablespoons olive oil
1 medium onion, peeled and chopped
2 cloves garlic, peeled and minced
1 pound beef stew meat, cut into 1" pieces
3 tablespoons all-purpose flour
¼ teaspoon salt
¼ teaspoon ground black pepper
2 cups beef broth
1 pound sliced button mushrooms
1 pound wide egg noodles
½ cup low-fat plain Greek yogurt

SERVES 6	
Per Serving:	
Calories	446
Fat	13g
Protein	19g
Sodium	721mg
Fiber	4g
Carbohydrates	63g
Sugar	5g

1 Press the Sauté button on the Instant Pot® and heat oil. Add onion and cook until soft, about 5 minutes. Add garlic and cook until fragrant, about 30 seconds.

2 Combine beef, flour, salt, and pepper in a medium bowl and toss to coat beef completely. Add beef to the pot and cook, stirring often, until browned, about 10 minutes. Stir in beef broth and scrape any brown bits from bottom of pot. Stir in mushrooms and press the Cancel button.

3 Close lid, set steam release to Sealing, press the Manual button, and set time to 10 minutes. When the timer beeps, quick-release the pressure until the float valve drops, open lid, and stir well. Press the Cancel button.

4 Add noodles and stir, making sure noodles are submerged in liquid. Close lid, set steam release to Sealing, press the Manual button, and set time to 5 minutes.

5 When the timer beeps, quick-release the pressure until the float valve drops. Open lid and stir well. Press the Cancel button and cool for 5 minutes, then stir in yogurt. Serve hot.

Bulgur and Beef–Stuffed Peppers

If you prefer, you can bake these peppers in the oven. Place them in a baking dish, top with the cheese, and bake at 350°F for 20 minutes, or until cheese is melted and peppers are tender.

½ cup bulgur wheat

1 cup vegetable broth

2 tablespoons olive oil

1 medium white onion, peeled and diced

1 clove garlic, peeled and minced

1 medium Roma tomato, seeded and chopped

1 teaspoon minced fresh rosemary

1 teaspoon fresh thyme leaves

½ teaspoon salt

½ teaspoon ground black pepper

½ pound 90% lean ground beef

4 large red bell peppers, tops removed and seeded

½ cup marinara sauce

1 cup water

½ cup grated Parmesan cheese

1 Add bulgur and broth to the Instant Pot® and stir well. Close lid, set steam release to Sealing, press the Rice button, adjust pressure to Low, and set time to 12 minutes. When the timer beeps, quick-release the pressure until the float valve drops. Open lid and fluff bulgur with a fork, then transfer to a medium bowl and set aside to cool.

2 Press the Sauté button and heat oil. Add onion and cook until tender, about 5 minutes. Add garlic, tomato, rosemary, thyme, salt, and pepper. Cook until garlic and herbs are fragrant, about 1 minute.

3 Add ground beef and cook, crumbling well, until no longer pink, about 5 minutes. Press the Cancel button.

4 Add beef mixture to bulgur and mix well. Divide mixture between bell peppers, making sure not to compact the mixture too much. Top each pepper with marinara sauce.

5 Clean out pot, add water, and place rack in pot. Carefully stand peppers on rack. Close lid, set steam release to Sealing, press the Manual button, and set time to 3 minutes. When the timer beeps, quick-release the pressure until the float valve drops. Open lid and carefully transfer peppers with tongs to plates. Top with cheese and serve immediately.

SERVES 4

Per Serving:

Calories	346
Fat	17g
Protein	20g
Sodium	977mg
Fiber	4g
Carbohydrates	29g
Sugar	7g

STUFFING PEPPERS

When selecting bell peppers for a stuffed pepper recipe, make sure they are firm and unblemished. If the skin of the pepper is wrinkled or soft, the stuffed pepper will turn out mushy. Make sure the peppers are large enough to hold a good amount of filling. Small peppers are not ideal for a stuffed pepper. And always be sure to cook meat thoroughly before filling the peppers. Peppers will insulate the filling somewhat while cooking, and meat will not come to a safe temperature unless cooked beforehand.

Savoy Cabbage Rolls

SERVES 10

Per Serving:

Calories	117
Fat	3g
Protein	6g
Sodium	337mg
Fiber	0g
Carbohydrates	15g
Sugar	1g

These small cabbage rolls are a little labor-intensive and do require some patience. However, if you are up for the challenge, the end result is amazing. Give yourself a pass on the first two rolls, but once you get into the swing of things, you'll love the end result.

1 medium head savoy cabbage
3 cups water, divided
½ pound ground beef
1 cup long-grain rice
1 small red bell pepper, seeded and minced
1 medium onion, peeled and diced

1 cup beef broth
1 tablespoon olive oil
2 tablespoons minced fresh mint
1 teaspoon dried tarragon
1 teaspoon salt
½ teaspoon ground black pepper
2 tablespoons lemon juice

1. Remove the large outer leaves from cabbage and set aside. Remove remaining cabbage leaves and place them in the Instant Pot®. Pour in 1 cup water.

2. Close lid, set steam release to Sealing, press the Steam button, and set time to 1 minute. Press the Adjust button to change the pressure to Low. When the timer beeps, quick-release the pressure until the float valve drops and then open lid. Press the Cancel button. Drain cabbage leaves in a colander and then move them to a kitchen towel.

3. In a medium mixing bowl, add ground beef, rice, bell pepper, onion, broth, olive oil, mint, tarragon, salt, and black pepper. Stir to combine.

4. Place the large uncooked cabbage leaves on the bottom of the Instant Pot®.

5. Remove the stem running down the center of each steamed cabbage leaf and tear each leaf in half lengthwise. Place 1 tablespoon ground beef mixture in the center of each cabbage piece. Loosely fold the sides of the leaf over the filling and then fold the top and bottom of the leaf over the folded sides. As you complete them, place each stuffed cabbage leaf in the pot.

6. Pour remaining 2 cups water and lemon juice over the stuffed cabbage rolls. Close lid, set steam release to Sealing, press the Manual button, and set time to 15 minutes. When the timer beeps, let pressure release naturally for 10 minutes. Quick-release any remaining pressure until the float valve drops and then open lid.

7. Carefully move stuffed cabbage rolls to a serving platter. Serve warm.

Giouvarlakia Soup

This hearty Greek meatball soup is a one-pot meal.

1 pound lean ground beef
1 medium onion, peeled and grated
3 large eggs, divided
⅓ cup plus ½ cup Arborio rice, divided
1 teaspoon ground allspice
⅛ teaspoon ground nutmeg
¾ teaspoon salt, divided
¾ teaspoon ground black pepper, divided
8 cups low-sodium chicken broth
1 tablespoon all-purpose flour
2 tablespoons water
3 tablespoons lemon juice

SERVES 6	
Per Serving:	
Calories	262
Fat	5g
Protein	25g
Sodium	670mg
Fiber	0g
Carbohydrates	18g
Sugar	5g

1 In a large bowl, combine beef, onion, 1 egg, ⅓ cup rice, allspice, nutmeg, ¼ teaspoon salt, and ¼ teaspoon pepper. Roll the mixture into 1" balls. Set aside.

2 Add broth, meatballs, remaining ½ cup rice, and remaining ½ teaspoon each salt and pepper to the Instant Pot®. Close lid, set steam release to Sealing, press the Manual button, and set time to 5 minutes. When the timer beeps, let pressure release naturally for 10 minutes. Quick-release any remaining pressure until the float valve drops. Press the Cancel button and open lid.

3 In a large bowl, whisk together flour and water to form a slurry. Whisk in lemon juice and remaining 2 eggs. Continuing to whisk vigorously, slowly add a ladle of soup liquid into egg mixture. Continue whisking and slowly add another 3–4 ladles of soup (one at a time) into egg mixture.

4 Slowly stir egg mixture back into the soup.

5 Allow the soup to cool for 5 minutes and then serve it immediately.

Wedding Soup

The name "wedding soup" comes from minestra maritata, *an Italian phrase meaning "married soup." This refers to the flavor produced by the combination or "marriage" of greens and meatballs. Because of its name, the soup has become a wedding tradition, especially in the northeastern United States.*

3 (1-ounce) slices Italian bread, toasted

¾ pound 90% lean ground beef

1 large egg, beaten

1 medium onion, peeled and chopped

3 cloves garlic, peeled and minced

¼ cup chopped fresh parsley

1 tablespoon minced fresh oregano

1 tablespoon minced fresh basil

1 teaspoon salt

½ teaspoon ground black pepper

½ cup grated Parmesan cheese, divided

2 tablespoons olive oil

8 cups low-sodium chicken broth

5 ounces baby spinach

1 Wet toasted bread with water and then squeeze out all the liquid. Place soaked bread in a large bowl. Add ground beef, egg, onion, garlic, parsley, oregano, basil, salt, pepper, and ¼ cup cheese. Mix well. Form the mixture into 1" balls.

2 Press the Sauté button on the Instant Pot® and heat oil. Brown meatballs in batches on all sides, about 3 minutes per side. Transfer meatballs to a plate. Press the Cancel button.

3 Add broth to pot, stirring well to release any browned bits. Add meatballs and stir well. Close lid, set steam release to Sealing, press the Manual button, and set time to 10 minutes. When the timer beeps, quick-release the pressure until the float valve drops. Open lid.

4 Add spinach and stir until wilted, about 1 minute. Ladle the soup into bowls and sprinkle with remaining ¼ cup cheese.

Greek Meatball Soup

This recipe is adapted from a Greek soup (youvarlakia avgolemono) and is thickened with a little corn flour, or masa harina. The traditional version doesn't have the vegetables added to the broth, but those vegetables make this soup a one-pot meal. Serve with feta cheese and crusty bread.

1 pound 90% lean ground beef

¼ pound ground pork

1 small onion, peeled and minced

1 clove garlic, peeled and minced

6 tablespoons long-grain white rice

1 tablespoon dried parsley

2 teaspoons dried dill

1 teaspoon dried oregano

½ teaspoon salt

¾ teaspoon ground black pepper

3 large eggs, divided

6 cups low-sodium chicken broth, divided

1 medium onion, peeled and chopped

1 cup baby carrots, each cut into thirds

2 large potatoes, peeled and cut into pieces

1 stalk celery, diced

2 tablespoons masa harina (corn flour)

⅓ cup lemon juice

SERVES 6	
Per Serving:	
Calories	408
Fat	17g
Protein	29g
Sodium	693mg
Fiber	2g
Carbohydrates	27g
Sugar	5g

1 In a large bowl, mix beef, pork, onion, garlic, rice, parsley, dill, oregano, salt, pepper, and 1 egg. Shape into small meatballs and set aside.

2 Add 2 cups broth to the Instant Pot®. Add meatballs, onion, carrots, potatoes, and celery, and then pour in remaining 4 cups broth to cover meatballs and vegetables. Close lid, set steam release to Sealing, press the Manual button, and set time to 10 minutes. When the timer beeps, let pressure release naturally, about 25 minutes. Open lid. Use a slotted spoon to move meatballs to a soup tureen. Cover and keep warm. Press the Cancel button.

3 Press the Sauté button and bring liquid to a simmer. In a small bowl or measuring cup, beat remaining 2 eggs and then whisk in masa harina. Gradually whisk in lemon juice. Ladle in about 1 cup of hot broth from the Instant Pot®, doing so in a slow, steady stream, beating continuously until all of the hot liquid has been incorporated into the masa harina mixture. Stir this mixture into pot. Stir and simmer for 5 minutes or until mixture is thickened. Pour over the meatballs and serve.

Rosemary Pork Shoulder with Apples

SERVES 8	
Per Serving:	
Calories	394
Fat	25g
Protein	33g
Sodium	393mg
Fiber	1g
Carbohydrates	5g
Sugar	4g

For a sweeter sauce, use apple juice for all or part of the white wine. Substitute water for the wine if you want the apples to remain tart. Serve with fried potatoes, a steamed vegetable, and crusty bread or dinner rolls.

1 (3½-pound) pork shoulder roast
3 tablespoons Dijon mustard
1 tablespoon olive oil
½ cup dry white wine
2 medium tart apples, peeled, cored, and quartered
3 cloves garlic, peeled and minced
½ teaspoon salt
½ teaspoon ground black pepper
1 teaspoon dried rosemary

1 Coat all sides of roast with mustard. Press the Sauté button on the Instant Pot® and heat oil. Add pork roast and brown on all sides, about 3 minutes per side.

2 Add wine and scrape up any browned bits sticking to the bottom of the pot. Add apples, garlic, salt, pepper, and rosemary. Press the Cancel button.

3 Close lid, set steam release to Sealing, press the Manual button, and set time to 45 minutes. When the timer beeps, let pressure release naturally, about 25 minutes.

4 Open the lid. Transfer roast to a serving platter. Tent and keep warm while you use an immersion blender to purée sauce in pot. Slice roast and pour the puréed juices over the slices. Serve.

CHAPTER 14

Fruits and Desserts

Stewed Cinnamon Apples with Dates

SERVES 6

Per Serving:

Calories	111
Fat	2g
Protein	1g
Sodium	2mg
Fiber	4g
Carbohydrates	26g
Sugar	20g

FIRM APPLES

The best apples for baking, stewing, or braising are firm-fleshed varieties. Firm apples are the apples that are most crisp when eaten raw. While a softer apple may be more appealing as a snack to eat out of hand, firmer apples hold up to cooking or baking and don't turn mushy. Granny Smith apples are among the firmest apples, but if you like a sweeter apple, try a Pink Lady instead.

Dates are naturally sweet, so you do not need to add any sugar to these apples. You can serve this dish hot, or let it cool and serve over cold Greek yogurt.

4 large Granny Smith or Pink Lady apples, peeled, cored, and sliced
½ cup water
¼ cup chopped pitted dates
1 teaspoon ground cinnamon
¼ teaspoon vanilla extract
1 teaspoon unsalted butter

1 Place apples, water, dates, and cinnamon in the Instant Pot®. Close lid, set steam release to Sealing, press the Manual button, and set time to 3 minutes.

2 When the timer beeps, quick-release the pressure until the float valve drops. Press the Cancel button and open lid. Stir in vanilla and butter. Serve hot or chilled.

Spiced Poached Pears

This dessert is elegant and easy. To double the number of servings to eight, just slice the poached pears in half with a sharp paring knife and remove core with a melon baller.

2 cups water	**2 cinnamon sticks**
2 cups red wine	**1 star anise**
¼ cup honey	**1 teaspoon vanilla bean paste**
4 whole cloves	**4 Bartlett pears, peeled**

1 Place all ingredients in the Instant Pot®. Stir to combine. Close lid, set steam release to Sealing, press the Manual button, and set time to 3 minutes.

2 When the timer beeps, quick-release the pressure until the float valve drops. Press the Cancel button and open lid. With a slotted spoon, remove pears to a plate and allow to cool for 5 minutes. Serve warm.

Cranberry Applesauce

A little bit of butter adds richness to this applesauce, but you can omit it if you prefer. Enjoy this applesauce as is, or use it as a side dish for roasted pork or chicken.

1 cup whole cranberries	**¼ cup granulated sugar**
4 medium tart apples, peeled, cored, and grated	**1 tablespoon unsalted butter**
4 medium sweet apples, peeled, cored, and grated	**2 teaspoons ground cinnamon**
	½ teaspoon ground cloves
1½ tablespoons grated orange zest	**¼ teaspoon ground black pepper**
¼ cup orange juice	**⅛ teaspoon salt**
¼ cup dark brown sugar	**1 tablespoon lemon juice**

1 Place all ingredients in the Instant Pot® and stir well.

2 Close lid, set steam release to Sealing, press the Manual button, and set time to 5 minutes. When the timer beeps, let pressure release naturally, about 25 minutes.

3 Open the lid. Lightly mash fruit with a fork. Stir well. Serve warm or cold.

Blueberry Compote

This blueberry sauce is perfect as a topping for frozen yogurt or oatmeal, or enjoyed as it is for a simple yet wholesome dessert. Think blueberry pie without the crust!

1 (16-ounce) bag frozen blueberries, thawed
¼ cup sugar
1 tablespoon lemon juice
2 tablespoons cornstarch
2 tablespoons water
¼ teaspoon vanilla extract
¼ teaspoon grated lemon zest

SERVES 8	
Per Serving:	
Calories	57
Fat	0g
Protein	0g
Sodium	0mg
Fiber	2g
Carbohydrates	14g
Sugar	7g

1 Add blueberries, sugar, and lemon juice to the Instant Pot®. Close lid, set steam release to Sealing, press the Manual button, and set time to 1 minute.

2 When the timer beeps, quick-release the pressure until the float valve drops. Press the Cancel button and open lid.

3 Press the Sauté button. In a small bowl, combine cornstarch and water. Stir into blueberry mixture and cook until mixture comes to a boil and thickens, about 3–4 minutes. Press the Cancel button and stir in vanilla and lemon zest. Serve immediately or refrigerate until ready to serve.

Dried Fruit Compote

Add a little sugar to this compote if you find it's not sweet enough. Add it one teaspoon at a time before the fruit has cooled so that it can be stirred into the fruit mixture until it dissolves.

8 ounces dried apricots, quartered
8 ounces dried peaches, quartered
1 cup golden raisins
1½ cups orange juice
1 cinnamon stick
4 whole cloves

SERVES 6	
Per Serving:	
Calories	258
Fat	0g
Protein	4g
Sodium	7mg
Fiber	5g
Carbohydrates	63g
Sugar	49g

1 Place all ingredients in the Instant Pot®. Stir to combine. Close lid, set steam release to Sealing, press the Manual button, and set time to 3 minutes. When the timer beeps, let pressure release naturally, about 20 minutes. Press the Cancel button and open lid.

2 Remove and discard cinnamon stick and cloves. Press the Sauté button and simmer for 5–6 minutes. Serve warm or allow to cool, and then cover and refrigerate for up to a week.

Chocolate Rice Pudding

If you love chocolate, then this recipe is made just for you. When the pudding is served warm, the chunks of dark chocolate melt and swirl into each bite.

2 cups almond milk
1 cup long-grain brown rice
2 tablespoons Dutch-processed cocoa powder
¼ cup maple syrup
1 teaspoon vanilla extract
½ cup chopped dark chocolate

1 Place almond milk, rice, cocoa, maple syrup, and vanilla in the Instant Pot®. Close lid, set steam release to Sealing, press the Manual button, and set time to 20 minutes.

2 When the timer beeps, let pressure release naturally for 15 minutes, then quick-release the remaining pressure. Press the Cancel button and open lid. Serve warm, sprinkled with chocolate.

Fruit Compote

Serve compote with a dollop of whipped cream or use it as a topping for plain or lemon yogurt.

1 cup apple juice
1 cup dry white wine
2 tablespoons honey
1 cinnamon stick
¼ teaspoon ground nutmeg
1 tablespoon grated lemon zest
1½ tablespoons grated orange zest
3 large apples, peeled, cored, and chopped
3 large pears, peeled, cored, and chopped
½ cup dried cherries

1 Place all ingredients in the Instant Pot® and stir well. Close lid, set steam release to Sealing, press the Manual button, and set time to 1 minute. When the timer beeps, quick-release the pressure until the float valve drops. Press the Cancel button and open lid.

2 Use a slotted spoon to transfer fruit to a serving bowl. Remove and discard cinnamon stick. Press the Sauté button and bring juice in the pot to a boil. Cook, stirring constantly, until reduced to a syrup that will coat the back of a spoon, about 10 minutes.

3 Stir syrup into fruit mixture. Allow to cool slightly, then cover with plastic wrap and refrigerate overnight.

Stuffed Apples

You can replace the sugar with maple syrup or brown sugar if desired. Serve with a scoop of vanilla frozen yogurt, or drizzle with Greek yogurt sweetened with a touch of honey.

½ cup apple juice
¼ cup golden raisins
¼ cup chopped toasted walnuts
2 tablespoons sugar
½ teaspoon grated orange zest
½ teaspoon ground cinnamon
4 large cooking apples
4 teaspoons unsalted butter
1 cup water

SERVES 4	
Per Serving:	
Calories	432
Fat	16g
Protein	3g
Sodium	5mg
Fiber	6g
Carbohydrates	72g
Sugar	62g

1 Put apple juice in a microwave-safe container; heat for 1 minute on high or until steaming and hot. Pour over raisins. Soak raisins for 30 minutes. Drain, reserving apple juice. Add nuts, sugar, orange zest, and cinnamon to raisins and stir to mix.

2 Cut off the top fourth of each apple. Peel the cut portion and chop it, then stir diced apple pieces into raisin mixture. Hollow out and core apples by cutting to, but not through, the bottoms.

3 Place each apple on a piece of aluminum foil that is large enough to wrap apple completely. Fill apple centers with raisin mixture.

4 Top each with 1 teaspoon butter. Wrap the foil around each apple, folding the foil over at the top and then pinching it firmly together.

5 Add water to the Instant Pot® and place rack inside. Place apples on the rack. Close lid, set steam release to Sealing, press the Manual button, and set time to 10 minutes.

6 When the timer beeps, quick-release the pressure until the float valve drops and open the lid. Carefully lift apples out of the Instant Pot®. Unwrap and transfer to plates. Serve hot, at room temperature, or cold.

Cinnamon-Stewed Dried Plums with Greek Yogurt

SERVES 6

Per Serving:

Calories	301
Fat	2g
Protein	14g
Sodium	50mg
Fiber	4g
Carbohydrates	61g
Sugar	33g

Dried plums have a smooth, silky texture when they are stewed. Here, they are stewed with whole cinnamon sticks to add a spicy richness. Serve over tangy Greek yogurt.

3 cups dried plums
2 cups water
2 tablespoons sugar
2 cinnamon sticks
3 cups low-fat plain Greek yogurt

1 Add dried plums, water, sugar, and cinnamon to the Instant Pot®. Close lid, set steam release to Sealing, press the Manual button, and set time to 3 minutes.

2 When the timer beeps, quick-release the pressure until the float valve drops. Press the Cancel button and open lid. Remove and discard cinnamon sticks. Serve warm over Greek yogurt.

Vanilla-Poached Apricots

SERVES 6

Per Serving:

Calories	62
Fat	0g
Protein	2g
Sodium	10mg
Fiber	1g
Carbohydrates	14g
Sugar	13g

This recipe is perfect for apricots that are too hard or not ripe enough to eat yet. Their firm flesh will become tender while cooking in your Instant Pot®, but it won't get so soft that it turns to mush.

1¼ cups water
¼ cup marsala wine
¼ cup sugar
1 teaspoon vanilla bean paste
8 medium apricots, sliced in half and pitted

1 Place all ingredients in the Instant Pot®. Stir to combine. Close lid, set steam release to Sealing, press the Manual button, and set time to 1 minute.

2 When the timer beeps, quick-release the pressure until the float valve drops. Press the Cancel button and open lid. Let stand for 10 minutes. Carefully remove apricots from poaching liquid with a slotted spoon. Serve warm or at room temperature.

Creamy Spiced Almond Milk

Nut milk bags are available at most natural food stores and online. These finely woven bags allow all the liquid to drain out, leaving the nut pulp behind in the bag.

1 cup raw almonds
5 cups filtered water, divided

1 teaspoon vanilla bean paste
½ teaspoon pumpkin pie spice

1 Add almonds and 1 cup water to the Instant Pot®. Close lid, set steam release to Sealing, press the Manual button, and set time to 1 minute.

2 When the timer beeps, quick-release the pressure until the float valve drops. Press the Cancel button and open lid. Strain almonds and rinse under cool water. Transfer to a high-powered blender with remaining 4 cups water. Purée for 2 minutes on high speed.

3 Pour mixture into a nut milk bag set over a large bowl. Squeeze bag to extract all liquid. Stir in vanilla and pumpkin pie spice. Transfer to a Mason jar or sealed jug and refrigerate for 8 hours. Stir or shake gently before serving.

Poached Pears with Greek Yogurt and Pistachio

Pears are an excellent source of potassium, which can help if you are looking to lower your blood pressure. They are also an excellent source of fiber, which is great for your heart.

2 cups water
1¾ cups apple cider
¼ cup lemon juice
1 cinnamon stick

1 teaspoon vanilla bean paste
4 large Bartlett pears, peeled
1 cup low-fat plain Greek yogurt
½ cup unsalted roasted pistachio meats

1 Add water, apple cider, lemon juice, cinnamon, vanilla, and pears to the Instant Pot®. Close lid, set steam release to Sealing, press the Manual button, and set time to 3 minutes.

2 When the timer beeps, quick-release the pressure until the float valve drops. Press the Cancel button and open lid. With a slotted spoon remove pears to a plate and allow to cool to room temperature.

3 To serve, carefully slice pears in half with a sharp paring knife and scoop out core with a melon baller. Lay pear halves on dessert plates or in shallow bowls. Top with yogurt and garnish with pistachios. Serve immediately.

Peaches Poached in Rose Water

Rose water (a liquid containing water and the distilled essence of dried rose petals) is available in natural food stores, and in Middle Eastern or halal markets. In this recipe it adds the scent and flavor of traditional Middle Eastern desserts. Outside of the kitchen, you can use rose water as a facial toner before you moisturize.

1 cup water
1 cup rose water
¼ cup wildflower honey
8 green cardamom pods, lightly crushed
1 teaspoon vanilla bean paste
6 large yellow peaches, pitted and quartered
½ cup chopped unsalted roasted pistachio meats

1 Add water, rose water, honey, cardamom, and vanilla to the Instant Pot®. Whisk well, then add peaches. Close lid, set steam release to Sealing, press the Manual button, and set time to 1 minute.

2 When the timer beeps, quick-release the pressure until the float valve drops. Press the Cancel button and open lid. Allow peaches to stand for 10 minutes. Carefully remove peaches from poaching liquid with a slotted spoon.

3 Slip skins from peach slices. Arrange slices on a plate and garnish with pistachios. Serve warm or at room temperature.

SERVES 6

Per Serving:

Calories	145
Fat	3g
Protein	2g
Sodium	8mg
Fiber	2g
Carbohydrates	28g
Sugar	25g

ROSES IN COOKING

You may be more familiar with roses as the centerpiece of the dining table as opposed to the centerpiece of the meal, but roses have a long history as an ingredient in cooking. In the Middle East, rose petals are used to flavor many dishes and beverages, and dried petals are added to spice mixes. Rose can be a nice addition to poultry and lamb dishes, as well as sweet dishes. If you choose to cook with fresh roses, be sure they were not treated with pesticides or other chemicals. It is best to talk to your local florist about untreated varieties instead of buying a dozen from your local floral market.

Brown Betty Apple Dessert

Brown Betty, a cross between a cobbler and a bread pudding, is a classic American dessert. It is usually made with apples, but pears or berries are also a great choice.

2 cups dried bread crumbs
½ cup sugar
1 teaspoon ground cinnamon
3 tablespoons lemon juice
1 tablespoon grated lemon zest
1 cup olive oil, divided
8 medium apples, peeled, cored, and diced
2 cups water

1   Combine crumbs, sugar, cinnamon, lemon juice, lemon zest, and ½ cup oil in a medium mixing bowl. Set aside.

2   In a greased oven-safe dish that will fit in your cooker loosely, add a thin layer of crumbs, then one diced apple. Continue filling the container with alternating layers of crumbs and apples until all ingredients are finished. Pour remaining ½ cup oil on top.

3   Add water to the Instant Pot® and place rack inside. Make a foil sling by folding a long piece of foil in half lengthwise and lower the uncovered container into the pot using the sling.

4   Close lid, set steam release to Sealing, press the Manual button, and set time to 10 minutes. When the timer beeps, let pressure release naturally, about 20 minutes. Press the Cancel button and open lid.

5   Using the sling, remove the baking dish from the pot and let stand for 5 minutes before serving.

Blueberry Oat Crumble

Is there anything better than warm fruit crumble? You can also make this with fresh diced apples, pears, or a mix of blueberries, raspberries, and blackberries.

1 cup water
4 cups blueberries
2 tablespoons packed light brown sugar
2 tablespoons cornstarch
1/8 teaspoon ground nutmeg
1/3 cup rolled oats
1/4 cup granulated sugar
1/4 cup all-purpose flour
1/4 teaspoon ground cinnamon
1/4 cup unsalted butter, melted and cooled

1 Spray a baking dish that fits inside the Instant Pot® with nonstick cooking spray. Add water to the pot and add rack. Fold a long piece of aluminum foil in half lengthwise. Lay foil over rack to form a sling.

2 In a medium bowl, combine blueberries, brown sugar, cornstarch, and nutmeg. Transfer mixture to prepared dish.

3 In a separate medium bowl, add oats, sugar, flour, and cinnamon. Mix well. Add butter and combine until mixture is crumbly. Sprinkle crumbles over blueberries, cover dish with aluminum foil, and crimp edges tightly.

4 Add baking dish to rack in pot so it rests on the sling and close lid. Set steam release to Sealing, press the Manual button, and set time to 10 minutes.

5 When the timer beeps, let pressure release naturally for 10 minutes, then quick-release the remaining pressure until the float valve drops. Press the Cancel button and open lid. Carefully remove dish with sling and remove foil cover.

6 Heat broiler on high. Broil crumble until topping is golden brown, about 5 minutes. Serve warm or at room temperature.

SERVES 8

Per Serving:

Calories	159
Fat	6g
Protein	2g
Sodium	2mg
Fiber	2g
Carbohydrates	26g
Sugar	17g

BLUEBERRIES

The majority of the health benefits from blueberries comes from anthocyanin, which is the same compound that gives them their color. This compound is a powerful antioxidant, which research has shown can help increase bone strength and skin health, and may help improve blood pressure and overall heart health.

Red Wine–Poached Figs with Ricotta and Almond

SERVES 4	
Per Serving:	
Calories	597
Fat	21g
Protein	13g
Sodium	255mg
Fiber	9g
Carbohydrates	56g
Sugar	37g

Dried figs are available all year, so you can have the ingredients on hand to make this dessert anytime you want.

2 cups water	12 dried mission figs
2 cups red wine	1 cup ricotta cheese
¼ cup honey	1 tablespoon confectioners' sugar
1 cinnamon stick	¼ teaspoon almond extract
1 star anise	1 cup toasted sliced almonds
1 teaspoon vanilla bean paste	

1 Add water, wine, honey, cinnamon, star anise, and vanilla to the Instant Pot® and whisk well. Add figs, close lid, set steam release to Sealing, press the Manual button, and set time to 1 minute.

2 When the timer beeps, quick-release the pressure until the float valve drops. Press the Cancel button and open lid. With a slotted spoon, transfer figs to a plate and set aside to cool for 5 minutes.

3 In a small bowl, mix together ricotta, sugar, and almond extract. Serve figs with a dollop of sweetened ricotta and a sprinkling of almonds.

Apple and Brown Rice Pudding

SERVES 6	
Per Serving:	
Calories	218
Fat	2g
Protein	3g
Sodium	54mg
Fiber	4g
Carbohydrates	51g
Sugar	25g

This rice pudding is perfect to eat on crisp fall days. The brown rice adds extra fiber, and the raisins contribute a rich, caramel sweetness. If you are making this for vegans, replace honey with maple syrup.

2 cups almond milk
1 cup long-grain brown rice
½ cup golden raisins
1 Granny Smith apple, peeled, cored, and chopped
¼ cup honey
1 teaspoon vanilla extract
½ teaspoon ground cinnamon

1 Place all ingredients in the Instant Pot®. Stir to combine. Close lid, set steam release to Sealing, press the Manual button, and set time to 20 minutes.

2 When the timer beeps, let pressure release naturally for 15 minutes, then quick-release the remaining pressure. Press the Cancel button and open lid. Serve warm or at room temperature.

Vanilla-Spice Pear Butter

Bartlett pears are the light green pears that are especially prevalent in the Pacific Northwest. They have hearty flesh that yields a smoother pear butter. Serve this luxurious spread on scones or on toasted English muffins.

6 medium Bartlett pears, peeled, cored, and diced
¼ cup dry white wine
1 tablespoon lemon juice
⅓ cup sugar
2 orange slices
1 lemon slice
2 whole cloves
1 vanilla bean, split lengthwise
1 cinnamon stick
¼ teaspoon ground cardamom
⅛ teaspoon salt

MAKES 2 CUPS	
Per Serving (2 tablespoons):	
Calories	56
Fat	0g
Protein	0g
Sodium	20mg
Fiber	2g
Carbohydrates	14g
Sugar	10g

1 Add pears, wine, and lemon juice to the Instant Pot®. Close lid, set steam release to Sealing, press the Manual button, and set time to 8 minutes.

2 When the timer beeps, let pressure release naturally for 10 minutes. Quick-release any remaining pressure until the float valve drops and open the lid. Press the Cancel button. Transfer fruit and juices to a blender or food processor, and purée until smooth.

3 Return purée to pot and add sugar. Press the Sauté button and cook until sugar dissolves, about 1 minute. Stir in orange slices, lemon slice, cloves, vanilla bean, cinnamon stick, cardamom, and salt. Cook until mixture thickens and mounds slightly on spoon, about 25 minutes.

4 Remove and discard orange and lemon slices, cloves, and cinnamon stick. Remove vanilla pod and slice in half. Use the back of a knife to scrape away any vanilla seeds still clinging to the pod and stir them into the pear butter. Cool and refrigerate covered for up to 10 days or freeze for up to 4 months.

Lemon Zest Olive Oil Cake

SERVES 8

Per Serving:

Calories	167
Fat	12g
Protein	3g
Sodium	171mg
Fiber	0g
Carbohydrates	13g
Sugar	9g

STEAMED CAKE

Steamed cakes—or sponges as they are sometimes called—yield moist, tender, and utterly luscious results. While it may seem odd to steam a cake, it is a popular technique in Europe and Asia. In the United Kingdom, steamed cakes—or puddings—are served for holidays and are a traditional favorite. In Asia, cakes and breads are steamed to ensure a soft, fluffy texture. When making cakes with less oil or fat, steaming is an excellent way to preserve richness and flavor.

Steamed cakes are incredibly moist and tender. You can make this in a standard cake pan that fits inside your Instant Pot®, but a glass bowl or rounded cooking pot will give the cake a unique look. Serve with Greek yogurt on the side if you like.

1 cup water
6 tablespoons olive oil
⅓ cup sugar
2 large eggs
1 tablespoon grated lemon zest
1 teaspoon vanilla extract
1⅓ cups all-purpose flour
1½ teaspoons baking powder
½ teaspoon salt
½ cup whole milk, at room temperature

1 Spray a 1-quart heatproof glass bowl or cooking dish with nonstick cooking spray. Add water to the Instant Pot® and place rack inside. Fold a long piece of aluminum foil in half lengthwise. Lay foil over rack to form a sling.

2 In a large bowl, cream together olive oil and sugar until completely combined. Add eggs, one at a time, and blend well. Add lemon zest and vanilla and stir to incorporate.

3 In a medium bowl, sift together flour, baking powder, and salt. Add dry ingredients alternately with milk to creamed olive oil and sugar, starting and ending with the flour. Do not overmix.

4 Pour batter carefully into the prepared bowl. Cover bowl with aluminum foil, crimping the edges tightly.

5 Place bowl on the rack so it rests on the sling, close lid, set steam release to Sealing, press the Manual button, and set time to 35 minutes. When the timer beeps, let pressure release naturally for 10 minutes, then quick-release the remaining pressure. Press the Cancel button and open lid.

6 Carefully use sling to remove pan from pot. Uncover bowl and set aside to cool 10 minutes, then turn out onto a serving platter and serve warm.

Cornmeal Cake

SERVES 8	
Per Serving:	
Calories	226
Fat	12g
Protein	4g
Sodium	43mg
Fiber	1g
Carbohydrates	24g
Sugar	9g

Serve warm with maple syrup or make a maple-infused butter by whisking pats of butter into heated maple syrup. Eat leftovers for breakfast by crumbling the cake into a bowl of milk.

2 cups whole milk
¼ cup light brown sugar, packed
1 teaspoon grated orange zest
½ cup fine yellow cornmeal
1 large egg
2 egg yolks
2 tablespoons unsalted butter, melted
2 tablespoons orange marmalade
1 cup water

1 Spray a 1-quart soufflé dish or heatproof glass dish with nonstick cooking spray.

2 Bring milk to a simmer in a saucepan over medium heat. Stir in brown sugar; simmer and stir until milk is at a low boil. Whisk in orange zest and cornmeal. Simmer and stir for 2 minutes. Remove from heat. Whisk together egg, egg yolks, butter, and orange marmalade. Stir into cornmeal mixture. Pour batter into prepared pan.

3 Add water to the Instant Pot® and place the rack inside. Fold a long piece of aluminum foil in half lengthwise. Lay foil over rack to form a sling. Place soufflé dish on the rack so it rests on the sling. Close lid, set steam release to Sealing, press the Manual button, and set time to 12 minutes. When the timer beeps, let pressure release naturally for 10 minutes. Quick-release any remaining pressure until the float valve drops and open the lid. Use the sling to transfer the soufflé dish to a wire rack. Serve warm or at room temperature.

Steamed Dessert Bread

Serve this dessert bread with sweetened cream cheese or butter. Toast leftovers by placing slices directly on the oven rack or on a baking sheet in a 350°F oven for 5 minutes.

½ cup all-purpose flour
½ cup stone-ground cornmeal
½ cup whole-wheat flour
½ teaspoon baking powder
¼ teaspoon salt
¼ teaspoon baking soda
½ cup maple syrup
½ cup buttermilk
1 large egg
1 cup water

SERVES 8	
Per Serving:	
Calories	175
Fat	1g
Protein	4g
Sodium	102mg
Fiber	2g
Carbohydrates	37g
Sugar	13g

1 Grease the inside of a 6-cup heatproof pudding mold or baking pan.

2 Add flour, cornmeal, whole-wheat flour, baking powder, salt, and baking soda to a medium mixing bowl. Stir to combine. Add maple syrup, buttermilk, and egg to another mixing bowl or measuring cup. Whisk to mix and then pour into the flour mixture. Mix until a thick batter is formed.

3 Pour enough batter into prepared baking pan to fill it three-quarters full.

4 Butter one side of a piece of heavy-duty aluminum foil large enough to cover the top of the baking dish. Place the foil butter side down over the pan and crimp the edges to seal.

5 Add water to the Instant Pot® and place the rack inside. Fold a long piece of aluminum foil in half lengthwise. Lay foil over rack to form a sling. Place pan on rack so it rests on the sling.

6 Close lid, set steam release to Sealing, press the Manual button, set time to 1 hour, and press the Adjust button and set pressure to Low. When the timer beeps, let pressure release naturally, about 25 minutes.

7 Open lid, lift pan from Instant Pot® using the sling, and place on a cooling rack. Remove foil. Test bread with a toothpick. If the toothpick comes out wet, place the foil over the pan and return it to the Instant Pot® to cook for 10 additional minutes. If the bread is done, use a knife to loosen it and invert it onto the cooling rack. Serve warm.

STANDARD US/METRIC
MEASUREMENT CONVERSIONS

VOLUME CONVERSIONS

US Volume Measure	Metric Equivalent
⅛ teaspoon	0.5 milliliter
¼ teaspoon	1 milliliter
½ teaspoon	2 milliliters
1 teaspoon	5 milliliters
½ tablespoon	7 milliliters
1 tablespoon (3 teaspoons)	15 milliliters
2 tablespoons (1 fluid ounce)	30 milliliters
¼ cup (4 tablespoons)	60 milliliters
⅓ cup	90 milliliters
½ cup (4 fluid ounces)	125 milliliters
⅔ cup	160 milliliters
¾ cup (6 fluid ounces)	180 milliliters
1 cup (16 tablespoons)	250 milliliters
1 pint (2 cups)	500 milliliters
1 quart (4 cups)	1 liter (about)

WEIGHT CONVERSIONS

US Weight Measure	Metric Equivalent
½ ounce	15 grams
1 ounce	30 grams
2 ounces	60 grams
3 ounces	85 grams
¼ pound (4 ounces)	115 grams
½ pound (8 ounces)	225 grams
¾ pound (12 ounces)	340 grams
1 pound (16 ounces)	454 grams

OVEN TEMPERATURE CONVERSIONS

Degrees Fahrenheit	Degrees Celsius
200 degrees F	95 degrees C
250 degrees F	120 degrees C
275 degrees F	135 degrees C
300 degrees F	150 degrees C
325 degrees F	160 degrees C
350 degrees F	180 degrees C
375 degrees F	190 degrees C
400 degrees F	205 degrees C
425 degrees F	220 degrees C
450 degrees F	230 degrees C

BAKING PAN SIZES

American	Metric
8 × 1½ inch round baking pan	20 × 4 cm cake tin
9 × 1½ inch round baking pan	23 × 3.5 cm cake tin
11 × 7 × 1½ inch baking pan	28 × 18 × 4 cm baking tin
13 × 9 × 2 inch baking pan	30 × 20 × 5 cm baking tin
2 quart rectangular baking dish	30 × 20 × 3 cm baking tin
15 × 10 × 2 inch baking pan	30 × 25 × 2 cm baking tin (Swiss roll tin)
9 inch pie plate	22 × 4 or 23 × 4 cm pie plate
7 or 8 inch springform pan	18 or 20 cm springform or loose bottom cake tin
9 × 5 × 3 inch loaf pan	23 × 13 × 7 cm or 2 lb narrow loaf or pate tin
1½ quart casserole	1.5 liter casserole
2 quart casserole	2 liter casserole

Index